FROM
BOURASSA
TO
BOURASSA

FROM
BOURASSA
TO
BOURASSA

A PIVOTAL
DECADE
IN CANADIAN
HISTORY

L. IAN MacDONALD

HARVEST HOUSE

Deposited in the Bibliotheque Nationale of Quebec, 4th quarter
1984

Typography and cover: Marie Gilbert

Printed in Canada

Canadian Cataloguing in Publication Data

MacDonald, L. Ian
From Bourassa to Bourassa

Includes index
ISBN 0-88772-030-7 (bound). –
    ISBN 0-88772-029-3 (pbk.)

1. Bourassa, Robert, 1933-   2. Quebec (Province) —
Politics and government — 1976-   3. Canada —
Politics and government — 1963-   . I. Title

PC2925.2M32 1984   971.4'04   C84-090197-6
F1053.2.M32 1984

For Andrée
For Everything

"A week is a long time in politics. And a year is an eternity." — Robert Bourassa, as he often quoted Harold Wilson.

CONTENTS

PREFACE

The period of 1976 through 1984 has been a tumultuous and historic time in the life of the Quebec Liberal party, of Quebec, and of Canada. The party lived through two leadership crises, the province through two important elections, and the country as a whole lived through the referendum experience.

Along the way, there were many unexpected twists and turns. Robert Bourassa, driven from public life in 1976, came back only seven years later to replace the man who succeeded him. And Claude Ryan, acclaimed as the savior of the federalist cause in 1977, found himself utterly alone after his defeat in the Quebec election of 1981. Watching these events, in a not altogether disinterested way, were the cousins, the federal Liberals of Pierre Trudeau in Ottawa. Trudeau, born again in the 1980 election, came home to Quebec to play an important role in the referendum of 1980. He then kidnapped the result, demanding patriation of the Constitution as a ransom. Ryan always believed the timing of the Trudeau patriation package delayed the call of a 1980 provincial election, and contributed to his defeat. Bourassa's loss in the 1976 election had made Claude Ryan possible as a political figure. And Ryan's defeat in 1981 allowed Bourassa to complete one of the most remarkable comebacks in the annals of elective politics.

Thus, *From Bourassa to Bourassa*, an attempt to tell that story within the framework of the party they both led, and in the context of the referendum experience, the story of a lifetime for any journalist, and the story of our lives for those of us who lived through it.

There are many people to be thanked. More than 100 persons gave generously of their time for personal interviews. Claude Ryan, a difficult man to get to sit down and talk, finally granted two long sessions late in 1980. In his office, Jacques Hudon, Michèle Bazin, and Josette Poliquin opened the door.

Robert Bourassa was a willing and cooperative interview subject, who sat through many long sessions between 1980 and 1984 in the living room of his Montreal home, in a restaurant in Florida, and even on a train from Quebec to Montreal. Raymond Garneau was also generous with his time. At the Quebec Liberal party headquarters on Gilford street in Montreal, Pierre Bibeau was always available.

In Ottawa, Jean Chrétien made himself available for two lengthy interviews, and his executive assistant, Eddie Goldenberg, opened doors all over town. In the Prime Minister's Office, I'm indebted to speechwriter André Burelle, principal author of the memorable addresses delivered by Pierre Trudeau in the referendum, as well as to former Trudeau press secretary Patrick Gossage, a consummate professional.

In Montreal, I've been encouraged in this work by Mark Harrison, editor of *The Gazette*, who has given his political columnist the freedom to roam about two capitals, Quebec and Ottawa. Among my colleagues, one cherished friend, Robert McKenzie of *The Toronto Star*, has read the manuscript and made some pertinent comments. Bill Fox, formerly of The *Toronto Star* Ottawa and Washington bureaus, also read over part of the manuscript.

Thanks are also due to Agnes McFarlane and her staff at the incomparable *Gazette* library, as well as to Michel Roy who, when editor-in-chief of *Le Devoir*, granted access to that newspaper's Ryan file.

Among those who lent a hand with the sifting and sorting of interview materials, I have to thank June Thompson, Alison Burns and Nancy Southam for typing up transcripts, just about the most time-consuming and thankless of the essential tasks in a job like this. As for lining up interviews, there is no one anywhere to match *The Gazette*'s chief switchboard operator, Millie Thompson, who once tracked down a colleague to a bar in Vienna simply by having the presence of mind to get the hotel doorman into a transatlantic conversation about the names of the local watering holes.

As for source material, all the interview quotes in this book, unless otherwise attributed, are from interviews with the author. Translations of excerpts of articles from *Le Devoir* are, with a few exceptions, also the author's handiwork, and any errors are his own. However, the translations of Pierre Trudeau's referendum speeches are from official texts furnished by the Prime Minister's Office.

Much of the material in chapter 8, dealing with the origins of the Catholic Action movements in Quebec, is from a research paper written for this project by Sandra Wheaton Dudley, and I wish to acknowledge her special contribution.

On the production of the manuscript, I'm grateful to Kim Mullin, Johanne Simetin and Robert Roll of Perspectra Inc. in Montreal, who were always willing to liberate one of their Micom machines to furnish me with fast printouts and chapter corrections.

In Toronto, my friend and attorney Sam Wakim, took the time and trouble to believe in this book. His faith in the project was undiminished over the years. In Ottawa, Jason Moscovitz and Vincent del Buono also showed an interest in finding a publisher. It is to the latter that I am indebted for securing the enthusiastic participation of Harvest House of Montreal and of its editor, Maynard Gertler.

Most of all, I'm indebted to Andrée Dontigny, who provided encouragement, good humor and boundless love, through the long and occasionally difficult period of researching and writing this book. It is her book, too.

October 29, 1973: Robert and Andrée Bourassa arrive at Liberal headquarters in Montreal to claim the greatest victory in the annals of Quebec politics. In fact, it is a pyrrhic victory, the beginning of the end. . . (Montreal *Star* photo)

1
"A CHANGE MAY BE IN THE ORDER OF THINGS"

The deadline was closing in with the darkness of the November afternoon. But it was his custom to leave the lead editorial until the end of the day. As always he wrote quickly, and later he said the conclusions came to him only as he was doing the piece. One of the things that struck people about Claude Ryan was his capacity to write the most arduous and closely reasoned editorials with the speed of a wire-service reporter filing a bulletin. In a little more than an hour he would knock out a 1,500-word article that would fill three wide columns over half a page in the next day's paper.

For Ryan, this was the easy part of the job at *Le Devoir*: the summing up of a situation. The policy of the paper might be arrived at by a tortuous route of consultations, but once a decision was taken, the logic of a Ryan editorial fell easily into place. There would be many who would not comprehend, and many more who would loudly disagree, but everyone who cared about public policy in Quebec would know about a position taken on an important matter by the Montreal daily, whose political influence far exceeded its modest circulation. It was a newspaper with a vocation and he, as its all-powerful editor and publisher, was equally a man with a calling. Only the fourth "director" since the paper's founding in 1910, Ryan was the full-blooded journalistic heir of its founder, Henri Bourassa, a moral authority in the affairs of French Canada.

Now, three days before the 1976 Quebec election, Ryan was at last prepared to pronounce on the foremost question of the day: with considerable misgivings, he would endorse the Parti Québécois. He had tipped his hand in an editorial which appeared that morning. "In Quebec, after twelve years of Liberal rule since 1960," he had concluded, "a change may be in the order of things if the goal of independence can truly and satisfactorily be put in parentheses."

Even then, Ryan had left the question hanging for the conclusion of the two-part editorial, characteristically guarding his options until the very end. Many readers wondered if he would go through with the paper's prospective endorsement of the PQ. To be sure, he was a firm Quebec nationalist, but always within the context of the federal Canadian framework. It was the tradition of the paper, the fleur-de-lys and the maple leaf. Henri Bourassa's legacy. Claude Ryan's inheritance. It was not something he treated lightly.

He took everything seriously as concerned *Le Devoir*, a marginally profitable enterprise that he administered with no frills. When he moved the paper into a gloomy old building on St. Sacrement Street in Old Montreal, he consulted an interior decorator who asked how he would like his office done. "In white," Ryan replied. In this spacious but cheaply furnished room that looked more like a principal's than a publisher's office, he was beginning to write the concluding endorsement when his younger brother stuck his head in the doorway.

"I don't want to disturb you," said Yves Ryan.

The older brother waved him in. "Sit over there," Claude said, "I'll begin typing the article and I'd like you to see it as I write it."

They might go months without seeing each other. But now Yves, mayor of the distant suburb of Montreal North, said he just happened to be in the neighborhood of the old city during a Friday afternoon rush hour and decided to drop in. "You worried a lot of people this morning," he said. "You're taking a very serious risk."

The director of *Le Devoir* replied that he thought it was a risk worth taking. But he would say so in the most prudent and ambiguous of terms, covering himself every paragraph inch of the way. The PQ was supportable, he indicated, because its chief campaign plank was the promise of good government, with the assurance that its option of independence would be submitted to the people in a referendum. Between the apparently discredited Liberal administration of Robert Bourassa and the leap into the unknown with René Lévesque, the director concluded that it was better "to open the door on the future."

But even as he did so, Ryan left the door open for himself to go the other way. Buried in the middle of the editorial that would be quoted back to him hundreds of times in dozens of contexts, there was a paragraph of which no one later took any notice. "In those ridings where the Liberals or other federalist parties offer superior candidates to those of the PQ," he wrote, "a voter of federalist convictions should have no hesitation in voting for them."

Ryan was thinking particularly of his own riding of Outremont, and nearly said so. But as he was writing, he concluded it was better not to mention names. Reading this as the editorial came out of the typewriter page-by-page, Yves was reasonably satisfied that his brother had covered himself for any political eventuality. "He takes the long way home," the mayor would later say of his brother, "But he always gets there safely."

In spite of his qualified endorsement of the PQ, Ryan would personally take the way out he offered himself. The following Monday, November 15, he would vote for Liberal candidate André Raynauld, whom Bourassa had recruited from the chairmanship of the Economic Council of Canada, and whom Ryan had known for a quarter of a century since Raynauld, like so many other members of Quebec's political elite, had worked with him in the Catholic Action movements of the post war period.

Afterward, Ryan never volunteered this information on his own behalf. And no reporter ever bothered, or dared, to ask.

Robert Bourassa always had the first edition of *Le Devoir* delivered to him and when the paper came out that Friday night in November, he was taping some last-minute, last-ditch commercials at an English-language television station.

"Ryan is recommending a vote for the PQ," he was informed by campaign aide Jean-Pierre Ouellet.

"That's their problem," Bourassa replied with a rare note of sarcasm in his voice.

He did have other things on his mind that night. He was trying desperately to patch up the governing Liberal coalition of the French-speaking middle class and the English-speaking minorities, who gave every indication of deserting him in droves before the election was called and remained surly as the morbid campaign entered its final weekend. Given the high degree of dissatisfaction with the government and the widespread personal antipathy towards the premier — one of his own backbenchers had recently called him the most hated man in the province — it was doubtful the voters would heed Bourassa's dire warnings of the separatist peril, as they had in the two previous elections. Moreover, a proud Quebec electorate was susceptible to the blandishments of the PQ that autumn after experiencing a summer-long backlash in the rest of Canada against bilingual air-traffic control over the skies of Quebec. The wounds were still fresh in September when bilingual announcements were roundly booed at Toronto's Maple Leaf Gardens during the Canada Cup international hockey series. Ryan himself had written in his endorsement that "for English Canada, the election of a Péquiste government would have the effect of a salutary shock."

If Bourassa was not surprised by the editorial posture of *Le Devoir*, he must have been disappointed. From the beginning of his premiership, he had assiduously courted the favor of the director. Not only did Ryan enjoy being consulted by politicians, he practically required it as a condition of his support. For he was not merely an occupant of a splendid editorial tower, but an active participant in the brawling main street of Quebec politics. Nor did he have any qualms about the normal ethical proprieties that kept journalists at a certain distance from their sources. "There are those," he had once written, "who see the press as a sort of sanctuary which attends and reports events without being associated with those who make them." For himself, he was for the larger conception of journalism, "as incarnated in the United States by men like Walter Lippmann and James Reston and in Canada by men like George Brown, John Dafoe, and Henri Bourassa." The pundit as participant. This was not very humble. But it happened in Ryan's case, as in the others he had named, to be true. Ryan had stature. And he was not to be easily ignored. Robert Bourassa had done so only once, in 1972, when he shuffled his cabinet without consulting Ryan. The result, Bourassa would recall many years later, was an editorial with the headline, "The Triumph of Mediocrity."

So long as he was premier of Quebec, Bourassa would never again make that mistake. He attached such importance to *Le Devoir*'s support that when he recruited Yves Ryan as a prospective candidate and cabinet minister before the 1973 election, the premier first had someone check with the publisher to ascertain if he would have an ethical problem writing about a government of which his brother was a member. Claude Ryan sent word back that he would probably have to resign as director of *Le Devoir*. Bourassa quickly informed Mayor Ryan that while he was most welcome as a member of caucus, he could not enter the cabinet. Ryan declined, not without a touch of bitterness that his activities should be limited by those of his brother. But for Bourassa, it was an easy choice between the Ryan brothers.

"I found that Ryan was a valuable man," he said later. "He was one of the few intellectuals who was supporting us."

Bourassa still considered it important to have Ryan with him, if at all possible, as he pondered the calling of an early election in 1976, only three years after his election to a second term by a landslide of historic proportions that gave the Liberals all but eight ridings in the 110-seat

Quebec National Assembly. But the social and political climate had soured since 1973. The once moribund Union Nationale was resurgent in the polls, gathering an important protest vote. If Bourassa could not reverse the trend, he would lose the next election whenever he called it. And to nip the new Unionist coalition of old-line rural Quebec nationalists and disaffected English-speaking city-dwellers, Bourassa was inclined to gamble on an election sooner rather than later. That, as he confided to his Outremont candidate, André Raynauld, among others, was the real reason for the calling an election in the fall of 1976. The pretext upon which he seized in public, however, was the necessity of receiving a fresh mandate to negotiate new constitutional arrangements between the provinces and Ottawa. In the jargon of the day, Prime Minister Pierre Trudeau was threatening unilateral "patriation" of the British North America Act, it having occurred to Ottawa's mandarins that "repatriation" of the constitution was a contradiction in terms, since it had never resided in Canada.

On a visit to Canada late that September, British Prime Minister Jim Callaghan informed Bourassa that if Trudeau petitioned Westminster for patriation, he would have no alternative but to comply. As Bourassa walked with the British prime minister around the grounds of the Quebec government lodge at Lac à l'Épaule, where Jean Lesage had made the decision to call an election over the nationalization of the hydroelectric companies in 1962, it occurred to the premier that he had the election issue he needed. "In my view this was a determining factor," he said later. "Without it, I would not have called an election. Because historically Quebec fought unilateral patriation."

So he informed Ryan in early October during a private lunch at the premier's corner office on the 17th floor of the Hydro-Québec building in Montreal. Ryan later said he was not persuaded by the premier's arguments, and warned Bourassa "that he would lose an election if he called it that fall."

Bourassa had no such recollection: "He never told me anything like that; I would have remembered." Bourassa did recall that Ryan had said, as he wrote in the paper the very next day, that an early election "could be justified more easily today because of the extremely quick rhythm which characterizes social and political change."

But whether Ryan warned Bourassa in private that he would lose an autumn election, he did so in his editorial of the following day. Not only did the polls indicate trouble for Bourassa, Ryan noted, but he was getting it from his own private sources, in whom he placed a higher faith. He wrote of attending a banquet just the previous evening to mark the 75th anniversary of one of Quebec's leading financial institutions. Many of those in attendance, who by no means fit the PQ voter profile, spoke to him of their dissatisfaction with the Bourassa regime and their intention to support Lévesque in the event of an election. As an editorial touch, this was pure Ryan, a man who liked to say he was in contact with his readers, in touch with his world. He also noted that he had attended a meeting in Montreal's important Italian community, a bedrock of Liberal support, where a Péquiste panelist received warm applause while two Liberal participants were roundly booed at the very mention of Bourassa's name. As for Quebec's English-speaking community, another vital Liberal constituency, they were practically apoplectic over the the government's Bill 22, the 1974 law which made French the official language of the province and introduced proficiency tests as a condition of admittance for immigrants to English-language schools. Noting that Bourassa's three English-speaking ministers seemed to be in difficulty in their own ridings, Ryan wondered how Bourassa could turn all this around within the space of a few short weeks. Ryan was already sniffing the wind, and carefully weighing his own options. It remained to be seen, he ventured when the election was called a week later, whether the voters would prefer to return the present government "rather than saying yes to a leap into the unknown."

From the outset of the campaign, Ryan had signaled his disposition to consider an endorsement of the PQ more seriously than he had in the previous elections of 1970 and 1973. There was the PQ's solemn undertaking to hold a referendum on independence. There was its social-democratic orientation, which Ryan thought was a considerable service to the cause of democracy in Quebec. And there was the high level of dissatisfaction, as Ryan himself had noted in his own travels, with the Bourassa government.

But Ryan was also a politician, with his own constituency, the intelligentsia as well as the bourgeoisie. The intellectuals had all but given up on him after his endorsement of Bourassa for a second term in 1973, and it may have struck Ryan that this was an opportune moment to recoup. So it seemed to Gérald Leblanc, one of his senior political reporters, and an avowed independantist. "In the previous eighteen months he had become tougher and tougher on Bourassa," Leblanc later observed; "he thought that Bourassa had served the federalist cause, which was his own, badly."

Years later, Ryan said as much himself. "I kept looking at things and had grown frustrated with the Bourassa government, because I felt they were not delivering the goods," he said. "In the social field, Bourassa had lost his credibility; for right or wrong reasons, he was no longer credible. And we heard more and more stories to the effect that his hold over his cabinet had considerably weakened. Finally, I had difficulty trusting his word as a public figure at that time. At the end of six years in office he would skate all over the place and refuse to face up clearly to an issue. I thought to myself, this is not the kind of leadership to which Quebecers are entitled. And Lévesque, on the other hand, gave exactly the opposite impression. He gave the impression of a man who would tackle the issues squarely. And since they had decided to put their constitutional option between brackets for that election, it appeared to me that it would be a good time to recommend that the people vote for the Parti Québécois."

But it was not until November 9, six days before the election, that Ryan was convinced the PQ was likely to win it. On that Tuesday morning, Ryan and his editor-in-chief, Michel Roy, went over to the St. Antoine Street office of *The Gazette*, where in a fifth-floor boardroom they received the results of a public-opinion poll jointly commissioned by the two Montreal papers, *Le Soleil* of Quebec City and *The Toronto Star*.

Maurice Pinard was doing most of the talking. A McGill sociologist, Pinard was explaining how he and his colleague Richard Hamilton had worked over the numbers obtained by l'Institut de cueillette de l'information (INCI), which had been in the field the previous week. The PQ led the Liberals by an astonishing 2 to 1 margin, 52 to 26, among decided voters. Among those decided and leaning, the numbers were virtually unchanged. Even with the most favorable Liberal hypothesis, assuming undecided voters broke the way they did in the 1973 landslide, the PQ still led 42 to 35.

The numbers spoke for themselves: only the pollster's margin of error could save Bourassa. And Pinard knew that was unlikely. Fully two-thirds of his respondents, all across the broad but thin spectrum of Quebec's four million voters, said they were dissatisfied with the government.

"Bourassa thought an anti-separatist surge could turn the tide for him as it had in '73," Pinard later said. "But the tide had already been turned in '73. It had nothing to do with separatism, but with their satisfaction with the government, which was then very high."

Ryan was impressed. He knew Pinard was solid, knew his methodology was deep and that his extrapolations of the undecided and "discreet" vote were based on long-established voting patterns. Pinard was also a federalist, one of the Group of Seven that included Pierre Trudeau and Marc Lalonde who drafted the so-called "Canadian Manifesto" in 1964. Moreover, Pinard was a founding member of the Social Research Group, a 1950s outgrowth of the Catholic Action movements in which Ryan had spent half his adult life. Even so, Ryan later said he was taken aback. "It went beyond my expectations at that stage of the campaign," he said. "I hadn't thought it would be that severe against the government."

Pinard was reluctant to say how sweeping the trend might be in terms of seats. Robert McConnell, then assistant to *Gazette* publisher Ross Munro, asked if the figures didn't translate into a range of 70 seats for the PQ. Yes, Pinard allowed, if everything broke the right way. "I must say they were all very surprised," Pinard would recall, "not at the results, but at the predictions." Throughout most of the meeting, Ryan sat pokerfaced at one end of the table, chatting with *Gazette* editorial page editor, Tim Creery. In light of the projected results of the election, Michel Roy argued forcefully that the papers should simultaneously publish the second part of the poll, which indicated that a clear majority of respondents was against independence for Quebec. With an occasional word of support from Ryan and Creery, Roy carried the day. At the end of the meeting, Munro and Ryan withdrew to an adjacent boardroom. Munro, practically seized by panic, thought Ryan looked stunned. "But I was so flabbergasted myself, maybe my feelings colored his," Munro later remembered. Ryan recalled only that Munro was shattered by the poll, "that he could hardly believe it."

Long afterward, many wondered whether the tidings Professor Pinard bore that Tuesday morning tipped the editorial scales at *Le Devoir* in favor of the PQ. "I had the feeling it was important," Pinard said later, "but that's all I can say." For his part, Michel Roy, Ryan's closest professional associate, thought "it might have played a little bit. It had been a factor that had come into play in the past." It reminded him, Roy said, of a visit he had made to Tokyo, where he had spoken to editorialists who explained to him that the polls helped them take a position in elections. "I was quite struck by that," Roy said. "And I found a bit of that with Ryan."

Did the Pinard poll give Ryan a decisive push towards the PQ? "No, I really don't think it did," he said more than four years after the fact. "Frankly I think if you read all the articles I wrote in the month before the election, there was a strong trend toward the conclusion that was arrived at. But the very conclusion was arrived at only at the writing of the second article."

In fact there were those at *Le Devoir* who shared Gérald Leblanc's impression that far from encouraging him in that direction, the Pinard poll actually pulled him back from the brink and that until the last minute he was inclined to change his mind. "There's one thing you have to remember about Ryan," said Michel Roy, who worked with him for all of his fifteen years at the paper, "and that is that he has deep convictions on the national question, on the constitutional future of Canada and Quebec.

"And he was unreservedly opposed to the fundamental thesis of the PQ. But he was also quite convinced that we needed a bit of a cleaning up in the Quebec government. So he was ready to take the risk of supporting the PQ, on condition it wouldn't be for independence, but only for good government."

As the polls closed on November 15, the premier of Quebec was beginning the ritual of his daily swim. Nearly every day he was in office, wherever he was, he would swim between a quarter and a third of a mile. For some reason he had always refused to join a private athletic club, and insisted on swimming at public pools, as he did this night at the Centre Notre Dame on Queen Mary Road in the West End of Montreal. His critics thought it was typical of his obsession with his image. His friends thought it might have more to do with his working-class roots in his East-Central Montreal riding of Mercier, a marginal Liberal seat which he refused to abandon, in spite of all advice before calling this election, in favor of the safe Liberal fortress of Outremont. He would pay for that *hubris* later in the evening, going down to personal defeat.

But by then he fully expected to lose his seat. Only the day before, an aide had shown him a specially commissioned Gallup poll which indicated he would be defeated in his own riding by Gérald Godin, the radical journalist and poet who would go on to become Lévesque's immigration minister and unofficial ambassador to English-speaking Canada. What Bourassa thought, as he slipped into the pool on the evening of November 15, was that he had a chance, "not much of a chance, but a chance," of forming a minority government and forging a coalition with Union Nationale leader Rodrigue Biron.

He wasn't long in having his answer. When he came out of the pool at 7:30, his 16-year-old son François informed him of the early returns: the PQ elected and leading in six seats to the Liberals' one. Bourassa knew that an early election night trend is seldom if ever reversed. "It's finished," he told his son. The PQ would finish the evening with a 41 to 34 lead in the popular vote and a clear majority of 71 seats to the Liberals' 26. Professor Pinard's projections and predictions were to prove eerily and unerringly accurate. Half an hour later, as Bourassa's Cadillac made its way downtown to his headquarters at the Queen Elizabeth Hotel, there was already dancing in the streets.

Presently, a celebration was also underway at *Le Devoir*. "In the newsroom, they were joyful," Ryan later recalled. "They were exuberant, I was not. I thought it was a good outcome, but I was not especially exuberant." One celebrant was Ryan's former ace police reporter, Jean-Pierre Charbonneau, who had run in the election for the PQ and to his very great surprise had been elected in the Montreal-area riding of Verchères. "I can't share your enthusiasm," Ryan told him, "because I supported that party for other reasons than you." Spending a good part of the evening in the newsroom, Ryan had a special word with Gérald Leblanc, the former priest from Acadia who now declared Quebec to be his country. "You won't believe this," Ryan

November 15, 1976: Three generations of Bourassas watch the election returns. Adrienne Bourassa does not know that her son, the premier, is a beaten man. Her grandson François, having informed his father of the early returns as he climbed out of a swimming pool, is all too aware of what is about to happen. (Photo by Gerry Davidson)

told him, "but in the end I'm glad the PQ is in power. In opposition everything has been so easy for them. Everyone thinks they're so wonderful. Now we'll see what they can do." Nevertheless, Ryan appraised the election of the PQ as "the most important political event in Quebec since the end of the Second World War."

In a previously scheduled address the next day at the Chambre de Commerce, Ryan set an agenda for the incoming government, and warned that he would hold the PQ to its promises. The organizers of the luncheon had sold only a few hundred tickets before the election, but on the morning after, over one thousand persons turned up, jamming every corner of the hotel ballroom. They seemed to hang on Ryan's every word. Already, the search for a moral figure, if not a savior, had begun.

Ryan had a few parting shots for Bourassa. The defeated government, he said, was composed of a bunch of schoolkids. The outgoing premier, he suggested, should immediately resign the Liberal leadership. It was a theme he took up in the Wednesday edition of *Le Devoir*. Sitting alone in his Quebec office, the body still warm, as he later said, Bourassa heard this on a radio news report. This was one subject, he thought, on which he needed no advice from Ryan. He had already made up his mind to quit the leadership at year's end, and told his wife on the night of his defeat that he would go to Europe to study and teach for at least a year.

And so it ended for Bourassa. He had gambled and lost it all, apparently washed up at the tender political age of 43. And thus it began for Ryan. Because of Bourassa's fatal miscalculation, the Quebec Liberal party would be searching for a new leader who could respond to the political context created by the accession of the PQ.

Ryan had written as much in the final lines of his November 13 editorial endorsement of the PQ. "To defeat the Liberals," he had concluded, "would force them to profoundly revise their leadership and policy with a view to some of the most demanding confrontations ever seen in Quebec."

How far the Liberal party would go in that direction, how far it would carry him along with it, was not something Ryan could ever have imagined then.

2
THE LIBERAL ESTABLISHMENT: PICKING UP THE PIECES

It was not the first time Philippe Casgrain had been host to a series of informal meetings at the Club St. Denis. Ten years earlier, following the Liberal party's previous defeat in June of 1966, Casgrain had convened the leading lights of the party at this citadel of the bourgeoisie.

René Lévesque, then still a year away from breaking with the party over his constitutional option, was a regular participant in Casgrain's soirees. Another occasional guest was Robert Bourassa, the 33-year-old former secretary of a Quebec royal commission on taxation, now a freshman backbencher with an opportunity to make a name for himself as opposition finance critic.

Other Liberal legislators and activists would join the group as they talked vaguely about policy directions for the party, but seldom did they discuss what was really on their minds: the leadership of the party in the post-Lesage era. The Quiet Revolution was over. Its patron was tired. The final months of his six-year premiership had become something of an imperial reign. But no one dared to tell Jean Lesage that his political life was nearing an end. He lingered nearly four years in opposition, serving as a transitional figure who paved the way for his successor to restore the Liberal dynasty. When he retired from politics in 1970, it was with exemplary grace. Since the public phase of his life was now over, he made no further appearances in public, content to serve as a highly paid legislative counsellor to the new Bourassa government. In the last years of his life, Lesage slipped comfortably into the role of the party's elder statesman, whom everyone addressed as "M'sieu Lesage." But in 1966, even in defeat, he was still very much a force, a figure of considerable moral authority who was not to be lightly crossed.

And so as they sat around the St. Denis Club in the fall of 1966, they talked their way warily around the edges of the leadership question. Philippe Casgrain, then as later, was nothing more or less than a member in good standing of the Liberal establishment. A senior partner in the boardroom law firm of Byers, Casgrain, he was then married to Claire Kirkland-Casgrain, the first woman to hold cabinet rank in Quebec history. He was not the sort who was around very much when the party was in office, usually refusing "government mandates," as patronage work is known in Quebec law firms, saying it wasn't worth the trouble. All he wanted, when the party was in power, was to be able to make the big phone call on behalf of an important client.

A decade later, as the Liberals began to pick up the pieces after the shattering defeat of November 1976, Casgrain would again become an important figure in the renewal of the party. The interim leader, Gérard D. Lévesque, was a Quebecer who went to Montreal as infrequently as possible and was not well-connected within his own party there. It made sense that he should reach out to someone like Casgrain, as he did one night in the early winter of 1977, to organize a policy convention as a first step on the long road back. Extremely sociable, highly opinionated, capable of talking a blue streak in two languages, Casgrain knew nearly everyone who counted in the party in Montreal. And since he had no political ambitions of his own, he was a natural instigator for the renewal process.

He was by no means alone. The group he gathered around him at the St. Denis was one of many informal Liberal committees, most then unaware of the activities of the others, who would eventually coalesce in the choice of the new leader. But of the many groups meeting after hours in Montreal boardrooms and drawing rooms, the Casgrain committee was the most high-powered and influential. For starters, it had a mandate from the interim leader to pull together a policy meeting of the party, which he was determined should be held prior to a leadership convention. A wily parliamentary veteran of the Lesage and Bourassa administrations, Gérard D. Lévesque was in no rush to accommodate the panic-stricken members of the party who clamored for an early leadership congress. After twenty years on the front bench of the National Assembly, the interim leader knew the rhythms of Quebec politics, knew the Liberals were at an ebb, knew the flow was with the PQ, knew that a leader should be chosen only after the government's high tide had receded. By persuading the party to busy itself with preparations for a policy meeting in the fall of 1977, Lévesque could delay the leadership convention until the following year.

That sat well with the members of the Casgrain committee, who in their surgical post-mortems of the events of November 15 agreed that the party had given itself as a hostage to the previous leader. Analyzing the causes of the electoral debacle, they agreed it was vitally necessary to determine a policy orientation that would be binding on the new leader.

Apart from its policy mandate, the St. Denis group was terribly important by virtue of its composition. There were eight of them in all, four "ministerial" level members of the party and another four from its ranks of executive assistants. The senior members of the group besides Casgrain were Fernand Lalonde, Thérèse Lavoie-Roux and André Raynauld. Lalonde, solicitor-general in the defeated government of his law school classmate Robert Bourassa, had withstood the onslaught of November 15 and retained his seat in the legislature. Lavoie-Roux and Raynauld, though only first-term members of the National Assembly, had been the most prestigious recruits of the defeated premier. Lavoie-Roux had been the head of the Montreal Catholic School Commission. Raynauld had been chairman of the Economic Council of Canada. They gave the party a badly needed semblance of intellectual legitimacy.

The junior members of the group, all in their late twenties or early thirties, were to become its operatives in the organization and manipulation of the policy convention in the fall of 1977. Jean-Pierre Ouellet, a Rhodes scholar who had worked in Bourassa's office before entering private law practice in Montreal, was considered the intellectual of the foursome. The legmen were José Dorais, formerly a ministerial aide in the provincial justice department, and Charles Bélanger, a young courthouse administrator who would become executive assistant to Secretary of State Francis Fox upon the federal Liberals' return to office in 1980. But the key player was Richard Mongeau, later counsel to the McDonald Royal Commission into wrongdoing by the Royal Canadian Mounted Police. Before the defeat of the Bourassa regime in 1976, Mongeau had been executive assistant to Social Affairs Minister Claude Forget. Running the day-to-day affairs of the largest department in the Quebec government, Mongeau had developed and maintained a vast network of contacts across the province. Moreover, he was well-connected with the federal Liberals through his brother, Jean-Pierre Mongeau, then director-general of the Liberal Party of Canada's Quebec wing.

Jean-Pierre Mongeau was a new breed of back-room boy. Dispensing patronage was of little interest to him. A terrible administrator, he was a master of political intrigue. A one-time junior aide to the prime minister in the early Trudeau years, Mongeau had been executive assistant to Marc Lalonde before returning to Montreal to mastermind political intelligence for the federal Liberal party. Talking incessantly on the telephone, he cultivated his own province-wide network of contacts who kept him abreast of developments in all political circles, not the least in those of the new PQ government.*

---

* Jean-Pierre Mongeau, who worked as a senior aide to the secretary of state after the federal Liberal restoration of 1980, was later named a full-time member of the Canadian Radio-Television and Telecommunications Commission (CRTC).

The defeat of the Bourassa government had hardly been declared before J. P. Mongeau's phone began ringing. Though the federal and provincial parties had separated into autonomous entities in the mid-sixties, largely so that each would feel free to develop its own constitutional policy, they were effectively one and the same party at the grass-roots level. One of the residual Liberal strengths was that, though the provincial party was now out of power, its membership could turn to the "cousins," very much in power in Ottawa. "When one leg is cut off," as pollster Maurice Pinard has suggested, "it still has another leg to stand on."

Never was this source of Liberal strength more apparent than in the days after the triumph of the PQ. And never were the party rank and file more in need of sustenance and comfort. Seldom were they more susceptible to take-over by the cousins. For Lalonde, who had a well-earned reputation as a political hardball player, the temptation to move in on the provincial Liberals may have been difficult to resist. Jean-Pierre Mongeau later said he had "an enormous debate," with Lalonde and Trudeau's chief Quebec organizer André Ouellet, who were "a bit worried" about the evident disarray in provincial Liberal ranks and "tried to take control" of the party and dominate the leadership convention.

As Mongeau later recalled his discussions with Lalonde and Ouellet, he tried to persuade them that their role was to be supportive of the provincial party until it could again support itself, not to attempt a takeover while it was in a weakened state. Ouellet later denied this. "You mustn't exaggerate," Ouellet said, pointing out that he was an early exponent of the view that the provincials should turn for leadership to an outsider. "My own idea from the outside," Ouellet later maintained, "was that as long as the Liberals didn't choose someone who was a former minister or federal minister," they would be well placed to win the next election. Among others, to Ouellet's way of thinking, this eliminated his colleague, Jean Chrétien, the minister of finance.

Within the Casgrain group as elsewhere, the idea of Chrétien or anyone else from the federal cabinet as a prospective leader, was dismissed much more quickly than it was by the news media, or for that matter, by Chrétien himself. "There was a lot of resentment against the feds at those meetings," recalled Jean-Pierre Ouellet. "We figured they had cost us three or four points in the campaign." Indeed, the provincial Liberals were still simmering with resentment over Trudeau's Quebec City speech in March of 1976, in which he denounced Bill 22 as politically stupid. Earlier that day, as he entered the lobby of Bourassa's office, the prime minister had replied to a reporter's casual question about their luncheon menu by saying he imagined they would be having hot dogs, because "everyone knows Mr. Bourassa likes hot dogs." The headline, with Trudeau calling Bourassa a "mangeur de hot dog," did the premier considerable damage. The provincial Liberals were also bitter over the federal government's wishy-washy solution to the *Gens de l'Air* dispute over bilingual commercial flight controls in Quebec during the summer of 1976. While Trudeau went on television to describe the situation as the gravest threat to Canadian unity since the conscription crisis of the Second World War, he was able to defuse the situation only to the extent of naming a commission of inquiry, which eventually reported its findings that bilingual air traffic control was perfectly safe. But that was not until 1979, long after the damage had been done on the provincial hustings in the fall of 1976. Any gains the Bourassa government might have made with moderate nationalists over Bill 22 went down the drain in the *Gens de l'Air* crisis.

But perhaps most damaging of all had been the federal government's policy of tightening milk production quotas in the summer of 1976. This enraged Quebec's dairy farmers, many of whom relied entirely on milk production for their incomes. A delegation of militant Quebec farmers went to Ottawa that summer and splattered milk all over the face of Agriculture Minister Eugene Whelan. The feds still didn't get the message and the angry farmers took it out on Bourassa at the polls that fall. "That milk policy," said Jean-Pierre Ouellet, "cost us badly in the Eastern Townships. Everywhere there were cows, we got murdered."

But most of all, in circles like the St. Denis group, Quebec Liberals knew they had mostly themselves and Bourassa to blame. While the former premier took up temporary exile in Brussels that winter to study the economic federalism of the European Common Market, his one-time adherents were harsh in their judgments of him for events that got out of control during his second term. After the excellent technocratic reforms of his first administration, including a massive consolidation of hospital services, Bourassa's second government was plagued by a series of public-service strikes, a succession of minor scandals, and runaway spending at the James Bay and Olympic construction sites. As the government lurched from one crisis to the next, the premier seemed to be its principal crisis manager. With few other ministers in public view, the government appeared weak. Its leader looked irresolute and obsessed with his standing in public opinion polls.

Drawing on these perceptions of the causes of their defeat, Quebec Liberals gradually sketched a rough composite of the kind of leader they needed in the post-Bourassa era.

First, they wanted someone with proven intellectual credentials to do battle with the PQ in the coming referendum. Second, they had to find someone with no links to the past, specifically with the discredited Bourassa administration. Third, they were looking for a leader of unquestioned moral integrity. "Everyone," as Jean-Pierre Ouellet later put it, "was very sensitive about the public morality issue."

Quebec Liberals were looking for someone, as Jean-Pierre Mongeau summarized it, "who was free of the past, someone who wasn't a puppet of Ottawa." Above all, they were looking for someone who could win the referendum for the federalist side. These stringent criteria effectively eliminated prospective candidates from Ottawa like Chrétien, and otherwise attractive leadership possibilities such as Raymond Garneau, the able minister of finance in the Bourassa government. Widely liked within the party, Garneau was written off by the Liberal establishment because of his links with the defeated government.

Before very long, in the Casgrain group as in other informal gatherings, the emerging consensus was that the party must look for an "outsider." The name of Montreal Mayor Jean Drapeau came up and was quickly discarded because of his association with the scandalous Olympic cost overruns and because he was known to be a political loner.

Among all the prospective candidates, one stood out: Claude Ryan. His name was mentioned in the Casgrain group as early as January of 1977. It would be a few months before the various members of the Liberal establishment in Montreal would get around to discussing it with Ryan. But the idea immediately took hold, and the fact that he had so recently endorsed the PQ was not considered an important obstacle to his candidacy. As Casgrain cheerfully told Ryan in their preliminary discussions months later, "if anything, you made the same mistake as thousands of others."

This was a tribute to the Liberals' capacity to put the past behind them, to say nothing of their pragmatism. For Quebec Liberals, who considered themselves born to rule, the instinct for power quickly reasserted itself in the winter of 1977. There would be a long, twilight struggle, but already they were confident of emerging victorious. As for their defeat, it was quickly rationalized as an opportunity for renewal. The victory of the PQ soon came to be regarded as an accident of history.

Claude Ryan did not think so. At least, if he thought so, he did not then say so. As early as a speech before the Canadian Club of Montreal in late November of 1976, and the next month in a column for *Maclean's* magazine, he maintained that the PQ victory was neither an accident "nor the erratic product of spontaneous growth." Rather, he asserted, "it marks the return to power in Quebec of a school of thought that has always played a key role in our collective life." The fundamental difference between René Lévesque and his nationalist forebears such as Honoré Mercier and Maurice Duplessis was that "the new party in power in Quebec not only questions the federal structure but is resolved to replace it with a structure in which the first and ultimate locus of power will reside in Quebec."

Just so. And though Ryan was soon quarreling with the new government, he sent up a number of friendly signals at the very beginning of the Lévesque era. On the day after the cabinet was unveiled by Premier Lévesque, Ryan wrote a positively lyrical commentary in *Le Devoir* about the "impressive dignity" of the televised ceremony from the old Legislative Council chamber of the National Assembly. "Clear and incisive as always, calmer and graver than he is usually is," Ryan wrote of the new premier, "Mr. Lévesque dominated, as he should have, this first day of his new government."

But Levesque either failed to receive the warm message or failed to be moved by it. In either case, he wasted none of his time consulting Ryan. It was the premier's first step on the road to making an important adversary for his government. "I've been used to governments who would have a great respect for the paper, and myself in particular, who would heed my opinions to a large extent," Ryan later said with a characteristic lack of modesty that nevertheless accurately described his role in those years.

"But we rapidly realized with the Lévesque government," he continued, "that it was going to be somewhat different, you know, and they would like to keep their distance. And they would like, in effect, to ignore what would be written. Especially by myself."

In short, Ryan's feelings were hurt. He would marshal his criticisms and bide his time, awaiting the right moment to unload on the new administration.

He did not have long to wait. Only two months after the swearing-in of the new government, on January 25, 1977, the premier flew to New York for an important engagement before the Economic Club of New York, a forum for Wall Street movers and shakers. Quoting extensively from the American Declaration of Independence, Lévesque delivered a finely crafted but poorly observed address that squarely stated the separatist aims of his party. Understandably, the audience was unmoved.

And at least one member of the audience, Claude Ryan, was very angry. "I felt we were being betrayed," Ryan recalled. "You know, after all the assurances they had given that their constitutional option would be put between brackets, for the premier to come up on such a formal occasion and assert as clearly as he did the option for independence of his party as implicitly as he suggested, was very shocking to me. And I said to myself, I won't let that go that way, because the thing I had always been afraid of in Quebec would be the kind of drift that would lead us to a conclusion we didn't want, because of our indifference or passiveness. I thought to myself, I will not be an accomplice to that. Being editor of *Le Devoir*, I felt it was my duty to react in the way which I felt I should, regardless of the mood of the time."

Back in Montreal the next day, Ryan wrote his first substantive criticism of the new regime. In an editorial entitled, "Why the New York trip was a failure," Ryan leveled Lévesque for misreading his audience, and for saying things he had lacked the candor and the courage to say at home. "Though Mr. Lévesque's vigorous and original personality made a favorable impression on his hosts," Ryan concluded, "the message he delivered did quite the opposite: it contributed to prolonging, rather than ending, the anxious state they are now in, due to new sources of tension in a country of which they are quite fond." As for Lévesque's subsequent charge that an "Anglo-Canadian fifth column" of businessmen had infiltrated the audience to sabotage his welcome, Ryan later acknowledged that many Canadians attending Lévesque's address greeted his speech with "excessive abruptness." But from there, "to infer, as Mr. Lévesque did, that these elements were responsible for the skeptical reactions to his address, is to twist the truth unashamedly, and to credit the premier's American hosts with less intelligence than they possess."

But it wasn't until April, when Cultural Development Minister Camille Laurin published the Charter of the French Language, that Ryan declared an abrupt end to the government's honeymoon. "In its present form," he wrote of what was then Bill One, and would later be enacted as Bill 101, "the Lévesque government will have succeeded in saddling Quebec with some of the most stifling restrictions ever seen in linguistic and administrative matters. At first glance, the shocking thing about this bill is the rigid, dogmatic, possessive and authoritarian manner with which it attempts to decree the exclusive use of French." And that was just the beginning. His criticisms of the Laurin bill were withering and unrelenting.

"Starting from there," said *Le Devoir* editor-in-chief Michel Roy, "the campaign of editorials hostile to the PQ was unceasing, and reached a crescendo that lasted until his departure. I found the tone a bit excessive. But by then it was evident that the battle, not the battle but the war, against the PQ had begun."*

In the beginning, at least, Ryan found that it was a lonely fight. The government was riding the wave of its popularity and paid no attention to Ryan's criticisms. "I think I was perhaps the most persistent and active opponent of that piece of legislation," he said. "But they would speak and act as if I just did not exist. As if nothing had been said. You know, they were continually invoking that atmosphere of unanimity which allegedly existed around their legislation. And I said to myself, 'I hope to God that Quebec will never drift into such a state of intellectual conformity.' "

Ryan was particularly hurt that he was not invited to debate the language legislation on Radio-Canada. It was on English-language television, on the CBC regional program "Decision," that he finally had a memorable dustup

---

* In 1982, Roy became editorial-page editor of *La Presse.*

with Dr. Laurin in early June. The argument continued for many minutes after the conclusion of the program. If Laurin wouldn't introduce generous amendments to the bill, Ryan warned his longtime acquaintance, "you'll force me to go into politics, and I wouldn't like that at all."

But by then a lot of Liberals had the same idea, and in those days they liked it a lot. In a way, Ryan had already become leader of the opposition in Quebec. And the drafting of Claude Ryan for the Liberal leadership, over the summer and into the fall of 1977, was simply confirmation of the obvious.

Ryan couldn't be exactly sure, but afterwards he thought Pierre Mercier might have been the first person to broach the idea of the Liberal leadership with him. It was one day in May or June and Ryan, true to his frugal nature, was having lunch as he often did at Murray's restaurant near the newspaper in Old Montreal.

A corporate lawyer whose own office was nearby, Mercier was one of those establishment Liberal figures who, like Casgrain, surfaced after a defeat. A good deal more discreet than his colleague, Mercier remained completely in the background, practically unknown to political reporters. In fact, he played a critical role in persuading Ryan to enter the leadership race.

Mercier had married into the Liberal party. His father-in-law, Elie Beauregard, had been speaker of the Senate in the St. Laurent era. It was much the same family history with Gilles Hébert, who would become the other key fund-raiser in the Ryan campaign. A successful municipal lawyer in his own right, he was the son of G. René Hébert, a lumber magnate and for many years the provincial Liberal bagman in Montreal. The elder Hébert actually carried a little black book with all the right phone numbers in it. Like father, like son. One of Gilles Hébert's neighbors, a couple of blocks over in the upper reaches of Outremont, was Pierre Mercier. Contemporaries at the University of Montreal law school in the mid-fifties, they had quietly been scouting leadership prospects in the spring of 1977. It occurred to them, as it had to the members of the Casgrain group, that Ryan was an intriguing possibility.

"He was the man of the moment," Mercier later said of the Draft Ryan period in 1977. But at the beginning, the notion seemed so preposterous, even to those people behind it, that they didn't quite know how to bring it up with Ryan. When he bumped into Ryan at Murray's that day, Mercier casually asked if his brother Yves might be interested in the leadership and would the publisher have a word with him about it. When they met again a few days later, Ryan brusquely informed Mercier that he should find another intermediary if he wished to initiate serious conversations with the mayor of Montreal North. "I was kidding the other day," Mercier replied, "It's you some people will be after. I want you to think about it. I'm dead serious."

Ryan had a busy round of speaking engagements that spring, and he was beginning to hear the same thing from people who came up to him after meetings. It was a season when voters wanted to hear new ideas on the constitutional question. And wherever people began talking seriously of renewed federalism and a third option, Ryan was invariably a keynote speaker or a panelist who stood out from the rest. Before long, Liberal activists began to match his face with the constitutional issue.

At a spring seminar sponsored by the young federal Liberals in Montreal, Ryan shared the stage with Claude Forget; the Quebec Liberal constitutional critic, Gérald Beaudoin, dean of the University of Ottawa law school who would later serve on the Task Force on Canadian Unity; and Jean-Paul L'Allier, the former communications minister in the Bourassa government and a leading spokesman for the nationalist wing of the Liberal party. And there was Ryan, who somehow seemed better prepared, who seemed to have thought things through as he talked about how to renew the Canadian link. Sitting in the first row, Lucette St. Amant turned to former federal cabinet minister Jean-Pierre Goyer and said: "Our chief, we've found him."

Lucette St. Amant could start a leadership campaign all by herself. As a young woman, she had come to Montreal from Rouyn-Noranda nearly twenty years before to work as a publicist in the election that vaulted Jean Lesage to office. She had worked in every election since. Lesage thought enough of her to have her fly back from Paris, where she was studying, to run the publicity side of his 1962 election on the nationalization of electricity. The natural resources minister, Réne Lévesque, met her at Dorval Airport, and briefed her on the nationalization plans. She knew Robert Bourassa well enough to warn him that if he called an election in the fall of 1976, he would be a private citizen by Christmas. Like Casgrain, Mercier and Hébert, she had never looked for rewards when the party was in office, and so was around to help pick up the pieces after a defeat. She was a formidable woman, an organizational whirlwind and a non-stop talking machine who wasn't the least bit shy about approaching Ryan. She marched right up to him after the meeting and planted herself squarely in his path. "Everyone is wondering what we're going to do for a leader," she told him. "Well, we've found him."

Ryan laughed at the suggestion, as he was inclined to do whenever it was made, but in fact he rather fancied the idea. Before long he was discussing it with some trusted friends and associates. "From the summer of '77 on," recalled Michel Roy of Le Devoir, "hardly a day passed that he didn't speak to me about it. He spoke of it constantly. One sensed that it was a major preoccupation for him. Some days he was enthusiastic and talked of the things he could do, and other days he saw the danger of the Liberal party, and thought it would never change. He thought, 'no I'm wasting my time with that, I'm better to remain in journalism.'"

Ryan discussed the possibility of his candidacy with at least one important visitor to Le Devoir, Finance Minister Jean Chrétien, himself a prospective candidate. In Montreal to attend a baseball game one night in June, Chrétien and his trusted aide Eddie Goldenberg called on Ryan. They had a wide-ranging discussion that eventually settled on what was on both their minds: "I see three possible candidates," the director said. "Claude Castonguay, you and me." Chrétien thought he was hearing things. Goldenberg told him he had heard right. Several years later, reminded of the incident and asked if he had been joking, Ryan gave a cryptic one word reply: "Probably."

There is no question that in the summer of 1977, Chrétien rather fancied his own chances. At the age of forty-three, "Le p'tit gars de Shawinigan" had already come a long way in national politics. He was the first finance minister of French-Canadian origin in Canadian history. But he could reach no higher in Ottawa. Trudeau, riding the crest of his popularity on the national unity issue that summer, was certainly in no hurry to retire. And even when he did leave, the road to the Liberal succession appeared blocked to Chrétien by the party's tradition of alternating French and English-speaking leaders. Chrétien liked to say, then as later, that it hadn't prevented eight English-speaking candidates from running against Trudeau for the leadership in 1968. But Chrétien must have known that many of his own caucus colleagues from Quebec were among the most determined that the principle of alternation be maintained after Trudeau's retirement, so that they could put in a claim for one of their own the next time around.

And so Chrétien was looking around in 1977, quietly scouting his own prospects. The fact that he was from the federal side was considered a serious obstacle to his candidacy, especially among journalists and intellectuals. But hadn't Jean Lesage himself, father of the Quiet Revolution, come from Ottawa in 1958 after a stretch in the St. Laurent government as minister of Indian affairs? That, said the intellectuals, was twenty years ago. Besides, Chrétien was too closely aligned with the centralist policies of Trudeau. He was also sneered at for his "My Rockies" speeches, so well received in Western Canada but an embarrassment to some people at home who saw him as some kind of performer in a minstrel show.

Still, there was a vacuum of leadership in the Quebec Liberal party in 1977, and Chrétien was prepared to step into it if he could be sure of having no serious rivals at the convention. He was not without important support in the business community, notably from his friends at

Power Corporation, where his former executive assistant John Rae now worked as an executive in Paul Desmarais' holding company. Desmarais was Chrétien's kind of guy, a brash kid from a small town who had made it big in a world that had formerly been considered an exclusively English-speaking domain. More than that, Chrétien and Desmarais were fast friends.* If and when Chrétien decided to go for the leadership, he could count on important moral and financial support from the influential Desmarais circle in Montreal. Moreover, after Trudeau himself, no federal minister was more popular than Chrétien among Montreal's English and minority ethnic communities, core constituencies for the Liberals. He was the only big name to turn up at a Forum rally organized early that summer by some nervous English-speaking residents of West-End Montreal who wanted to show the flag at the height of the separatist scare. Chrétien also had some prominent supporters in the National Assembly caucus, notably Michel Gratton, the Gatineau MNA and founder of the Quebec-Canada movement, and John Ciaccia, who represented Trudeau's silk-stocking district of Mount Royal in the National Assembly and who had been Chrétien's assistant deputy minister of Indian affairs.

But that wasn't enough. And as Chrétien well knew, none of these elements represented the establishment wing of the Quebec Liberal party. They would come to him only if there was no one else, only if the overtures to Ryan proved fruitless, only if someone like Claude Castonguay turned them down. Castonguay, who had been minister of social affairs in the first Bourassa administration, had an immense and possibly inflated reputation as its only intellectual before he left government to go into business in Quebec City in 1973. Now head of a large Quebec insurance firm, Castonguay's reputation had

---

* In May of 1981, they would be bound by family ties when Chrétien's daughter, France, married one of Desmarais' sons, André, who had gone to work for the justice minister as press secretary.

grown, if anything, in the years since he quit politics. He was not much of a public speaker — even Ryan's speeches were stemwinders by comparison — but he was cerebral, competent and clean, the qualities the Liberals were looking for. Often in touch with Ryan, Castonguay made it clear that he was interested in the leadership only if Ryan wasn't. And there was aiways André Raynauld, who had come from Ottawa to be sure, but had been an independent figure as head of the Economic Council. He, too, met the intellectual criteria and qualified as an outsider. The establishment would have preferred either Castonguay or Raynauld to Chrétien.

If Chrétien were to consider seriously leaving Ottawa to run for the Liberal leadership in Quebec, the active opposition of *Le Devoir* would be the last thing he needed among intellectuals and establishmentarians. And so he went to Ryan a second time in the month of June and made it clear that he would be available under the right circumstances. Chrétien later claimed this was a private and confidential conversation in Ryan's confessional, as some people called his office at the newspaper. But Ryan, being a newspaperman and perhaps wanting to test the climate of Chrétien's prospective candidacy against his own, gave the story to Michel Roy. After checking the story with his own sources in Ottawa, Roy wrote it himself and ran it prominently on page one the following day. It created no boomlet for Chrétien and the finance minister was forced to issue an angry denial that he had any intention of leaving Ottawa.

That cleared the way for Ryan. By the time he went on vacation in the Laurentians north of Montreal, the newspaper publisher had some serious thinking to do. He spent a good deal of his leisure time reading a copy of the correspondence between Robert Baldwin and Louis-Hippolyte LaFontaine, the two great unifying figures of the United Canadas in the 1840s. Ryan may have thought he could play such a role himself. Though he was still inclined not to enter the undeclared leadership race, he found the pressures on him mounting.

For one thing, the members of the Casgrain group had decided to make him the central figure of the party's November policy convention by inviting him to give the keynote address. The invitation was conveyed over lunch before Ryan went on vacation in early July by the convention chairman, Michel Robert, whom Casgrain had recommended for the job to Gérard D. Lévesque. A young law professor and labor lawyer who was also known as the "silver-tongued advocate" in courthouse circles, Robert was himself considered an attractive longshot possibility for the leadership. "We discussed thoroughly what would be his participation in the congress," Robert remembered, "but at the end he himself started to ask me about the subject of the leadership. I think he was basically interested to know if I was a candidate. I told him I was not interested and that he would make a good candidate. I think he was pleased with that. I think in hindsight the important part of the lunch was the last five minutes."

With Ryan's appearance set for the November convention, the ground was now prepared for Casgrain to go public with the Draft Ryan movement. It turned up for the first time on the front page of *The Gazette* in mid-September. Suddenly, Ryan was beseiged by callers assuring him of their support. He was forced to issue a statement in his own newspaper saying the story was essentially true, and that he was seriously considering running for the leadership.

Thus began what would later be known as Ryan's first period of reflection.

3

"THIS DAMN WORD IRREVOCABLE"

From the time Ryan was named publisher of *Le Devoir* in 1964, hardly an election passed without his being approached to run for office at one level or another, for one party or another. Mike Pearson was the first to go after him before the 1965 federal campaign, when the prime minister was trying to put together a team of new faces from Quebec that would be led by labor leader Jean Marchand, newspaper editor and columnist Gérard Pelletier, and a wealthy but obscure law professor named Pierre Elliott Trudeau.

Except for the fact that he was a loner by nature, Ryan might have been persuaded to join them. And so to Pearson and other federal or provincial leaders who courted him as a candidate, Ryan's answer was always the same. Though he was undoubtedly flattered by the attention, he was too deeply involved in his work, and wouldn't even consider it. He didn't exclude the possibility of entering politics one day. But if that time ever came, as Aurelien Leclerc noted in an early study of Ryan, he hoped to be chosen by the voters rather than imposed by a party.

When Ryan's moment finally arrived in the fall of 1977, when he was being offered not just a seat but the leadership on a silver platter, the difficulty was not in persuading him that he could be chosen by the people so much as in convincing him that he could be imposed on the Quebec Liberals. And in those months, even some of his staunchest supporters entertained serious doubts about his suitabililty for a political career.

As he vacillated for weeks, Ryan seemed hopelessly incapable of making up his mind. His self-proclaimed period of reflection became an agony of indecision. Ryan made things worse for himself by announcing deadlines for deciding whether he would run, and then pushing them back. Finally, he was determined to make his intentions known before the policy convention where he was scheduled to give the keynote address on November 19. In this, he ignored the advice of Casgrain, Gilles Hébert, and others who had implored him not to decide one way or another before attending the convention where he could measure his reception against the confident assurances he had been receiving from his supporters.

They were under the impression that he was coming through a maze of consultation to a positive decision for making the leadership race. By early November it was generally assumed in Montreal journalistic and political circles that he had gone too far down the road to turn back, that he had compromised his professional purity at *Le Devoir*. Suddenly, almost impulsively, Ryan announced on November 7 that he would not run. His decision, he concluded in a statement published in his own paper the next day, was "firm and irrevocable."

It was the word "irrevocable" that slammed the door on the Liberal party. And, as Ryan would soon discover, his own foot was caught in it. Later, when the draft started up again, he would wonder if there was a way of getting out of "this damn word, irrevocable."

Before issuing the statement, Ryan showed it to his editor-in-chief, who urged him to take it out. "But it was a guarantee against himself," Roy surmised. "He wanted to raise a barrier against himself." Ryan himself would later admit that this was exactly what he had in mind.

Ryan's decision not to run in November had its origins in his conviction that he could not win the convention without the support of the Liberal establishment. And he had profound doubts, despite the frantic efforts the establishment was making on his behalf, that it was really supporting him.

Then, as his brother Gerry Ryan observed, the draft was still spontaneous and uncoordinated, lacking an organizational core. "Up to then the organizational efforts had not been very inspired," said Judge Ryan, a member of the Quebec Superior Court and the oldest of the three brothers. "They were more panic-inspired than anything else."

Moreover, Ryan was for some reason terribly concerned about the sullied financial image of the party, which had always subsisted on corporate donations. Such donations were being outlawed by the Lévesque government, but Ryan still wondered about financial skeletons in the Liberal closet that might come back to haunt him later on. "He was terribly worried," as Michel Robert recalled, "about the finances of the party that may have been obtained in an improper or even illegal way."

In sum, Ryan was afraid the Liberal party would not support someone like him, in spite of the new, democratic procedures that had been adopted by a general council of the party in Sherbrooke that September. The new ground rules required that one-third of the delegates be Young Liberals, and another one-third women. There would be twenty-four delegates from each of the 110 ridings, 2640 delegates in all. Even sitting members of the National Assembly would have to get themselves elected in their own riding associations.

Most significantly, there would be no delegates-at-large, a break with custom in most Canadian parties. This would make it almost impossible to pack the convention, as the party's former chief organizer, Paul Desrochers, had done for Bourassa in 1970. Then, some 300 delegates-at-large from the establishment ridings of Outremont, Westmount, Jean Talon, and Louis Hébert in Quebec, had voted en bloc for Bourassa, ensuring his first ballot margin of victory over Claude Wagner and Pierre Laporte. Wagner would later claim, with considerable justification, that the convention had been rigged against him. A very sore loser that January day, he practically had to be dragged to the podium.

Paul Desrochers was very much on Ryan's mind in November. Known as Bourassa's chief political fixer, Desrochers had left the former premier's service, as he liked to say, "on April 1, 1974," to take a job as a vice-president of Canada Permanent Trust, and claimed he had not been active in politics since then. While it was true that Desrochers had for the most part sat out the 1976 debacle, he remained a figure of mythic proportions within the party, widely admired and not a little feared.

Appointed chief organizer by Lesage after the 1966 defeat, the first thing Desrochers did was go off to the United States to see how the Kennedy and Rockefeller organizations ran modern-day elections. In addition to cultivating these sophisticated marketing techniques, Desrochers developed and maintained his own network to keep him informed of the mood of the province. Desrochers' eyes and ears across Quebec were insurance salesmen, brewery representatives, and his fellow members of the Knights of Columbus, the arch-conservative, lay Catholic organization.

Gradually, Desrochers developed a profile for the man who would eventually succeed Lesage. Quebecers wanted young leadership for the 1970s, and they wanted an economic manager at the helm. *Et voilà*, Robert Bourassa, only thirty-six when he was elected Liberal leader and later premier in 1970, a lawyer and economist, trained at Harvard and Oxford.

By the fall of 1977 it was no longer true, if it ever had been, that Desrochers was inactive within the party. Because of an old war wound that chronically bothered his back, Desrochers slept very little, and was usually at his desk in Montreal long before most people got out of bed. Constantly on the telephone, he had stayed in touch with the organizers whom he had brought along and installed in the Lesage and Bourassa years, and who were still in place in Montreal and across the province. And what he was hearing from them now was that something must be done.

On the last weekend in October, Desrochers gathered a few dozen of his faithful protégés together at the Dauphin Motel in Drummondville, midway between Montreal and Quebec. They talked, in a general way, about where the party should turn next. The Saturday meeting was really nothing more than a serious bull session. But though quite inconclusive, it was dramatic evidence of Desrochers's continuing influence within the party. And it was this wing of the party, the organizers as opposed to elite groups like Casgrain's, that made Ryan extremely nervous. He simply did not think he could prevail at a convention where the party professionals opposed him at Desrochers's bidding. And Desrochers's leadership preference, if he had one, was a mystery to Ryan.

This played on the profoundly suspicious side of Ryan's nature. He was spooked, as one of his prominent supporters, Claude Forget, would recall, "about the obscure, unknown and unpredictable forces." As all his supporters would eventually learn in one way or another, Ryan did not give his trust easily, and he was not the type to put himself in the hands of anyone.

"I was not sure of the party at all," Ryan said later. "I knew little about its structure. I knew little about the real people of influence in the party. I had my own impressions but I could not take them for very sure things, you know.

"So I think that my decision was probably influenced by the uncertainty in which I was about the state of the party, about what I could expect from it. I kept hearing organizers were extremely important and I did not want to become a thing in their hands. And I think I was repelled by that unconsciously."

And so it would be "No" to his seeking the Liberal leadership. Before putting out his statement, Ryan informed prominent supporters like Casgrain that the circumstances just weren't right. There was numbing disappointment and shock among Liberal activists who had built the November meeting around him. "After that," said Casgrain, "it was far from sure that he would even be invited. Lots of guys were mad as hell." Ryan himself offered to withdraw as keynote speaker to spare the party the embarrassment of his presence. But convention chairman Michel Robert insisted he appear anyway.

When some 2,000 Quebec Liberals gathered at Montreal's Bonaventure Hotel on the evening of Friday, November 18, the party managers were in something of a daze. It was one year and three days after the defeat. Time to begin the long march back. But they still hadn't found a leader to take them down the road.

With Ryan out of the leadership picture, the so-called Outremont Mafia turned their attention to the race for the party presidency. Their strategy was a simple one — to turn the convention into a holding operation to ensure that the party was not delivered into the hands of anyone else while the establishment resumed its search for a savior.

In the week before the convention, it appeared likely that the presidency would be won by a Quebec City marketing specialist, a longtime party activist named Guy Morin. He was a close friend and unwavering supporter of Raymond Garneau, the former finance minister who was regarded as the prospective leadership candidate of the old guard. The implications of Morin winning the presidency were all too obvious to the Montreal-based establishment crowd. For one thing, Morin would be able to control arrangements for the leadership convention, and could deliver the party into the hands of the old guard. For another, the Quebec City wing would take control of the party. It was too much. The Outremont crowd were determined to stop it. And so, late in the game, they invented a man named Lawrence Wilson.

It didn't matter that hardly anyone in the party knew Larry Wilson, a wealthy Outremont attorney who had been active before the 1976 election on the Liberal party's legal commission. He was the establishment candidate, and everyone was soon made to know it.

The gang of four "executive assistants," who had attended the Casgrain evenings, now swung into action with all deliberate speed. With Richard Mongeau masterminding the operation, Charles Bélanger ghosted an article for Wilson that appeared on *Le Devoir's* "Ideas" page on the eve of the convention. Mongeau also called in his brother, Jean-Pierre, and together they collected a lot of political debts. "I had a lot of IOUs in my pocket," Jean-Pierre Mongeau said. "And I took them out and cashed them and I wasn't the only one."

It was pure political hardball, an awesome display. As the delegates swept down the escalator to the convention hall, they would be met by one or the other of the two Mongeau brothers. They and their operatives reminded delegates that Wilson was a wealthy lawyer who wouldn't accept the $30,000 salary that went with the president's job. He would work for free. As a lawyer, which Morin was not, Wilson would be able to administer the financial affairs of the party. Finally, and most of all, he was against Garneau.

Wilson was shown around the convention hospitality suites by an organizer named Georges Boudreault, one of the most popular figures in the party. When the Liberals were in power, Boudreault had a licence-bureau concession in Montreal, and he favored his fellow organizers with small but important favors like low-numbered licence plates that impressed people in the neighborhood at the riding level. Moreover, he was a streetfighter. His territory was the tough East End of Montreal, the PQ heartland where Boudreault had to fight for every vote, even in the Bourassa sweep of 1973. But Boudreault was no mere political hack. He favored a renewal in the party and was an important link between the establishment and the rank and file. With his thatch of prematurely grey hair, habitual smile and ever-present Tiparillo cigar, Boudreault was instantly recognized everywhere on the floor. With Boudreault escorting him around the convention, Wilson didn't put a foot wrong. Guy Morin never had a chance.

The success of the Wilson campaign ensured that the pro-renewal wing in Montreal would keep control of the party for its own candidate. Perhaps Claude Forget or Claude Castonguay. Perhaps Michel Robert, if he made a big impression as convention chairman. Perhaps even Claude Ryan, if the Liberal party could yet persuade him to change his mind.

Ryan's mind was quite made up. But he may have felt a twinge of regret as he stood off to one side of the hotel escalator on that Saturday morning. What he was hearing from delegates as they streamed into the convention was not that they resented his decision, but that they regretted it. This was the sentiment wherever Ryan went in the day-long policy workshops. But it was nothing compared with the reception the Liberals had in store for him later on.

4
DRAFT RYAN

It was as if they were determined to change his mind for him. When Ryan was introduced to the convention on Saturday evening, he was engulfed in a wave of applause, a whistling, cheering, footstomping ovation that went on for three full minutes that altered the course of Ryan's life.

Long afterwards, Ryan would wonder if it had been spontaneous or laid on. "It was spontaneous," said Jean-Pierre Mongeau, "but if it hadn't been we would have arranged it." There was no claque as such. But a lot of people in the audience may have had the same idea as Philippe Casgrain. "Let's keep it going," he said to Jean-Pierre Ouellet as the ovation began to taper off. "Maybe we can make him change his mind."

It was certainly enough to set him thinking again. He was vain enough to be flattered, emotional enough to be moved, insecure enough to be shaken. The acclaim was quite authentic. It was an invitation to lead. And afterward, everyone, including Ryan, thought it was an important turning point.

After that, it didn't matter much what he said, and it didn't matter how he said it. The delivery of the speech was, for Ryan, routinely soporific. He wore his heavy glasses and bowed his head to the text he had written up in an hour or so during the afternoon.

It would be known later as the Third Option speech, mapping out a middle road that Quebec federalists were seeking between independence and the status quo. Ryan suggested the country could be reorganized into five regions: Atlantic Canada, Quebec, Ontario, the Prairies and British Columbia. He was more or less thinking out loud of a way the constituent parts of the federation could be regrouped into roughly coequal regions for a better functioning of the whole. It was Ryan's contention this would put each part of Canada on a stronger footing in dealing with Ottawa.

Among reporters, the speech would be remembered for Ryan's "Five Canadas," a notion which he threw up as a talking point and discarded the moment he became a serious politician. Nothing was ever heard of it again. It didn't matter to the Liberals that on this main point, Ryan was talking about something that sounded very neat in theory but was unattainable in practice, without first consulting the people of five provinces that would be wiped off the map, to say nothing of the five governments and premiers who would be put out of work.

For the delegates, what mattered was that Ryan had devoted a career to thinking about constitutional reform. He had both *civitas* and *gravitas*, a sense of public spiritedness and unmistakable substance.

And he left them on a note whose emotive quality could not be ruined even by his monotonous delivery. "No matter what the results are, after the referendum we will have to go on living together," he said to the hushed audience, who knew the importance of what he was saying from the divisions they were experiencing even then in their everyday lives.

"This very perspective," he concluded, "should lead us to conduct the struggle with utmost dignity, respect for facts and for the opponents' dignity; it is a struggle that promises to be the hardest and harshest in our history."

He sat down to another standing ovation. Madeleine Ryan, who rarely went to hear her husband speak, was in the audience that night because she "wanted to see what it was, the Liberal party."

The applause hadn't subsided when people who knew her, knew the discreet but profound influence she exercised on her husband, began lobbying with her to change his mind.

"He's the man we need," Pierre Mercier told her, entering a plea that rested on the immense ovation.

"Yes, but they're all Liberals," Madeleine Ryan replied, apparently unimpressed.

"Yes," Mercier conceded, "but a standing ovation."

Ryan himself heard the same thing as delegates button-holed him on his way out of the hall.

"After all that's happened here today," Boudreault told him, "that standing ovation; can you still refuse to be leader of the party?"

"Come and see me next week." Ryan replied as he went on his way.

The senior people in the abortive draft of Ryan caucused right there on the floor. "We've got to start up with Ryan again," Casgrain remembers one of them saying. And so they would. Only this time, when he challenged them about their ability to deliver, they would have answers for him.

"If we want to have Ryan," Gilles Hébert told a group of like-minded Liberals that weekend, "we'll have to prove to him that we can deliver, because with Ryan you have to do your homework; you have to prove to him that you're right."

First of all, as Claude Forget said, they "realized they needed someone to open the door again." Forget, as a prominent member of the parliamentary wing, and Hébert as a member of the party establishment, went to Ryan's home on Monday evening for a meeting that ran well past midnight.

Ryan lived in Outremont now. But he was not of Outremont. He had grown up in the underprivileged East End of Montreal and lived for nearly the first ten years of his marriage as a tenant in a very ordinary flat in East-Central Montreal, near the Gilford Street headquarters of the party he would one day lead.

Even now that he lived in Outremont, where the intelligentsia rubbed shoulders uneasily with the bourgeoisie, he occasionally reminded people that he didn't live "up there" on the northern slope of Mount Royal, with the likes of Bourassa and federal cabinet minister Jeanne Sauvé, or for that matter with Hébert and Mercier, two of his closest future advisers. No, Ryan lived "down below" in a modest duplex, just inside the Outremont line from Montreal, only a block away from polyglot Park Avenue.

And it was true. Ryan's house was sparely furnished. The carpets were threadbare. But it was his house, nearly all paid for by now, with an upstairs tenant. The one room he cared about was his study, with its brown leather armchair, the desk piled high with papers, and the walls lined with books. It was here that he received a stream of visitors over the years. And it was here that he greeted Forget and Hébert at the end of a long day at the paper.

Ryan's visitors told him they wanted nothing more than the chance to put together an organization chart that would give some indication of his support at all levels of the party, all across the province. "We'll make an *organigramme*," Hébert said, "and we'll be back to you within a week." All they wanted was Ryan's say-so and when they went away, well past midnight, they had it.

By morning, Georges Boudreault was on the phone placing calls to people he knew across Quebec. "I called all 110 ridings," he said later. "I called the man who was best at organizing, who was not necessarily the party's organizer in the riding." When Boudreault had obtained the commitments he wanted, he went to the home of Jacques Lamoureux, a young lawyer and chief organizer for André Ouellet in the federal riding of Papineau in East-Central Montreal. Lamoureux, who would become chief organizer of Ryan's leadership campaign, was known for his outer calm and inner toughness. By 3:30 on Wednesday morning, they had the *organigramme* which demonstrated deep commitment for Ryan everywhere in Quebec. They had something for Hébert to show Ryan. "It was then," as Lamoureux said, "that we began to structure the campaign."

With Ryan, as they learned, something had to be on paper as proof of its existence. The *organigramme* wasn't just a lot of loose talk and promises. It was tangible evidence that there was support out there for him. Ryan was impressed. Privately, he agreed to reconsider.

Meanwhile, he was playing out a demanding schedule of speaking engagements, and he was leading the league in standing ovations. In Quebec City, on the first Saturday of December, Ryan appeared as the keynote speaker at the founding meeting of the Pre-Referendum Committee, a fledgling coalition of federalist forces. There were fourteen organizations represented at the Château Frontenac, from the powerful federal Liberals to the right-wing fringe of the provincial Créditistes. There was no way for the Pre-Referendum Committee to fly as it was structured, with every party and unity group having a theoretically equal say of two votes under the umbrella. It was bound, in retrospect, to fail. But it was Créditiste Camil Samson, a gifted stump speaker who spoke in similes and metaphors, who summarized the commonly held hopes of that founding meeting. "When the house is on fire," he said, "it's not the time to fight over the choice of colors of the firemen's uniforms."

But Ryan was the principal attraction. As he rose to address the closing luncheon in the Château ballroom, he received another standing ovation. The job of the federalist forces, he said, was very simple. They had to find a way of turning a "No" at the referendum into a "Yes" for renewed federalism.

That would be quite a feat, and the founders of the umbrella committee thought Ryan would make an ideal chairman. In Montreal a few days later, a few of them took him to lunch and offered him the job. For a time, Ryan was sorely tempted, torn now between the prospect of becoming Liberal leader and head of the federalist forces, a nonpartisan position.

It was Jacques Lamoureux who presented the most compelling arguments for the Liberal leadership. "What good does it do to win the referendum," he asked Ryan, "if there is no one there to win the next election?" Ryan also knew that according to Bill 92, the enabling legislation for the referendum recently enacted by the Lévesque government, there would only be one official umbrella committee when the time came, controlled and directed by the leader of the opposition: that is to say, by the leader of the Quebec Liberal party. It did not take Ryan very long to discard the option of leading the Pre-Referendum

Committee outside the National Assembly. If he became Liberal leader, it would have to do his bidding anyway.

By mid-December, the news media had the story that Ryan was beginning a second period of reflection. He wasn't reflecting so much as consulting with everyone around him. Ryan was now completely preoccupied with the leadership question and the tension rubbed off on his colleagues at *Le Devoir*. But there were moments of black humor. At one point, Ryan showed a list of his supporters to his political columnist, Pierre O'Neill, who had worked for the Liberal party in the 1960s and had followed Lévesque into the independence movement as his press secretary for a time before joining *Le Devoir*. O'Neill knew the Liberal party inside out, and he knew most of the names on the list. "Mr. Ryan," said O'Neill, a sombre man with a permanent expression of brooding, "you're surrounded by a gang of crooks."

But Ryan's most serious consultations were with his wife and his two brothers. On a mid-December Sunday morning, the four of them met in Mayor Ryan's City-Hall office in Montreal North. All the brothers later agreed it was an important meeting. For two hours, Ryan reviewed his options and prospects with the three people he trusted most in the world, perhaps the only people he truly trusted.

"He made up his mind in excess of 50 percent at that meeting," Judge Gerald Ryan said later. "He consulted us because he knew he would get an honest gut reaction from us."

And Gerry Ryan noticed a change in Claude since he had last discussed the matter with him prior to the November policy convention of the Liberal party. "Before the November gathering, he put the emphasis on the negative factors," the judge said. "It's my conclusion that the reception he got in November plus renewed pressure from private sources led him to reconsider. I got the impression, and I think Yves did after that meeting, that he would go. But there was certainly no decision reached."

By now, the two brothers agreed that Claude should try for the leadership. It was the judge's view, as Claude recalled it, "that after fifteen years with *Le Devoir* I had made my contribution there and might have another contribution to make in another field." As for the mayor, a down-to-earth politician with his own network of contacts at the municipal level, he had changed his assessment of the situation and was now urging his brother to run. "You must go, you must," he said, as Claude recalled it. "I've gathered impressions and reactions and it's quite contrary to what I expected."

As it became evident that Ryan really might change his mind, there were many who wondered if he hadn't merely been testing the wind with his negative decision in early November. Some people who worked with him always thought so. But those who were closest to him never believed it. "That wouldn't have been entirely strange," said Michel Roy, "but the man wasn't as calculating as that. I think he thought after speaking with his wife, who was his principal adviser, and his two brothers, that it would be better not to go."

"He was happy where he was," said Madeleine Ryan. "He loved his work at *Le Devoir*. Then it was a big decision for him to take at the age our children were at." The five Ryan kids, then aged 10 to 18, were dead against their father's prospective entry into politics.

By Christmas, Ryan was finally moving towards an irreversible decision to seek the leadership. On December 27, Lucette St. Amant had a party for Ryan to which she invited the two dozen people who would form the core group of his campaign. Ryan kept insisting that there were problems. "We need a chief organizer," he said. Jacques Lamoureux was there. "We haven't got a financial chairman," Ryan said. Gilles Hébert agreed to take it on.

"That meeting was decisive," Ryan allowed later, "because they had made their own surveys with responsible people in the party. They felt we had a very strong chance of winning the convention if I made the decision to run."

When Ryan went home that night, the main elements of his campaign organization had apparently fallen into place. Even his fears about Paul Desrochers were allayed over the Christmas season when the former chief organizer visited Ryan and assured him that he would do nothing to thwart him, that indeed he would quietly support him.

Desrochers had taken thorough soundings of his own. At a second meeting of his friends at the Dorval Hilton on December 10, some 200 organizers cast a straw poll, in the form of a secret ballot, for the party's next leader. Desrochers had put five names on the ballot: Ryan, Jean Drapeau, Jean Chrétien, Raymond Garneau and Gérard D. Lévesque.

Georges Boudreault, who counted the ballots, later said that Ryan beat everyone else combined by a 2 to 1 margin. Desrochers also was aware of a preferential poll of delegates to the November convention after Ryan's speech, and that he was the overwhelming choice. Whatever Desrochers might think of Ryan, he was no fool. The director of *Le Devoir* was the clear consensus choice of the party. In mid-December, Desrochers called on Mercier and Hébert to assure them that he would play no role in the convention. "Paul was for Ryan," Mercier said, "and he understood that he had to be on the ouside, but he suffered from it."

Ryan spent New Year's with his in-laws at Lévis, across the river from Quebec. He consulted with old friends like caucus member Julien Giasson, a comrade from the Catholic Action days who agreed to serve as chief organizer for the eastern half of the province.

Back in Montreal after the holiday, Ryan went ahead with a final organizational meeting that had been scheduled for January 4. But before meeting with his supporters that Wednesday evening, he sat down at the manual typewriter in his office.

What he turned out in the next hour ran to his usual length of five or six pages double-spaced. And he wrote in his accustomed style, numbering all the points he wished to make. But it would not appear on the editorial page of the next day's paper. Instead, Ryan would read the text aloud to his assembled campaign team. To the two dozen people gathered at Montreal's Richelieu Hotel, it sounded rather like an ultimatum. In fact, it was. Ryan was posing what would later be known as the seven conditions of his candidacy.

"The organization of this campaign must not," Ryan recited, "be infiltrated, influenced, controlled or intimidated by any outside forces." He was thinking, though he did not name him, of Paul Desrochers, as he made clear a bit further on. "We don't need any kingmaker, and we must refuse any interference by those who would play such a role."

He went on to enjoin his supporters to refrain from "any dishonest methods, anything illegal, any intellectual trickery." He wanted a guarantee from his financial committee that it would not accept corporate donations, and so conform to the spirit of the Lévesque government's financing law which outlawed such donations and placed a $3,000 ceiling on individual donations. Though the law applied only to elections, leaving parties to manage internal affairs like a leadership campaign as they saw fit, Ryan wanted to comply with it anyway. He didn't want the PQ saying he was a creation of the bagmen and a creature of the corporate fatcats.

Furthermore, during the three-month leadership campaign, the organization would have to pay him the equivalent of his salary at *Le Devoir*. Moreover, in the event of losing the convention, he demanded the equivalent of his salary for a three to six-month period while he found other work, since going back to the paper was out of the question. Nobody was shocked by this condition, which everyone in the room thought eminently reasonable. What struck them as odd was the fact that Ryan insisted on putting it up front, and making such a big deal of it.

What no one present could understand at all was Ryan's drawn out shouting match with André Raynauld, the member for Outremont and former Economic Council of Canada chairman, over the economic resolution adopted at the November policy meeting. Among his seven conditions, Ryan said he would not be bound by the free enterprise resolution that called for a substantially reduced government role in the economy. The resolution had been Raynauld's baby. More to the point, perhaps, Raynauld had only recently decided that he would not himself be a leadership candidate, and Ryan may have wanted to test his loyalty. It was, as Ryan himself remembered it, "a tough exchange."

It was more than that. For Ryan's supporters, it was puzzling. For Raynauld it was humiliating.

"I had the impression," Raynauld said later, "that he wanted me completely on my knees. He spent a good part of the evening saying he wasn't sure he wanted to run because of a divergence of opinion with me."

Ryan's insistence that the party recognize the realities of a mixed economy was taken as a matter of course. It was the last thing on anyone's mind. But Raynauld, a certified intellectual who was not in the least intimidated by Ryan, said it was common knowledge he had a hand in writing the economic resolutions, and that he could not remain silent if Ryan insisted on attacking it. "But these aren't differences," Raynauld told him, "just slogans. I'll be loyal."

Years later, Raynauld would vividly recall this memorable dustup. "I found it very disagreeable," he said after leaving politics in 1980, "and a bit crazy for him to behave like that." It wasn't, as Raynauld said, enough to make him change loyalties in the leadership campaign, but he never forgave Ryan for the humiliation.

No one else who was there ever understood it, or forgot Ryan's adamant mood on the evening of the seven conditions. Even one of his own brothers, when he heard about it, was a bit taken aback. "Jesus Christ, you've got a lot of nerve," Gerry Ryan told him. "Don't humiliate them by telling them what they must accept."

But accept the conditions they did. Even so, over the final weekend, before his scheduled announcement, Ryan wavered again. And for most of the weekend, it seemed he wouldn't run. "He was," said Pierre Mercier, "a bit like a patient the night before his operation."

But there was more to it than pre-op jitters. On January 6, Paul Desrochers bumped into Brian Mulroney after a leisurely Friday lunch at the Beaver Club, the Montreal restaurant where senior executives went to be seen.

Mulroney, whom Ryan had enthusiastically supported for the Progressive Conservative leadership in 1976, was a longtime friend of the newspaper publisher. Though many years younger — Mulroney was then only 38 — the lantern-jawed Irishman from Baie Comeau had made it his business to know Ryan from his first days as a Tory activist. Mulroney had a hand in recruiting Yves Ryan as an unsuccessful Conservative candidate in the Trudeau-mania sweep of 1968. He remembered standing with Claude Ryan on the edge of a hysterical crowd of 40,000 who greeted Trudeau on the plaza at Place Ville Marie during the spring campaign of 1968. Since Ryan was endorsing Tory leader Robert Stanfield, the two men agreed, as Mulroney recalled, "that this was a very deplorable turn of events, and we immediately adjourned for a long lunch. "

After Ryan began to reconsider in December, he asked Mulroney for a list of do's and don'ts in the running of a leadership campaign. Mulroney, who still bore the marks and the bitterness of his defeat at the Conservative convention, drew up a fourteen-point handwritten memorandum that Ryan carried around in his pocket for weeks afterwards.

Whether Desrochers knew of Mulroney's friendship with Ryan, whether he wanted the exchange to get back to him, is not known. It's also possible Desrochers was just talking out his hurt at being a kingmaker without a king to crown. Mulroney thought he was talking straight. He was certainly talking tough. Desrochers denounced Ryan in the most categorical terms, and said there were many people in the party who didn't want it taken over by him. He thought Jean Chrétien might be the man to stop him. In any event, he left Mulroney with the clear impression that he would do anything to stop Ryan.

After he left Desrochers, Mulroney urgently phoned Ryan and asked to see him immediately at Le Parrain et La Marraine, a restaurant on Notre Dame Street up from *Le Devoir*.

"Who's Desrochers supporting?" Mulroney asked.

"He's supporting me," replied Ryan, explaining that "Mon Oncle Paul," as he was known with varying degrees of affection, had been to see him a few days before.

"He's got a funny way of showing it," said Mulroney, detailing his conversation with Desrochers. "You're having lunch at the wrong place, Claude. This is the big league now. The boys play rough. They're going to cut your throat."

Ryan was shocked. He went back to the newspaper and told Michel Roy he wasn't running. Roy who remembered the incident clearly as *Le Coup Mulroney*, said Ryan was "very upset, very agitated. Mulroney had told him, 'Watch out, Paul D. has sworn you won't be leader.'

"I remember," said Roy, "he was almost worn out, intellectually, morally, physically."

Ryan himself later acknowledged that he "wavered for about forty-eight hours," after his Friday afternoon meeting with Mulroney. "Brian had presented to me a very dark picture of all the prospects," he said. "It kept striking me that I probably could not overcome all those forces which were strongly entrenched in the party. It may have been a very illusory thought that some people had tried to develop in me."

Whatever, Ryan was a wild man, almost paranoid, that weekend. Since many of his own prospective advisers had been raised in politics by Desrochers, Ryan saw himself surrounded by enemies. Jacques Lamoureux, who had been a protégé of Desrochers, bore much of Ryan's suspicious wrath. Ryan thought he might be some kind of political mole who had been placed in the Ryan camp by Desrochers. Lamoureux quit on the spot after a very tough conversation with Ryan on Saturday night. It was Lucette St. Amant who finally talked some sense into Ryan. "If you want to play into Desrochers' hands," she told him, "you're going about it the right way if you let him scare you out." The next day, Ryan patched it up with Lamoureux.

But it was still far from certain that Ryan was running. There was still one more meeting over that Epiphany weekend at Ryan's house with his wife, his brothers and his 79-year-old mother, Blandine Ryan.

They agreed that Ryan should go, but only if his conditions were met. And on Sunday evening, he gathered his political advisers for one final run-through at his house. Hébert and Mercier were there with Boudreault. Julien Giasson had come down from Quebec. Claude Forget was in touch from his chalet in the Laurentians, although he did not come down to the city. "By that time I had grown a bit weary," he said, "not of fighting opponents, but of fighting him."

Ryan's advisers still had a fight on their hands. "I'm not going," Ryan told them, "our organization isn't strong enough, we have no money."

For three hours, they took him through it again. Finally, he agreed that he would go. When he came out of his study, his children were waiting for him.

"What's the decision?" one of them asked.

"It's yes," their father replied.

In the living room, Denys Pelletier was also waiting for Ryan's decision. A Montreal notary and son of *Le Devoir*'s second director, Georges Pelletier, he was president of L'Imprimerie Populaire, the trust that administered the newspaper.

When he had spoken with Ryan a few hours before, Pelletier had the strong impression that he would not run. Now Pelletier knew from the faces of the smiling party activists that "he had either changed his mind or had his conditions fulfilled."

Ryan introduced his advisors to Pelletier, who was a stranger to most of them.

"I want you," Ryan said to them, "to meet my former boss."

And so he had done it, at last.

5
INSIDER, OUTSIDER

Fromthe beginning, it was a case of insider versus
outsider, only the outsider was the insider, and the
insider was the outsider.

If ever the Liberal party of Quebec owed its leadership
to one man, that man was Raymond Garneau. Though
he was then only forty-three years old, Garneau had spent
all his working life in the Liberal party. He had risen
through the ranks, from assistant director of its Quebec
office, to economic researcher in Premier Lesage's office,
to chief of staff when Lesage was opposition leader after
the 1966 defeat. In 1970, Garneau had run for the new
Bourassa team in the Quebec City riding of Jean Talon,
a historic Liberal seat whose voters expected their member
to be in the cabinet.

They were not disappointed, as Garneau first became
a 35-year-old minister of state and then a 36-year-old minister of finance. Nor did they have any reason to be disappointed in his performance. In the 1973 election, Garneau
played a starring role, demolishing the PQ's economic
spokesman Jacques Parizeau and his "Budget of the Year
One," of independence. Because he was young and attractive, Garneau was one of the few members of the
administration welcome on campus in those days when
most students were ardent Péquistes. His star rose so
high during the second Bourassa government that he
became known as *le Dauphin*. As the premier's popularity
plummeted, Garneau's stock rose. Though he loyally refused to be a party to any intrigues, there was talk of him
succeeding Bourassa before the next election.

For a time, Garneau even shouldered a double load
as minister of education for a few months in 1975 after
the precipitous resignation of the moody Jerome Choquette.
Being minister of education at any time in Quebec is a

thankless task. Being minister responsible for implementing
Bill 22 in the schools, as the education provisions in the
language act came on stream, was a brutal burden for
Garneau to carry, in addition to the routinely onerous
finance portfolio at a time of heavy deficit-spending to
finance the Olympic Games. But Garneau did whatever
the premier asked. And he went wherever the party asked,
even to campuses in the bleak campaign of 1976.

When the Liberals left office, no survivor of the debacle
had more accumulated credits than Raymond Garneau.
He was young but experienced, loyal and talented. No
one had a more legitimate claim on the leadership.

He never had a chance.

For many Liberal activists, including some who may
have considered Garneau the obvious successor to Bourassa
when the party was in power, the choice of a new leader
was dictated by the circumstances in which the party
found itself. Once the heir apparent, Garneau was associated with an exiled and discredited regime. Since he
had the misfortune as finance minister to have responsibility for the liquor board and the provincial lottery, he
was tainted by association with a couple of minor scandals.
And he was still young, even baby-faced, at a time when
the party was trying to project an image of experience,
which he had in abundance.

Garneau was a man without important enemies in the
party. But more important, in the Liberal leadership race,
he was a man without important allies.

For many Liberals it was an affair *contre-coeur*, against
their own hearts, against their own better natures, and
for some of them eventually against their better judgment.
They thought it took someone like Ryan to win the referendum. And they told Garneau, in words that rained
on his heart.

"Raymond," Georges Boudreault had told him during
the November policy convention, "I would love to be
with you, but I can't. We need a renewal."

Garneau was hearing the same thing from establishment figures of the party who bluntly assessed his prospects. "You're a dead duck," Pierre Mercier had told him.

Within practically every influential quarter of the party, he was rudely rebuffed.

"They'd say, we like you," he recalled without a trace of bitterness years later when he had become president of the Montreal City and District Savings Bank. "Then they'd say, you'd do a good job as premier, but to win the referendum we need Ryan. That's what they'd tell me. I would answer, and I think my analysis was factual, that neither Ryan nor Garneau would win the referendum, but the cause, that in any event it would be an amalgamation of opposition forces."

And so the party's power brokers lined up against him, even though, of all the prospective candidates, Garneau was the one who spoke out of conviction for their interests. He was for individual rights as opposed to the collectivist vision of the PQ, a free-enterprising economist opposed to the interventionist policies of the new government, a staunch and strong federalist who made no apologies for saying as he always did that "Quebec is my home, but Canada is my country."

Yet they stood against him; the elites, the bourgeosie, the English, and the minority ethnic groups stood with a man who had endorsed the PQ in 1976. They were not looking for a candidate, as Garneau observed, "they were looking for a savior."

Most damaging to Garneau's hopes was the active opposition of the Liberal establishment. He couldn't define it with any precision, but he knew who comprised it.

"The establishment in any party is a moving concept," he later observed, "because it's not always the same people. But they're always found in groups that play a leadership role."

That's why, he said, you found the establishment in ridings like Louis Hébert in Quebec, and Outremont and Westmount in Montreal. "They are people who are very active, first of all," he said. "They have important jobs, they are interviewed on radio and television, they are invited to answer questions by the media. And, well that's the establishment, and they can build roads because of the access they have to public opinion."

Then why, with everything he had going against him, did Garneau run? "I have no choice," he told his friend Jean Chrétien in December of 1977. "I have to run because if I don't they'll say I have something to hide." Garneau was then referring to recurrent allegations that he was somehow mixed up in a patronage scandal. The veil of doubt was finally lifted from Garneau's head just before Christmas, when Lévesque's justice minister, Marc-André Bédard, formally and publicly absolved him of any wrongdoing during the Bourassa era.

And then, he really had no choice but to run, since he had nothing to hide. Damned if he didn't, Garneau was certainly damned if he did. He knew from the outset that it would be "very, very tough" for him, even if Ryan didn't come in.

Garneau knew a campaign would cost money, a lot of money, even though "we had none at the beginning of the campaign." By some kind of perverse symbolism, he rented a big storefront office on the ground floor of Place Dupuis, a spanking new office tower housing the Dupuis Frères department store that would go bankrupt later in 1978. He was not entirely without friends. Victor Goldbloom, who had been Bourassa's municipal affairs minister, was with him, but he could not deliver much support in the Jewish community. Paul Berthiaume, an able young cabinet minister who was defeated in 1976, served as campaign chairman.

It was Berthiaume who introduced Garneau to the Montreal news media when he announced his candidacy on the stormy afternoon of Monday, January 9. The sleet and snow closed the road from Quebec to Montreal, preventing some of his supporters in the capital from coming for the news conference. Still, as he announced his candidacy, it was a proud moment for *le p'tit gars de Plessisville*, who had come a long way in life from his Eastern Townships village, to the University of Geneva where he obtained his master's degree, to membership in the provincial cabinet. Now he sought to lead the federalist alliance in the referendum, and he hoped someday to become premier of Quebec. His hopes would rise no higher.

At that moment, only a mile or so away in Old Montreal, Claude Ryan was clearing out at *Le Devoir*.

On his last full day at the paper there was little time for reminiscing and no hint of regret at the prospect of his crossing the floor, in a sense, of his leaving journalism to enter politics. If anything, now that the agonizing was finally behind him, Ryan was serene.

When *Le Devoir*'s board of directors convened to receive his resignation, they also wanted his opinion on the succession. That was something they would have to work out on their own, Ryan told them. He had run the paper from stem to stern for more than a decade. Now it was their ship. He was not the type to waste much time in sentimentalizing over his departure. "Pain," as Michel Roy observed, "passes very quickly for him."

He had reserved the right in his letter of resignation only to publish one final editorial in which he could "take leave of the readers of *Le Devoir*." It was left to Roy to express the paper's gratitude to Ryan in an extraordinarily warm and well written tribute. "He not only served the institution," wrote the editor-in-chief, "in fifteen years he gave everything he had to this paper: his time, his health, all his intellectual resources, his passion." Comparing Ryan with the paper's illustrious founder, Henri Bourassa, Roy asserted that "none was greater than Bourassa, but Ryan was the greatest of his successors."

For Ryan, there was nothing more to do at *Le Devoir* but bid farewell to his staff and be on his way.

On January 10, a horde of reporters and a claque of supporters crowded into a salon of the Hotel Meridien to hear Ryan announce his candidacy. "Having given the matter serious consideration," he began, "I've decided I must put aside a career I was very attached to, right up to the end, and immerse myself in politics."

Explaining the reasons for the reversal of his "irrevocable" decision of only two months before to stay out of politics, Ryan said he was now convinced of the Liberal party's need for a leader of "new faith, familiar with the realities of the milieu, known for his reputation for integrity, and respected by his fellow citizens."

Typically, it wasn't a very modest advertisement for himself, but it was a fair summary of how the voters regarded the prospect of his candidacy. For Ryan felt he was responding to a very genuine draft, not just by the managers of the Liberal party, but by the electorate at large. By the likes of the bus driver who had taken him downtown the previous day, and the cabbie who drove him to a television interview earlier that afternoon. Wherever he went by now, his angular face was recognized. Though he was known as an intellectual, he had an easy and genuine rapport with ordinary working people. His reception on the street, he said later, "was stronger than I anticipated because I had never expected that much from the public at large. I knew I was respected. But I never expected this sort of moral draft to occur. And it was really that. You should have seen the reactions in those days."

Filing out of Ryan's press conference, some reporters noticed something on his first campaign poster. Alongside a broadly smiling Ryan, there was a long quotation he had found in Arnold Toynbee's last book, *Choose Life*. "If a democratic regime is to function satisfactorily," the political philosopher had written near the end of his life, "it needs a leader who is neither a trickster nor a demagogue, but a person of such ethical and intellectual worth that his fellow citizens will follow his lead without having to be either coerced or emotionally excited. Such a leader may be hard to find and, if found, may be reluctant to undertake the difficult and thankless task of guiding his fellow citizens. The leader's role is obviously of the greatest social importance; to undertake it for altruistic reasons requires a very high degree of public spirit and unselfishness."

It occurred then and there to some people covering Ryan that he really was going to be different from other politicians who devoted a great deal of their time to perfecting their thirty-second clips for television. There had never been anyone quite like him. Imagine, a politician quoting Toynbee on a campaign poster. Nobody had ever heard of such a thing.

That was how Ryan saw himself, answering a call. But there was a more apt description of him, though it had been written nearly three quarters of a century earlier about a prospective US presidential candidate named Woodrow Wilson. "Certain personal attributes are essential to successful candidacy," one George Harvey had written with the Princeton president in mind. "Known fidelity to high ideals. Unquestioned integrity. Veracity. Courage. Caution. Intellectuality. Wisdom. Experience. Achievement. Breadth of mind. Strength of body. Clarity of vision. Simplicity in manner of living. Eloquence. Human sympathy. Alertness. Optimism. Enthusiasm. Finally and practically: availability."

That was Ryan, right down to the ground. And now that he was available, he intended to run his own show, and he meant to score a smashing victory. "Right from the beginning," chief organizer Jacques Lamoureux said later, "the idea was to win big, so as to minimize the divisions in the party afterwards."

"Some of my people had that philosophy," Ryan acknowledged later on. He had a simpler explanation: "I have always tried to win big in all that I have attempted."

Ryan was determined from the outset to control his organization. "In those days," said Lucette St. Amant, who ran the publicity side of the leadership campaign, "Ryan listened to only one person: Ryan."

Since he first considered running in mid-1977, Ryan had an obsessive concern with the financing of his campaign, and a need to know that the party establishment was behind him. These concerns merged in the choice of Hébert as his bagman and Bernard Langevin as his treasurer. Hébert's father had been the Liberal fund raiser before him, just as Langevin's father, Hector, had been the party treasurer. Hector Langevin had also been a director of *Le Devoir*. His son Bernard, a man of Ryan own's generation, struck the candidate as reliable and trustworthy, as far as Ryan was willing to trust anyone with his campaign funds. "He followed it pretty closely," Langevin said much later; "I was giving him a report every day, how much was coming in, what went out and where it went."

As Hébert and Pierre Mercier had known, and as Ryan could never have known, they had no difficulty in raising money for him. Ryan had been terribly afraid that he would finish the campaign with a huge deficit. He knew they would spend the $350,000 permitted by the party. But he couldn't see how they could raise much more than $200,000. Even before entering the race, he obtained promises from his supporters that they would help shoulder an eventual deficit. "I had that pledge from that nucleus that we would share the responsibility for an eventual deficit," he said, "and I was very, very comforted by that."

Once his fundraisers set to work, as he later acknowledged, "we were never worried again." In their newly discovered enthusiasm for popular financing, Ryan's people left no possibility to chance. Every Tuesday morning, they would hold a fundraising breakfast in a restaurant of the venerable Windsor Hotel. One week it was the women of the Jewish community, the next it was the needle trade, then it was the lawyers and so on through the list of Montreal communities and professions. On Ryan's agenda, these were pencilled in as "PDBS," *Petits Déjeuners Bénéfices*, and he loved them because it was a way for him to meet community leaders in the metropolis.

If anything, the Ryan campaign had more money than it could reasonably or legally spend, and much more than the candidate was willing to spend. In the end, according to Langevin's statement on the leadership campaign, the Ryan campaign collected $529,863.26 and spent $422,793.59. This exceeded the party's $350,000 limit, but included Ryan's expenses and salary. In any event, there were no tag days for him afterwards, as his organization finished the campaign with a surplus of $106,899.67.

As late as March 20, less than a month before the convention, the Ryan campaign had spent only $120,000 over the first two months. That was because of the frugal nature of the man. The campaign headquarters was a sparsely furnished walk-up on the ninth floor of the Valiquette furniture building at the corner of Berri and St. Catherine Streets, only a block away from Garneau's highly visible storefront headquarters. Bernard Langevin owned Valiquette furniture and the building. He offered it free, and told Ryan he could pay a modest rent if he wanted. For Ryan, who had bought *Le Devoir*'s St. Sacrement Street headquarters for $65,000 cash, this smelled like a good deal.

If the leadership was a two-horse race, Ryan insisted on being both thoroughbred and jockey, as well as owner and trainer. He was extremely difficult to manage and suspicious of political professionals. They would discover, as he later said, that "people who try to organize me are anathema to me."

As if to underline his determination to remain his own man, Ryan insisted on driving himself to most meetings within easy commuting distance of Montreal. Often, Madeleine would come along, as she said, because it was the only time they could be alone together for a talk. If he was exceptionally tired after a late meeting somewhere in the boondocks, he would let her drive home while he curled up in the back seat of their Chevy sedan.

Finally, after a month, he permitted himself to be driven to an event in Drummondville. One of his supporters had insisted on sending a car for him. But he didn't know his man very well. Ryan was both amused and horrified when he saw the car, a purple Lincoln Continental. After that, it was back to the Chevy. Ryan had his reasons, even though he was a terrible driver who represented a threat to himself and thus to the federalist forces in those pre-referendum days. For a man of his humble origins, a car was a certain symbol of success. By driving himself, he signalled his intention to retain his independence and not be changed by politics. Besides, a chauffeur would overhear his conversations with other passengers. It was not until the 1980 referendum campaign that Ryan finally accepted the government-issue limousine that was his due as opposition leader. And in the 1981 election, it was still a bit strange to see Ryan being driven off in his big Pontiac. "You're getting used to the comforts," teased his brother Gerry, who nevertheless predicted that when Claude's time in politics was over, he wouldn't miss the perks.

So Ryan's organizers were never quite sure when or how he might turn up at a meeting, and they soon got used to waiting for his Chevy to pull up to the front door of some place like the junior college campus in Hull where the party staged the first of nine all-candidates debates on January 15.

There were only two candidates, and there would be only two if Ryan did his job properly. At this point, Chrétien was still ready to jump in if Ryan faltered badly in the first month. But it would have been very uphill for Chrétien. "I thought Chrétien in a battle against Ryan would have suffered the same result as Garneau," said André Ouellet, the federal Liberal chief organizer in Quebec, who knew the terrain well and knew the resistance to the idea of a candidate from Ottawa. "The reaction was we need an outsider and Ryan symbolized a new beginning."

Chrétien, Ouellet concluded, "would have had to declare himself much earlier and resign as a minister and run not as Minister Chrétien but as Citizen Chrétien." Chrétien's other major problem as a prospective candidate was that, as Garneau put it, "his clientele was the same as mine." Had Chrétien come in, he would have split his own vote with Garneau, while there was no other candidate of the establishment or youth wings of the party to divide Ryan's potential clientele. For a time, there was a possibility that interim leader Gérard D. Lévesque might come in, primarily to add some interest to the race. Because he was so well liked, Lévesque might have attracted considerable support. But there were more important considerations in his mind. "I know I can win the convention," he had told fellow MNA John Ciaccia during Ryan's second period of reflection. "But can I win the province?" The consensus was that he couldn't and Lévesque, who could usually be relied on to put the party's interest ahead of his own, stayed clear of the leadership campaign.

From the beginning then, it was a two-horse race, as it would remain to the end. For Ryan there were two challenges. First, he had to prove his capacity to perform under pressure in public. Second, he had to establish and maintain early momentum in the selection of delegates that would begin in late January and run through the end of March.

The prospective all-candidates meetings turned into a series of Ryan-Garneau debates, easy to organize, easy to follow, easy to score. In the news media, coverage of the meetings became a continuous metaphor of the boxing ring, with Ryan ahead in the early rounds, Garneau on the ropes in the middle rounds, with some serious questions as to whether he would go the distance or throw in the towel.

In fact, Garneau performed extremely well, demonstrating substance, a sense of history and a well-versed appreciation of the constitutional issue that was admittedly Ryan's strong suit. But the perception of Garneau, as a nice but essentially shallow man, had already been formed.

"The thing that insulted me the most in this campaign," Garneau said later, "was that I passed for a man without ideas, while the other guy passed for an intellectual who would conceive a new society."

By the very nature of a two-man race, there was bound to be considerable bad feeling between the two candidates. But it ran much deeper than that. "If you read Ryan's editorials over the years," suggested Jean-Claude Rivest, a former Bourassa aide who was then chief of staff in the opposition leader's office, "there weren't many bouquets in there for Raymond, because he never consulted Ryan between '70 and '76. Ryan thought then that Raymond was too junior." Rivest, who would succeed Garneau in his Quebec City riding of Jean Talon, thought that Ryan eventually came to recognize that Garneau was deeper than he had thought at the time.

"Garneau was never a person with whom I got along very easily," Ryan admitted long after the convention. "He's not an intellectual. He's a man who has grown from entirely different sources. His relations were mostly in Quebec and among the so-called professionals in the party. I could never get along with him easily. I never had a good conversation with him during the entire campaign, so I think we more or less grew apart as the campaign unfolded."

As the campaign progressed it got rough, as only Quebec politics can be, with each organization guilty of whispering campaigns about the opposing candidate. The Ryan campaign distributed a copy of an old newspaper article which asserted that Garneau had to be hospitalized for a minor nervous breakdown when he was finance minister in the Bourassa government. "Ask my colleagues if it's true," Garneau protested at a debate with Ryan in Rimouski at the end of February. Ryan apologized for his organization but, characteristically, not for himself.

On the other side, Garneau's telephone canvassers were working at one point from a "Perfect Salesman's Kit," a ridiculous catalogue of half-truths and distortions of many things Ryan had said or written over the years. While reminding Liberal activists of Ryan's endorsement of the PQ, the Garneau manual went on to claim that he was soft on separatism because René Lévesque had quoted some of his editorials in an early book. As for Ryan's seven conditions, the Garneau sales kit alleged that "only mercenaries pose conditions."

Despite frequent reminders of Ryan's position in 1976, his campaign for delegates went well from the beginning. Because it was a two-man race, the campaign translated itself at the riding level into the election of slates committed to one or the other candidate. Delegates would receive a list of the slates on their way into a hall and would vote accordingly. From the beginning, the Ryan forces were cleaning up. In some ridings, the score was 24 to 0 for Ryan. He even swept the riding of Louis Hébert, next door to Garneau's own in his supposed fortress of Quebec.

Before long, the party had a problem. Ryan was too strong. "At one point, most of the ridings were coming in about 4 to 1 in his favor," said convention chairman Louis Rémillard.

By mid-March, it was widely rumored in the party that Garneau would drop out of the race, and that only Gérard D. Lévesque had talked him into staying in. Both men vigorously denied it, "I didn't even talk to any organizers about that because I didn't want to discourage them," Garneau later claimed. "They were enthusiastic and I couldn't tell them that I myself had grave doubts. I was worried about coming out of it in debt, and I thought to myself of quitting because I knew I wasn't winning and I wished it would be over. But it would have caused considerable damage to the Liberal party if I hadn't persisted until the convention."

The way Ryan thought he heard it at the time, Garneau's organization was demanding that the party assume his debts as a condition of his staying in until the end to provide a good show at the convention. "Ryan told me that," said Michel Roy of *Le Devoir*, "and he told me that he obviously couldn't do it."

"There was never any question of that," Garneau said late in 1980. "I wouldn't have accepted, either. I would have paid out of my pocket first." In fact, Garneau ended the campaign with a $35,000 deficit, whereupon many of his friends, perhaps to assuage their guilt for having deserted him, rushed to cover his bills. He finished up with a $25,000 surplus and established a modest foundation for students. "It was probably the biggest consolation I had," he said, "to see that pack of friends who supported me after the convention."

But at the convention itself, Garneau had only two chances. Slim, and none.

6

SCARVES
AND BALLOONS

I t was the scarves that did it. It was the scarves, a sea of red Ryan scarves in the Quebec Coliseum, that told you for a certain fact that he had the numbers when it counted at the mid-April convention. It was the scarves, and Ryan's joining in the waving of them, that told you he had come down from the ivory tower of his newspaper into the brawling main street of Quebec politics.

The scarves had been Lucette St. Amant's bright idea. On a Ryan organization chart, she should have been in charge of gadgets. It was Lucette who had chosen the campaign's slogan, "Leadership." Actually it was picked out from several possibilities by her teenage son one night in the basement of her split-level home in the comfortable L'Acadie section of North-End Montreal.

In the single word, Leadership, several themes merged. For one thing, though it was an English word, it had become an accepted intrusion of *franglais* into the French political vernacular. Ryan himself had often referred in his editorials to the need for, or lack of, *le leadership*. Now he hoped to provide what he had so so often called for, a kind of moral leadership. As a slogan, it suited him down to the ground. It also fit in with what the party was looking for in the leadership campaign. There was something rather bald-faced about the Garneau campaign slogan, which promised to take the party back to power, "*Le Pouvoir*." Somehow it suggested that power was the only thing the Liberals stood for. And there was more than a grain of truth to that. But Liberal activists did not want to be reminded of it in the midst of a leadership campaign that was supposed to be about a higher purpose.

In Lucette's gadget kit there was to be a minimum of gadgetry that smacked of old-style convention hoopla. The Ryan convention kit consisted of a shopping bag with a few stickers. The convention mementos that people would keep around in drawers were the scarves and a reporter's notebook, complete with a history of the party and a crossword puzzle. The black notebook was Ryan's personal trademark, and had quickly become identified as such to delegates all over the province. Wherever he went in the leadership campaign, Ryan was still inclined to whip one out of his back pocket and begin ticking off his hand-written notes.

The scarves were another matter. They were clearly marked "Made in Japan." Which was sure to offend Quebec's struggling textile industry, not to mention the possibility of the press putting it out that Ryan had unilingual English scarves. St. Amant and a group of volunteers stayed up all through one night taking the labels off thousands and thousands of scarves. The ony thing she didn't have was balloons, and somebody wondered where they were. "I didn't order any goddamn balloons," she said. "I don't want to see one goddamn balloon."

The Liberals had planned to spend a bundle, about $750,000 to stage an American-style convention spectacular at the Coliseum in Quebec, the house that Jean Béliveau built. But there were a couple of fundamental problems, namely making sure that they had an arena and that Garneau stayed in until convention time to keep up the appearance of democratic suspense. The problem with the Coliseum was one of logistics, and assuring that Quebec's Nordiques, then of the old World Hockey Association, would not insist that the arena be reserved for their possible play-off dates in mid-April. This problem was rather easily resolved by the intervention of Jean Lesage. The patron of the Quiet Revolution, now a well-upholstered boardroom lawyer, also happened to be chairman of the board of the Nordiques. In effect, the party had their elder statesman make a phone call to himself. In any event, the problem of the Nordiques and the play-offs was worked out.

The matter of keeping Garneau in to the end was something else again. Garneau had been in politics long enough to know that his campaign was gathering no momentum.

"Among the people who had been expected to support us, 50 percent were voting for Ryan," recalled Garneau's chief organizer, Léonce Mercier, who later surfaced as director general of the federal Liberal party's Quebec wing. "At the beginning, our surveys showed we had 800 delegates, we didn't advance one vote in four months. And at the convention, people came with their minds made up."

Garneau had his reports from the riding conventions, and he knew his numbers didn't add up. He also knew from his own appearances, despite many fine performances, that the audiences weren't listening to him.

"There was a kind of wall," Garneau said much later, "they weren't reasoning, they weren't listening, and you couldn't argue very easily against that.

"That was very difficult for me," he said in late 1980, before Ryan's own defeat in the 1981 election, "and even today I look at that and say maybe I should have said this. But I'm still looking for the new ideas the Liberal party was supposed to benefit from under the leadership of Mr. Ryan. What does it stand for today in terms of political philosophy, the Liberal party of Quebec? "

As bitter as he would be in defeat, Garneau was quite resigned to his fate on the weekend of April 14 to 15, and quite determined to see it through. For above all else, Garneau was a party man. The party was all he had known, all his adult life. He had hardly stepped off the plane from the University of Geneva, when he went to work for the Quebec Liberal Federation, as it was then called, in Quebec City. It was the summer of 1963. Garneau was only 28 years old. Since the the ruling Lesage Liberals were then at the peak of their power, at the height of the Quiet Revolution, it was an exciting time to be in Quebec. And Garneau, as the assistant secretary general of the party in power, soon became known to, and relied on, by the men in power.

Before long, he was on Lesage's staff. When the premier went down to a stunning defeat in the 1966 election, a victim in a sense of his own *politique de grandeur*, Garneau stayed on with him in opposition. From a junior member of the premier's staff, he became Lesage's senior aide in opposition. He also became a kind of son to the former premier, who confided in Garneau as early as the summer of 1967 that it was his intention to leave politics. But he stayed on, and Garneau stayed with him, through the tumultuous departure of René Lévesque in the fall of that year, and through the next two years. Until Lesage decided to remove himself to the sidelines, Garneau had ample opportunity to observe a legislative master at work. Though the opposition stood the traditional two drawn sword lengths across from Daniel Johnson and his ministers, the Unionist government was often at sea on legislative drafting, and very much on the quiet they would often consult Lesage. Garneau would later recall one instance in which Lesage, truly the leader of Her Majesty's Loyal Opposition, wrote up a bill in his own hand in the presence of the clerk of the legislature. (In later years, he would receive more material rewards for his knowledge, when his Grande Allée law firm was retained by the Bourassa government to write much of its important legislation.)

And Garneau was with Lesage when the former premier decided he had finally had enough of the unseemly scheming for the leadership crown. "My decision is taken," Lesage told Garneau one day in 1969. "I'm quitting. I'm resigning tomorrow. I'm calling for a leadership convention. I want you to call so-and-so and so-and-so and ask them to come to my chalet at Lac Beauport, because I want them to know about it before I announce it." With Lesage until the end, Garneau stayed on in the lame duck leader's office during the fall of 1969 and into the convention of January 1970 that saw the election of Robert Bourassa, only a year older than himself. In the triumphs of the first Bourassa administration, Garneau played a considerable role as the energetic and capable young finance minister. And it was Garneau, in the darkest days of the second Bourassa administration, who stood loyally by his leader and played down speculation that he was the party's logical heir.

So having stayed a difficult course in the leadership campaign, he could at least stay in for his speech, and he could say with some conviction that Raymond Garneau would never conduct a campaign at the expense of Robert Bourassa, a line that brought down the house on both sides of the aisle. As he stood there before the Saturday afternoon vote, delivering one of the great speeches in the modern-day annals of Quebec politics, he was making the kind of impression that would count only much later on. For the speech was the sum and substance of all he stood for. He knew it by heart and it came from the heart. "Quebec is my home," he said, "but Canada is my country."

At that moment, Garneau had repaid any debts that might have been outstanding with the party.

But he was under no illusions about the impact it might have on the vote. "The speech did nothing," Garneau was to say years later. "It changed nothing. I'm convinced it didn't change one vote in the room. Because people weren't listening to me."

But by then, the convention organizers had themselves their television spectacular. As interim leader Gérard D. Lévesque got up to deliver the keynote address at the Friday night session, he could take some satisfaction from the fact that he had put the party back on its feet. From a nadir of 35,000 members at the time he picked up Bourassa's fallen mantle of leadership, the party membership rolls had doubled during the course of the four-month leadership campaign. The two candidates had performed well, aside from the obvious and bitter personal animosities that were bound to surface in a two-man race.

There was a clear difference between them on the important issues of the constitution and language rights. On the constitution, Ryan was the candidate of the third option, favoring a fundamental realignment of the Canadian federal system along the lines that would later emerge in his party's so-called "Beige Paper" issued in

January of 1980. Garneau also favored a renewed federalism, but was perceived as more of an orthodox federalist
than Ryan. On the language issue, both candidates favored
amendments to the Lévesque government's Charter of
the French Language, commonly known as Bill 101, which
would ease the restrictions on access to English-language
schooling for the children of Canadian citizens moving
in from other provinces. Both candidates also spoke of
amending the language law's controversial regulations
limiting the use of bilingual signs and advertising, even
in predominantly English-speaking neighborhoods. The
clear-cut intellectual divergences of the two candidates
restored a semblance of self-respect to the Liberals. No
longer did it seem that the Péquistes had a monopoly on
ideas or, for that matter, on virtue.

Gérard D. Lévesque's major achievement as interim
leader was getting the party to wait this long, seventeen
months to the day after its defeat, to select a new leader.
"There were certainly many, maybe a majority, who
wanted to go to a convention right away," he said later.
"They were looking for a magic way of revitalizing the
party right away. This is a normal reaction. But I was
convinced that time was necessary to get back to the grass
roots as much as possible."

It was not for nothing that Lévesque had been in the
legislature since 1956, and fought seven elections, of which
the Liberals had won four and lost three. He knew the
rhythms of politics, knew that 1977 was the year of the
PQ, and that time would be the best healer for the wounds
of his party. So the exercise of leadership in the interim
was largely a process of marking time.

At the first meeting of the Liberal general council at
the end of February 1977, Lévesque needed all the help
he could muster from the establishment wing of the party
to head off a move for an early convention. And then he
forced Liberal activists into the street in the first door-to-
door fundraising campaign in the party's history. It was
a bit of a disaster, raising only a few hundred thousand
dollars, but he thought it was important that rank-and-
filers get used to the idea of direct contact with the voter.

It was the best means of pulling in new members, and in any event it was the law of the land, since the Lévesque government's Bill Two, the new political parties financing act, simply abolished the corporate donations that had always been the principal means of support for the Liberals. So in that sense, Gérard D. 's fund-raising campaign was a qualified success. By the time Ryan became leader a year later, the party troops were ready to march on the first of several campaigns that raised more than $8 million for the referendum and the general election. By the time of Ryan's defeat in 1981, most of the money had been spent, a good deal of it on regional office staff to support his province-wide organization. By the time of his resignation in August of 1982, the party had also dipped into its substantial reserves. The Liberals, not to put too fine a point on it, were pratically broke. But that is getting ahead of the story.

When Louis Rémillard finally gavelled the leadership convention to order in Quebec eight months later, there were 2,640 delegates, twenty-four from each of the 110 ridings in the National Assembly as it was then constituted, of which twelve from each county were women and four were youth delegates under the age of 20. Finally, they were getting the show on the road. It began on the Friday afternoon with a sentimental appearance by Lesage, who was nominally reporting in for the Pre-Referendum Committee he had agreed to chair at the request of Gérard D. Lévesque.

But it was mostly for the applause. It had been twenty years since his own election as leader. But since his retirement in 1970, Lesage had made only one public appearance, the previous year, when he stood up at a meeting of the bar association in Quebec to register his disapproval of certain aspects of Bill 101. As Lesage made his way to the podium, it was apparent that the years had only improved his appearance. He looked more distinguished, more a premier, than ever. And when he spoke, in that distinctively deep voice of his, it was clear that he still had the magic. When he had come to power in 1960, it was the end of the era known as the *noirceur*, the darkness, meaning the age of Maurice Duplessis. Now Lesage spoke of another *noirceur*, in the option of separation or independence. It was a gloomy perspective but a powerful one. The Lesage appearance overshadowed the last direct confrontation between the two candidates, who took turns at the podium answering questions from the floor.

The Friday night session was to have been Gérard D. Lévesque's big moment, the moment for him to deliver one of his joyous stemwinders that made him a kind of Hubert Humphrey of Quebec politics. There is no doubt that Lévesque always left the impression of a happy warrior. "What a wonderful family," he began on a typical note. The only problem for Lévesque and the Liberals was that the CBC and Radio-Canada journalists covering the convention staged a walkout just as the networks went on the air. So while there was a picture and sound of the event, there was no commentary. As things turned out it was just as well. Lévesque was only a few minutes into his speech when the Garneau organizers released thousands and thousands of balloons from the ceiling of the arena. "At that point," said Ryan's chief organizer, Jacques Lamoureux, "we decided to bring out our scarves."

There they were, waves of red scarves, with Ryan's partisans chanting their campaign refrain, "Ryan, Ryan," to the tune of "Amen, Amen." What was going on, in the middle of a keynote address by the interim leader, with candidates' demonstrations expressly forbidden, were two full-fledged demonstrations for the candidates. The Ryan people were determined not to be outdone. Most neutral observers on the floor were horrified. "I was very shocked for Gérard D.," said Louis Rémillard. "I didn't see the TV. It looked terrific."

Indeed it did look terrific. In the absence of commentators to explain to viewers why pandemonium had broken loose on the floor, it looked to viewers as if Lévesque was hitting every applause line imaginable. He must have sensed this, because he got through his speech, even though no one in the crowd of 10,000 people was paying him the slightest attention.

And in the Ryan delegation, the most remarkable sight was the candidate himself, standing and waving a red scarf as enthusiastically as his followers. Afterwards, many observers thought it inappropriate, that he should have merely accepted the acclaim.

"Look, that's very simple," Ryan said. "I had a choice to make. I had to remain seated or participate with the other people. If I had remained seated, people would have said, he wants all this homage. So I chose the other way. I chose to become involved like the rest of my people. It's as simple as that. And I was never really overwhelmed by that."

But reporters who had worked with and covered Ryan over the years were startled by the complete transformation of the austere director of *Le Devoir* into the exuberant candidate, waving his scarf and even egging his people on.

Ryan had every reason to enjoy himself at the convention. His campaign had the *Garnistes* outnumbered, outorganized and outbussed right in Garneau's own backyard of Quebec. When Garneau's supporters arrived at the convention for the Friday night keynote, they were angered to find that a huge Ryan claque had already occupied most of the non-reserved spectators' seats. As the Ryan crowd arrived, they found two "Leadership: Ryan" posters beside each seat. "We had 20,000 posters spread around the arena," Lucette St. Amant said later. When it was pointed out that a crowd of only 10,000 people was expected, she said, "Well, they've all got two hands."

The dispersing of the posters all around the arena, to give the impression that the Ryan camp was everywhere, was something that was first tried at Pierre Trudeau's convention in 1968, and repeated at the Bourassa convention of 1970. This was not the only detail copied from the previous federal and provincial leadership campaigns, which was not suprising, since many of the same people who had worked in the Trudeau and Bourassa leadership camps, now turned up in the Ryan organization. The Ryan floor communications system was exactly the same one that had worked so flawlessly for Trudeau and Bourassa.

The Ryan campaign added its own wrinkle to check the delegate counts. Ryan campaign chairman Guy Saint-Pierre called it a "foolproof system of double *pointage*, one from regional coordinators, the other from riding sources who doubled-checked tallies after the election of the slates." By the time the Ryan forces arrayed themselves on the convention floor before the Saturday afternoon vote, chief organizer Lamoureux was ready to go on television with a firm prediction. He said that Ryan would win 1,750 delegates. The final result was actually 1,748 to Garneau's 804, a smashing majority and eerily close to Lamoureux's prediction. "We joked that two student delegates couldn't make it because they were studying for exams," Lamoureux said.

Since Ryan obviously had a lock on the convention, he had every reason to be looking serene as he sat, surrounded by his family and advisers in his box just down from the VIP loge, where Lesage was very much the guest of honor. Lesage was not the only former premier to be present. Another Friday night arrival was Robert Bourassa, accompanied by his wife, Andrée. Bourassa's European exile had come to an end. He had spent the better part of a year commuting between Brussels, Paris, Montreal and his winter condominium in Bal Harbour, Florida.

Practically on the morrow of his defeat, Bourassa sensed that one of the crucial tests of the PQ thesis would be the arguments for economic association after sovereignty. Bourassa determined to study the European model of economic association, the Common Market, headquartered in Brussels. He would go there and arm himself with rebuttals to the Péquiste argument. In the process, he hoped to begin a kind of rehabilitation, and perhaps in time even carve out a small but significant place for himself in the referendum debate. In Brussels, he immersed himself in everything from the European Economic Community's constitution, the Treaty of Rome, to the diverse factions composing the European parliament. It was neither a rest holiday nor a sightseeing tour. "Most people visit museums in Europe," commented a friend. "Bourassa visits parliaments."

By the spring of 1978, he was back in North America, commuting between Montreal and Washington, where he was a visiting professor at Johns Hopkins University's Institute of Canadian Studies. But his appearance at the leadership convention was his first public foray since his defeat. Many voices and eyebrows were raised in the Liberal establishment, where Bourassa was still considered a political leper. Finally, it was Gérard D. Lévesque, acting on his own, who decided that Bourassa should be invited as a simple courtesy. All the former leaders were being invited. Bourassa was a former leader, therefore the invitation included him. But he would not be asked to speak. He would appear with the other former leaders, Lesage, Georges-Emile Lapalme and George Marler, in a Friday night film short on the party's history.

That seemed enough for Bourassa, who was grateful just to be there. He arrived to polite applause, and an instant gathering of reporters, many of whom had gleefully savaged "Boo-Boo" during his years in power. He was, to most appearances, little changed in the last year and a half. He wasn't any heavier that you would notice. He kept in trim with his same old swimming routine. But the Bourassa bodyguard, who had doubled as the premier's hairdresser in the old days, was gone. He was no longer the carefully combed premier. There was something else. He had changed his severe horn-rimmed glasses for a pair of rounder glasses that softened his bony features. "I had to change my image," he told one reporter who asked him about it. "The other one wasn't very good."

It had been eight months since Bourassa had seen Ryan, in August of the previous year, when the former premier and his wife went to the Ryan family's rented summer cottage at the Chanteclerc compound at Ste. Adele, fifty miles north of Montreal. The dinner was at Ryan's invitation, as a courtesy to a forgotten man, and because he evidently wanted Bourassa's opinion on the tentative Ryan draft, which had started up during the summer. It was Ryan's first period of reflection, and Bourassa came away with the impression that he wouldn't do it.

"He said that he was not anxious to go into an unknown world," Bourassa later recalled. "That for him it was an unknown world. That is to say, a world he didn't know, a world in which he knew little of those things. He was very reluctant to enter a new world while he was at *Le Devoir*, which gave him a lot of security."

Be that as it may, Ryan did enter that unknown world the following January, and by the time of the convention he had impressed most observers with his performance under close scrutiny during the leadership campaign. But he remained fundamentally contemptuous of the way things were done in political campaigns. If his handlers told him to go in by one door, he would almost certainly go in the other, just to show them he was not their puppet. If he was urged to go directly to a podium, he was almost certain to linger in the back of the hall, shaking hands and kissing ladies on both cheeks.

"The candidate was not always easy to organize," acknowledged Ryan's campaign chairman Guy Saint-Pierre, the former Bourassa trade minister who was now a senior vice-president of Montreal's Ogilvie Mills, an outpost of the Brascan empire. "He could be unpredictable and stubborn. But for crowds he was surprisingly good. Very early in the game it became apparent that he was very effective in rural Quebec."

And why not? He had been traveling the province, not only for the last fifteen years as director of *Le Devoir*, but for more than fifteen years before that as the general secretary of Catholic Action. He was very much at home in the Louisevilles and the Victoriavilles of Quebec. "He touched on a lot of sensitive chords," as Saint-Pierre pointed out. "He touched on traditional values, sensible values."

Before a large audience in a big city, Ryan could be fatally boring, with his head down as he plowed resolutely through an arid text. But in those days people were listening to him, and he was being hailed, as Saint-Pierre said, "as a man who not only understood complex problems but could summarize them in a simple way."

Ryan was showing the press and the public another side of himself that had been rarely glimpsed outside the confidential precincts of *Le Devoir*. He had not the slightest hesitation in putting on the brass knuckles and getting down to a good old-fashioned political street fight.

Arriving late for a Quebec City news conference in the midwinter leadership campaign, Ryan blamed his tardiness on the "inexcusable negligence" of the PQ government in clearing the highways into the capital. Shades of Maurice Duplessis. There was even a passing physical resemblance, beginning with the lawyerly pose of the thumbs hooked into the vest, and ending with the beakish nose.

The emerging character of the streetfighter was seen in those days as a fascinating new aspect of Ryan's public personality. In time, the combative side of Ryan's nature would come to work against him. He would eventually be seen not as a streetfighter but as a bully. But back then, in the spring of 1978, he could do no wrong. What would later be identified as his *mesquinerie*, a certain meanness of spirit, was then perceived as proof that he had successfully made the jump from the intellectual world of his newspaper to the real world, the down and dirty world, of politics.

Yet it was for his ideas, in quantity alone, that Ryan very quickly made his mark. It wasn't enough just to talk of them from a platform. For Ryan, because of the world he came from, an idea didn't exist unless it was down on paper somewhere. Two weeks before the convention, he summoned reporters to his campaign office in Montreal where he put out a forty-page position paper called "Thoughts on the Challenge of the Future Years." When you held the paper up against the light, the authorship was as clear as a Rolland watermark. The Ryan touch was apparent throughout the original French version and the translation. The main points were enumerated, 2-a-b-c-d, just as in thousands of newspaper editorials he had written over the years. And the words spoke of his attachment to Quebec as a "truly distinct national community," and his commitment to Canada as a country that has "acquired the fundamental political liberties for its citizens."

To those who argued that Quebec's development had been stunted by the federal system, Ryan was able to reply that the flowering of fundamental freedoms in Quebec society "were not simply historical accidents, independent of our federal system. The diversity which characterizes the make-up of the Canadian population was also responsible for the climate of tolerance which favored the growth of these basic human freedoms."

It wasn't that such thoughts were entirely unheard of in Quebec in those days, it's just that Ryan lent them a certain intellectual currency. He was a forceful personality, celebrated for his intellectual rigor, and in the winter and spring of 1978 he was helping to make the federalist option respectable in Quebec again. For nearly a year and a half, the PQ had occupied most of the political space in Quebec, making the provincial Liberals appear almost like an irrelevant third party in its fight with the Trudeau Liberals in Ottawa. Ryan served notice during those weeks that he intended to be in the fray. In a later period, when it became fashionable to say that Ryan proved to be a bad leader, it was rather too easily forgotten in Liberal circles that in the space of a few months, he had helped the Liberals regain their self-respect.

Years later, when it was generally accepted that Ryan was in an impossible predicament as between Trudeau and Lévesque, it was also rather too easily forgotten that there had been a clamor for a "third option" that would satisfy the demands of Quebec for more autonomy within a Canadian framework. The comedian Yvon Deschamps had suggested in one of his more famous monologues that what the people of the province really wanted was a "free Quebec in a united Canada." To the amusement of some observers, Ryan called for exactly the same thing, "a free and open Quebec within a united Canada." He put it that way in his position paper of early April, and he repeated it from the podium of the convention two weeks later.

There were three significant aspects to the Ryan position paper, two of which received wide coverage and one of which was generally ignored. There was heavy reporting in the French media of Ryan's comments on constitutional arrangements, while the English media were more concerned with his statements on minority language rights. This was the usual dichotomy of the Montreal media, reporting the same story, in the same city, to different readers with different concerns. Both the English and the French news outlets missed the third aspect of the Ryan paper, namely his concept of public administration and its role in the Quebec economy. Even back then, Ryan was sounding a warning that the size of government, and the spending of government, were dangerously out of control.

"In the last fifteen years," Ryan noted, "the public and parapublic sectors have shown phenomenal growth almost everywhere in the world. In this respect, as in many others, Quebec is first in growth, even though its resources are more limited than others. From these factors stem the greater difficulties Quebec faces today and will face tomorrow." He pointed out that public expenditures in Quebec had risen faster in 1977 than the Gross Domestic Product of Quebec, by nearly 13 percent in the space of one year. "This means," he noted, "that the spending power of the private sector is reduced in favor of the public sector." These observations would later take on a prophetic quality when viewed from the perspective of the lean and mean 1980s. By then, incredibly, Ryan was gone from the scene.

But on April 15, 1978, Ryan looked very much like the savior the Liberal party had been looking for. The Liberals were quite certain they were selecting not only the leader of the federalist forces, but also the next premier of the province. He had said if he ever entered politics, he would never impose himself. And here he was, being acclaimed.

But it was going to be a long afternoon. First, each candidate had half an hour to address the convention, then the delegates would line up to vote, dropping a token into a slot beside the name of either contender. Then the convention organizers meant to take as much time as they could to stretch the afternoon broadcast of the convention on into evening prime time. Through most of it, Ryan sat in his box, surrounded by his family and closest advisers. When it came his turn to speak, following Garneau's heartfelt appeal for votes, Ryan made a speech that was also quite remarkable, not for its delivery, but for its content. For fifteen years at *Le Devoir*, he had been developing and articulating his position on Quebec's future. Now as he stood at center ice of the Coliseum, he had an opportunity not merely to express his views but to weld them onto the party that had sought him out. The Ryan outlook could be summarized as a nationalist perspective in a Canadian context. It was different from, say, the economic nationalism espoused by Robert Bourassa, in that Ryan began from historical premises. He was himself the intellectual heir of Henri Bourassa, the firebrand who had broken with Wilfrid Laurier to go off on his own and found *Le Devoir* in 1910. The newspaper was to play a pamphleteering role in Laurier's downfall at the polls the following year. Ryan was only the fourth in the line of *Le Devoir* directors, and never in the paper's history had the constitutional question been on the national agenda so much as during Ryan's own time. At all events, he tried, as he did this day, to stand for both the *fleur-de-lys* and the maple leaf.

"First of all, we are Quebecers," he told the convention. "We also want to enjoy all the desirable guarantees of freedom within the whole of Canada. We are equally Canadians. We are equally partisans of maintaining the Canadian link. It's in the Canadian path that Quebecers have the most opportunities to develop their freedom together."

When Ryan stepped down from the podium, it was all over but the voting. Because some of the delegates had difficulty dropping their tokens, it became one of those time-consuming timesavers that seem to haunt leadership conventions. By the time they finished counting the ballots, the convention managers had already used up their scheduled television period. But since they knew there was no way the networks could very well go off the air before the result was announced, they delayed the announcement for more than an hour, leaving Ryan fifteen minutes for an acceptance address. And so they figured to stay on the air, with millions of viewers, right up to the start of the Canadiens' playoff telecast at eight o'clock. What they didn't count on was Ryan going on for as long as he did, more than half an hour, talking right into the hockey game. Thus in his first act as leader, he managed to irritate a significant number of voters.

When Louis Rémillard finally appeared on the podium to announce the result, there was no great explosion. *Habemus papam*, he would say in as many words, and the result was no surprise. Ryan, 1748, Garneau, 807. Ryan had no advance word of the result. "I heard it the first time when it was given in public," he said. Only a few minutes before, he had turned to his wife and said that even if he lost he wouldn't mind because he had done what he had to do. He was not only *l'homme du Devoir*, but true to its slogan, *"fais ce que dois."*

"I would have done what I had to do," he said. "And then I would have done something else. I wouldn't have been a broken man at all."

As for Garneau, there was nothing for him to do but brace himself with a gallant smile and make his way to the podium for the traditional concession. But by the time he got there, it somehow turned out that Ryan spoke before him. This was the main reason Ryan's victory speech was remembered as the words of a sore winner, apart from its tending to put viewers to sleep. For there was certainly nothing ungracious about it. Though he referred to Garneau only as "my opponent," he was generous in his praise for him.

"First of all," he began, "I'd like to extend my thanks and congratulations to my opponent in this arduous contest. Only both of us can know all the difficulties of this race." It was, he continued, "a healthy rivalry, difficult for the candidates but good for democracy."

Years later, Ryan still rankled at the suggestion he had been mean to his opponent. Over Christmas of 1980, after viewing a tape of the sequence on his brother Yves's home-video recorder, he finally knew that he had been unfairly perceived. "First when Garneau walked up to the podium, you remember that he first shook hands with Gérard Lévesque and then I was waiting around for an opportunity to shake hands with him. He immediately came to me. I came to him. We both went to each other. We shook hands rather warmly. And in my speech, I referred to him, explicitly, at least four or five times."

He also referred to just about everyone else associated with his campaign, including his mother Blandine Ryan, who seemed to be enjoying her moment at his side. She had been, he said, "a Liberal militant from the turn of the century," and he apologized to her for "making her wait so long," before he joined up himself.

The challenge of the leadership, he said, "was beyond the capacity of my frail shoulders," but he accepted it "in a spirit of humility and docility. You may be surprised to hear those words from me. But they have been among the key words of my adult life." Of himself, he went on, "I'm sometimes told that I'm a bit arrogant. This is not true. It's a tendency toward candor. " By this time, someof the caucus members around him were barely suppressing yawns, but he was not finished. He wanted to speak to the rest of country. "To our fellow Canadians from other provinces who may be listening tonight," he said, "I want to say greetings. We won't wait until the next election before we start talking as brothers with leaders from other provinces. We will open conversations as free citizens have always been authorized to do." But he sounded a sober note. "I hope you won't be led to believe that because this convention took place and Claude Ryan was elected leader of the Liberal party that our problems have disappeared. Our problems have not disappeared. They won't melt away with a single leadership convention."

And so finally it was left to Garneau to have the last word, and the hall began to empty even as he spoke. In his dressing room a few minutes later, there were two visitors of note: Robert Bourassa and Paul Desrochers, come to congratulate him for staying in. Then he rounded up his wife Pauline and their two children. A car was waiting for them at the front entrance. "Come on," he said. "Let's go home." The convention of the scarves and the balloons was over.

April 15, 1978: In a ritual gesture the loser, Raymond Garneau, raises the arm of the victor, Claude Ryan, who "thanks my opponent in this arduous contest for the Liberal leadership," but neglects to mention him by name. It is the first time Ryan is perceived as a sore winner, and it will not be the last. . . (Photo by Paul Taillefer)

7
THE RYAN EXPRESS

R yan was not the sort to take vacations, never had been in thirty-five years of public life, and he wasn't about to start now in politics. "You'll understand there's no rest on the day after you become leader of a political party," Ryan told reporters after a series of meetings on the morrow of the convention. He meant to control the party he once called "a monster." He had feared it once, and may have had reason to fear it still, this party of insurance salesmen and lawyers, of management consultants and county organizers. If he really meant to make it over in his own image and his own ideas, then he had to take it over. And control it he would, from the party's two-storey office over a policemen's credit union in East-Central Montreal, to the lonelier outposts of Liberalism in the backacres of the province.

For Ryan, there were several compelling reasons to consolidate his hold on the party, and to do so quickly. First, there was his continuing concern, almost his obsession, with the sum and sources of the party's finances. There was no shortage of funds in the party's reserve held in account number 8-800 at the Montreal Trust, and administered by three trustees, including the redoubtable Paul Desrochers. It was not lost on Ryan that whoever controlled the party's cash reserve would have a very large say in the organization of an election and the organizers in place. Ryan surely remembered that Desrochers had made some rather threatening noises back in his January conversation with Brian Mulroney, perhaps nothing more than empty words at a chance meeting in a Montreal restaurant. Nevertheless, even the threat of Desrochers throwing his weight around had nearly been enough to derail The Ryan Express even before it left the station.

So here was Ryan, fresh from his triumph at the convention, with the party at his feet, and who should be holding the pursestrings but the legendary "Paul D." Moreover, Desrochers was a man with his own friends and protegés already in place, not only at the constituency level around the province, but at the heart of Ryan's leadership campaign and at the top of the party pyramid in Montreal. Ryan's chief organizer, Jacques Lamoureux, paid his dues to the party in Desrochers' time. At the party office in Montreal, the director general, Ronald Poupart, had been in place since before the 1976 election. And there was Pierre Bibeau, then organizer for the ridings between Montreal and Quebec City, who had been installed in the party's youth section at the beginning of the Bourassa years and had worked at Liberal headquarters ever since. Ryan was insecure to begin with, and he saw nothing to assuage his doubts as to the loyalty of the people he was inheriting.

But first he would have to deal with "Mon oncle Paul."

"My first action," Ryan later recalled, "was to suggest that I should have a contact with the trustees, who were in charge of the funds of the party.

"I think Paul Desrochers called me, or I called him, and he came to see me." The other trustees, also present, were Gilles Hébert who had become Ryan's financial chairman, and retired businessman Ted Ryan.

"We had a very cordial session," Ryan recalled. "At the end of it, Mr. Desrochers said to me, 'Mr. Ryan, I know that your regime is setting in. If you need my services, they will be available. If you don't need them, I will understand.'

"He could not have had a better attitude. I said to him, thank you very much, I will get in touch with you."

Quite understandably, Ryan decided that the services of Paul Desrochers could be dispensed with.

In Gilles Hébert, Ryan had someone who, it had developed, was his own man. And in the financial reserve, Gérard D. Lévesque was able to turn over some $3 million to the new leader. The Liberals, in other words, were flush. Ryan suddenly found himself with the means to install party functionaries whose loyalty he could rely on, since they would be dependent upon him to make a living. Ryan's staffing of party headquarters in Montreal and Quebec with professional employees, and his opening up of regional offices around the province, were sources of friction and controversy among his own advisers. "There were two concepts," said Jacques Lamoureux, "the volunteer concept and that of a paid staff. It was the latter that won out."

One of the losers in this organizational struggle was Lamoureux himself, who became one of the earliest of the dropouts around Ryan. He and Bibeau, representing opposite schools of thought, served briefly together as Ryan's representatives on the Pre-Referendum Committee. Thereafter, Lamoureux did not surface again until the referendum campaign of 1980, when he performed a few errands for his original patron, André Ouellet. In the 1981 election, the whiz kid of 1978 was relegated to the function of an assistant organizer for the South Shore of Montreal. Through it all, Lamoureux's small law practice was prospering in Old Montreal. Nor was it by coincidence that when Consumer Affairs Minister Ouellet set up an inquiry into the urea-formaldehyde insulation foam affair, it was his own organizer, Lamoureux, that he named as commissioner. Lamoureux did not regain Ryan's favor until the summer of 1982, when the leader was drawing the wagons in a circle in a desperate attempt to save his leadership. By then it was too late, and Lamoureux told him so.

With Lamoureux out, the organizational vacuum was very quickly filled by Pierre Bibeau, only 29 in the fall of 1978 when he was named director general of the party to succeed Ronald Poupart. Bibeau, as Ryan liked to kid him, looked more like a Péquiste than a Liberal, with his unclipped beard and unkempt appearance. But he had gained Ryan's confidence by making his tours outside Montreal run on time.

"I discovered that Bibeau was in charge of about forty ridings," Ryan said later. "He brought me to over thirty of those ridings during the fall months. I was struck with the precision of this boy's work. When he had said to me, 'At nine o'clock you will meet the mayor and his council. At 9:45 you will be at church for Mass. At 10:30 there will be a brunch. At 12:30 there will be a meeting with the local press. At 2:30 there will be a public meeting,' everything worked according to plan. There was never a deviation from the program he had set. So I said to myself, this guy must be strong.

"I was used to working with voluntary organizations and I knew they didn't always work according to plan. Because your people don't show up on that Sunday morning. And this guy let you down for this or that reason. Bibeau's people were there and he had a strong hold over them. He was not domineering, he would let them do their work. He would stand in the back of the hall and say nothing to anyone."

Ryan came back from his rural swing in the fall of 1978, "with a very, very solid grasp of the problems, resources and prospects."

More than that Ryan, not the type to be easily impressed by anyone's work, was convinced that Bibeau was "a very reliable man." Nor did it hinder Bibeau's prospects of advancement that he shared Ryan's prejudice in favor of a predominantly professional staff. Finally, Bibeau fit in with Ryan's plans to unload Ronald Poupart, a holdover from the Bourassa regime.

From the day Ryan entered the Gilford street head-quarters on the Tuesday following the convention, Poupart had put the resignations of the entire staff on the table. Since Ryan didn't even know his way to the washroom at that point, he naturally kept everyone on for the start-up period of his leadership. But by the fall, he was prepared to dump Poupart and install his own man.

"I did not get along well with Poupart because he was another sort of person," Ryan said. "He was very nice to me, he was very cooperative, but he just didn't have the kind of approach that I wanted. By the fall, I think it must have been in October, I told him frankly, 'we cannot work together.' "

But it did not take Poupart long to land on his feet as the operations director of the Pro-Canada Committee, the well-financed umbrella organization of federalist parties and unity groups. It was partially at Ryan's recommendation that Poupart was hired by Pro-Canada chairman, Michel Robert.

"At the time," Robert said later, "Ryan suggested to me that he wanted to hire Poupart. It turned out that he wanted to get rid of him. Poupart thought Ryan had confidence in him. He was happy to come and I was happy to have him. We learned later that Ryan wanted to get rid of him."

In any event, Ryan had not heard the last of Poupart, or Robert, or of the Pro-Canada Committee.

The Pro-Canada Committee was born as the Pre-Referendum Committee at a symposium organized by the Council of Canadian Unity at Quebec's Château Frontenac over the first weekend of December in 1977. The keynote speaker at the founding meeting was none other, it will be recalled, than Claude Ryan, then between periods of reflection on the leadership issue and still very much the director of *Le Devoir*. He hailed the meeting as an "historic event."

Exactly one year later, he set out to destroy the Pro-Canada Committee. What had happened to him in the meantime was that he had changed jobs, and perspectives. It was all right for Ryan, the newspaper editorialist, to praise the coordinated efforts of the federalist forces. One would have expected no less of him. It was another thing for the leader of the Quebec Liberals, who expected to be the uncontested leader of the federalist forces, to share that authority with others. One would have expected no less from the leader of any party.

As he told PRC vice-president Marcel Masse in the summer of 1978: "If I have responsibility for the federal presence, I need to control the machinery. I'm going to assume control. Besides, it's the law."

And so it was. According to Bill 92, the Lévesque government's enabling legislation for referenda, the National Assembly would divide itself into provisional committees which would later form "national" committees. As Ryan would eventually take his seat as leader of the opposition, he would be the leader of the provisonal No committee.

But Masse, a one-time Union Nationale stalwart who had the distinction of being the youngest cabinet minister in Quebec history, was aware that Ryan was not merely concerned with legal proprieties.

"He was afraid," Masse said, "that Pro-Canada would become a political movement to do a job that he wanted the Liberals to do. In that sense, it was in his interest to make it disappear."

And that is exactly what Ryan did, though not without a rather unseemly struggle.

In hindsight, it was clear what Ryan had in mind by the manner in which he dispensed with the Liberal party's own referendum committee, which Jean Lesage had agreed to chair in 1977 at the request of interim leader Gérard D. Lévesque. On the day after Ryan's election as Liberal leader, Lesage paid him a courtesy call in Quebec.

"I place myself at your disposal," Lesage said.

"Mr. Lesage," Ryan replied, "there's a contradiction here. We cannot have two structural networks, the referendum structure and the party structure. There's got to be one. It's got to be under the same authority. So I want to let you know there's a problem there."

As Ryan remembered it Lesage replied: "You're in charge. Whatever you decide, I will accept."

Getting rid of the party's own referendum committee, chaired by a man who entertained no further ambitions for himself, was one thing. Getting rid of the PRC, which its collection of very live political egos, was quite another. "It was extremely delicate," Ryan later admitted, "it took months before we could work things out to my satisfaction."

As Marcel Masse observed, "A machine like that was potentially dangerous for him," in that it could assume a role he had in mind for his party and for himself. Ryan had another concern, and that was the money, in the millions, being raised from corporate sources by the Pro-Canada Foundation. It was soliciting corporate donations, in contravention of the spirit though not the letter of the Lévesque government's Bill Two, the political parties' financing law, which outlawed corporate political charity. Since the Pro-Canada Foundation was not financing a political party, it did not fall under the terms of the act, and it felt free to solicit donations up to $75,000 from some of the big chartered banks and up to $50,000 from crown corporations like Air Canada and Canadian National. Some of the money was also coming in from corporate sources outside the province. It had the potential for a public relations nightmare. As Ryan remembered telling the PRC's first chairman, Claude Castonguay, "We have got to rid ourselves of that kind of thing."

In August of 1978, Castonguay decided to clear out of the PRC, and he called Michel Robert, urging him to take on the presidency of the revamped committee. Robert seemed to be the ideal candidate for the job. He was an articulate spokesman for any cause, and had proved his organizational capacities as chairman of the party's policy commission in putting together the successful convention of the previous November. More to the point, he was a charter member and an important influence in the Draft Ryan movement of the previous winter, and had lines into the federal Liberal network.

On vacation in the Laurentians, Robert drove over to St. Donat, where the Liberal leader had taken a cottage in the month of August.

"We spent the afternoon together," Robert would recall. "As I understood it, he wanted the Liberal party to take control of the movement again. The other thing was that he wanted the committee to assume control of the pre-referendum period."

At least that was the impression that Robert carried away with him that day and on August 25 he was unanimously elected president of the PRC.

"At the time of my arrival," Robert said, "it was as organized as a bordello. No, that's going too far. A bordello is organized." He was determined, he thought with Ryan's full approval, to whip the place into shape and devise an operations plan.

The first thing Robert did was to change the name of the umbrella group from the Pre-Referendum Committee, which he thought too ambiguous. He could not call it the Quebec-Canada Committee, since that could be confused with one of its member groups, the Quebec-Canada Movement, which had been at the heart of a squabble earlier that year for accepting a $265,000 grant from the feds. So Robert decided to state the umbrella's aims squarely. He had the name changed to the "Pro-Canada Committee."

"I decided to do that independently of Ryan," Robert said.

That was his first mistake.

As Robert later said of Ryan: "He often reproached me for that." Robert had been sent to the Pre-Referendum Committee as Ryan's man. Very quickly, on the revamped Pro-Canada Committee, he became the committee's man, and his own man.

"After a certain while," Ryan remembered, "it became clear that he was not working in unison with me." It developed that there was something else about Robert that Ryan didn't like. Robert was extremely cosy with the cousins in Ottawa. Because he practised labor law, a predominantly provincial field, because he had been bâtonnier of the provincial bar at the age of 36, because he taught law at the strongly provincialist University of Montreal, because he had been head of the Quebec Liberal policy committee, Robert gave the impression of being of the *Québec d'abord*, Quebec First, school of federalism. In fact, he was also closely linked with the feds. He was then representing Ottawa before the federal McDonald Commission and provincial Keable Commission into the activities of the Royal Canadian Mounted Police. Ryan later said he was unaware of the extent of Robert's relationship with the cousins.

"I was going to discover—hadn't known before," said Ryan, "that he had some very, very strong affiliations with the federal people."

But it was the Poupart plan that ruptured the appearance of solidarity among the federalist forces. Within weeks of going over to Pro-Canada from the Quebec Liberal party, Poupart had drawn up an extensive and expensive plan for the referendum. He laid it before the committee on November 17.

From even a cursory reading of the Poupart report, it was clear that its objectives and proposed plan of action were unacceptable to Ryan. "The gathering of the federalist forces in Quebec under the umbrella of the Pro-Canada Committee is an accepted fact," the report began. "Pro-Canada constitutes the only tool, means, and leadership available to partisans of the federalist cause."

Right away, Ryan must have been clearing his throat. But what he was really unable to swallow was Poupart's organizational concept, which would have seen a central office of fourteen paid employees directing a volunteer organization in each of the province's 110 ridings. And in each of those ridings, each of the Pro-Canada Committee's fourteen member organizations would be entitled to two persons on the executive. From these 28-member executive committees on up to the head office, Poupart dubbed his campaign plan a "vertical structure." It was vertical all right, about as vertical as the Tower of Babel. Quite apart from the practical impossibility of having 28-member local executive committees, Ryan also noted that each riding committee would be presided over by a sitting MP or Member of the National Assembly. In those days, there were barely two dozen Liberal MNAs in Quebec, and over five dozen Liberal MPs in the federal capital. Ryan may not have been a mathematician, but he could count, and he was not greatly enamored of the idea of such a highly visible federal presence.

Finally, Ryan was horrified by the budgeting of the Poupart plan, which came in at $1,325,000 for 1979, which everyone then expected would be the referendum year. The Poupart budget included generous allocations of

$625,000 for the headquarters staff, $200,000 for travel expenses and a further $200,000 for the preparation and dissemination of campaign materials and propaganda. These were not the sorts of things the parsimonious Ryan was known for spending money on.

"As concerns its expenses and budget, the Pre-Referendum Committee should proceed with more care," Ryan wrote in a memorandum to his party executive on December 7. "It should take initiatives that truly respond to the needs expressed by its member organizations, rather than creating a vast machine which is going to run up excessive costs."

At all events the Pre-Referendum Committee — it is perhaps significant that Ryan did not acknowledge the change of name — should take no decision without the unanimous approval of its 28-member board, including his two delegates. As for the Liberal party of Quebec, it would "complete its own organization down to the poll level."

This was on Pearl Harbor Day, and it was certainly the torpedoing of the Poupart plan.

Robert tried to patch things up in two lengthy meetings with Ryan on the 14th and 15th of December. As Robert put it in a private memorandum to his foundation president, Pierre Côté, he tried to explain to Ryan "that in my view the rule of unanimity would render the committee completely unworkable," and that in any event, "other important member organizations of the committee, like the federal Liberal party," were not prepared to grant the Quebec Liberals "the equivalent of a veto."

On the evening of December 15, the full Pro-Canada Committee met to formally consider the Poupart plan. It was accepted by a vote of 20 to 2, only Bibeau and Lamoureux dissenting. This time, the Quebec Liberals had their instructions from the leader. Ryan ordered Bibeau to "make no compromises in any way." And so even as the plan was accepted it was doomed. Or as Robert put it, it lacked only two votes out of twenty-eight, but "Ryan won, 27 to 26."

Much later, Robert was prepared to admit that "maybe he was right, because we would have given a base to the Union Nationale or any third party. If 60 percent of the vote was federalist, Ryan wanted it to be indivisible" later on.

Over the Christmas period of 1978, Robert's outlook was hardly so sanguine. But he was the first to realize what was happening to him. Ryan was in the process of shutting him down.

Ryan went back a long way, all the way back to the Catholic Action period, with Marc Lalonde, who was the undisputed boss of the Trudeau Liberals in Quebec. Ryan was able to persuade Lalonde, and through him Trudeau, that the Poupart operational plan was wholly impractical. It was also agreed in Ottawa that Ryan had to appear to be the leader of the federalist forces in the referendum. With the powerful federal Liberals lining up with Ryan against the Poupart plan, the position of Pro-Canada became quite untenable. Then Ryan administered the coup de grâce. He saw to it that Pro-Canada's funds dried up.

Ironically, it was the man who had raised the potentially troublesome millions who set in motion the process of turning off Pro-Canada's tap.

"I was the guy who was the sort of bagman," said Reford MacDougall, a Montreal stock broker and scion of the old Golden Mile establishment. After cheerfully lowering the boom on every important chief executive officer in town, MacDougall just as cheerfully switched roles and got Ryan together with Pierre Côté for the purpose of cutting off the money.

"It was a typical case of Ryan being right and everyone else being wrong," MacDougall said, "though everyone was pretty sore about it at the time."

The combination of Lalonde pulling out the cousins, and Côté cutting off the money, brought the Pro-Canada follies to their inevitable conclusion the following February 25. "I called a meeting and folded the shop," Robert said simply. He dismissed the option of fighting on against formidable odds. "If I had wanted to be leader of the party," Robert told his staff, "I would have been a candidate. Ryan is the chief."

And with that, Pro-Canada closed its office at 550 Sherbrooke Street West, paid off its debts and disappeared. Of the $2.7 million raised by MacDougall, some $2.2 million remained with the foundation and would be spent later in 1979, largely on a billboard and advertising campaign, *Le Canada, J'y suis, j'y reste*; Here I am, Here I'll stay. The billboards became controversial when a couple of them were blown up in the run-up to the referendum campaign.

As for the Pro-Canada Committee, it had spent the other $500,000 and had exactly nothing to show for it. What Ryan had to show for the episode was who was in charge.

The last and by his own admission the least of Ryan's concerns was his relationship with his caucus in Quebec City. This may have been why, almost from the beginning, things seemed to go badly between him and his parliamentary wing.

First, there was the matter of healing the rift with Garneau. Ryan thought he had made the appropriate gestures in his victory speech. A lot of people who saw it thought otherwise. But if Ryan was not going to be in the House himself, and he was plainly in no hurry to get himself a seat, then it stood to reason that he did not want Garneau to be too prominently spotlighted when the Assembly proceedings went on television in the fall of 1978. Ryan was quite determined that if Garneau were to stay on, it would be on the leader's terms.

"I anticipated very early his coolness toward Garneau," said Ryan's campaign president, Guy Saint-Pierre. "Long ago he had started discussing the role of the other MNAs. I could see he was very determined that the number two man in the campaign would not be the second-in-command of the party." Ryan kept referring to the fate of Robert Winters, who finished second to Pierre Trudeau in the 1968 federal Liberal convention, only to disappear over the political horizon. In effect, Saint-Pierre recalled, Ryan was saying that "Garneau would have to fall back into the ranks."

Then, when Ryan met his caucus for the first time for dinner at Quebec's Reform Club in May, the vacationing Garneau was conspicuously absent, and the press made much of it. There was an awkward moment during the meeting when Victor Goldbloom, a man of great decency, considerable eloquence, and a charter Garneau supporter, stood up and made an impassioned plea for party unity. Instead of responding in kind, Ryan simply moved on to the next person who wanted to speak. It was a missed opportunity, and typical of Ryan's difficulty in making the magnanimous gesture.

Weeks went by without Ryan and Garneau meeting. Finally, at Ryan's request, they got together one day for about fifteen minutes. Afterwards, Garneau always had the impression that the only purpose served by the encounter was that Ryan could tell reporters he had met with his defeated opponent, and so got that little monkey off his back. Nevertheless, Garneau availed himself of the occasion to offer Ryan some advice.

"Mr. Ryan," Garneau began, "you're going to be premier, you're going to be whether you want to or not, because it's written in the heavens. The Liberals were re-elected on the morning of November 16, the day after the PQ's victory."

Garneau also said he advised Ryan to be careful about publishing a detailed and complex constitutional position before the referendum, one that federalists could not be unanimous on, one that the PQ could obviously attack. Finally, Garneau suggested that Ryan should start thinking about getting himself a seat, though not Notre Dame de Grace, a predominantly English-speaking riding in West-End Montreal that had come open with the resignation of Bryce Mackasey a few days after the leadership convention. There were also rumors floating around that Robert Burns was about to resign the PQ stronghold of Maisonneuve in East-End Montreal. Garneau told Ryan that if he was thinking about Maisonneuve for himself, he shouldn't, that it was too big a risk. "It's a risk you don't have the right to run," Garneau said. And that, after fifteen minutes or so, was that.

There was nothing to be done about the awkwardness that existed between them. When Garneau's ailing mother died a few months later, Ryan neither visited the salon nor did he send flowers. Instead he sent his executive assistant, Pierre Pettigrew, and a Mass card. Much was made of that by the unconverted *Garnistes*.

"He asked me to go," Pettigrew explained. "He said, 'That family has been hurt a lot, hurt by my election, I don't want them to be reminded by my presence of these wounds.' Then people said Ryan didn't send flowers. He offered Masses instead because he's a practising Catholic, and Garneau's a practising Catholic, he thought that more appropriate."

While these whispers of Ryan's alleged lack of grace made the rounds of the caucus, the leader was usually elsewhere. "I would go and meet them about once a week, once every two weeks," he said in 1980. "I had told Gérard Lévesque, 'You handle that side of the operation. 'I had not too much interest in it; to be frank with you, I felt my work was elsewhere."

Ryan's neglect, benign or otherwise, was to lead to his first major blowup with the caucus in November over two issues, the matter of his getting into the House, and the question of appointing a new chief organizer for the party.

Ryan listened to about two hours of this and promised a reply the following week. When he met his deputation the next time, Ryan minced no words. "The answer to your first question is a categorical no," he said. "There will be no chief organizer at this point. We will structure the party and stop having all authority rest with one individual. Those days are finished. I will tolerate no more discussion on that."

As for the matter of Ryan getting into the House, he was under a lot of pressure because the proceedings were televised for the first time in the fall of 1978. For many Liberals, it was urgent that he be there. "In the minds of some people perhaps," Ryan said later, "not in my mind particularly."

He had some eminent advice to the contrary, from Jean Lesage for one, who told him "to stay away from that hole" until the next election, as Lesage himself had done after his own accession to the leadership in 1958, free to concentrate on his electoral responsibilities.

But Lesage's day had been before television, before a televised referendum debate. The consensus was that Ryan had to be there, but as he himself pointed out to his caucus, no one was offering his seat.

"You're all talking about it," he told them, "but I haven't heard one member here suggesting that he might be willing to resign his seat in my favor. So there's no vacancy, no seat available, don't talk about it. And I won't tolerate any talk unless there's something we can discuss."

After that, Ryan said, his caucus "realized for the first time the kind of guy they'd be dealing with."

Perhaps in more ways than he knew.

8

OBSERVE, JUDGE, ACT

"**H**e's a foreign body with the Liberals," observed eminent journalist and commentator Jean-V. Dufresne, who knew both the man and the party well. "They've got a fantastic reflex for rejecting the transplant until they've taken power."

In 1981, when Ryan unexpectedly lost an election he was supposed to win, the patient did reject the transplant. But for three years, from his election as leader until his defeat at the polls, Ryan held absolute sway over the party. "This guy's going to be another Duplessis," ventured one charter member of the Draft Ryan movement at the time. "He needs us now to win the leadership. Afterwards, he'll get rid of us."

For the people who had seen his leadership campaign close-up, it was astonishing how many insiders were soon out of the picture. From the campaign hierarchy, the young campaign director Jacques Lamoureux was squeezed out in an office power play within six months. A young Montreal lawyer named Jean Masson, who had served as Ryan's tour director, discovered that Ryan didn't even remember his name. He never worked for him again. Like many disillusioned members of the rank and file, they remained convinced that Ryan was the man of the moment, but in their own moments they wanted nothing more to do with the man.

On the policy side, most of the original braintrusters eventually fell out with Ryan. This was brutally emphasized by the composition of the federal delegation at the 1980 constitutional summit. If Ryan was watching the proceedings, he could not have failed to notice the presence, over PierreTrudeau's shoulder, of Michel Robert and Raynold Langlois. Robert, who arranged for Ryan's critical appearance at the 1977 policy convention, never got along

with Ryan after their split over the Pro-Canada Committee
in early 1979. Langlois, a Grande Allée lawyer and scion
of one of Quebec's oldest political families, served Ryan
as late as 1980 as chairman of the party's important constitutional commission which in January of that year produced the "Beige Paper." Barely eight months after its
publication, its principal author had in a sense gone over
to the other side, since the Trudeau option was substantially
different from the constitutional perspectives of the "Beige
Paper" (on days when he was trying to distance himself
from the document, Ryan would occasionally refer to it
as the Langlois Report. When he spoke of it in approving
terms, it was the "Beige Paper," for the color of the book's
cover). In the parliamentary caucus, Ryan got off to a bad
start at his first meeting when he ignored Victor Goldbloom's conciliatory speech. He even managed to alienate
some of his own charter supporters like André Raynauld.
With Raynauld, matters with Ryan came to a head over
the leader's criteria for candidates, issued at a general
council at Sherbooke in the fall of 1979. The criteria listed
things like financial integrity, a college degree, and a
model domestic life. The newspapers had a field day.
And intellectuals like Raynauld, who had their own ideas
of organizing in a liberal democracy, were simply appalled.
"I was so furious I couldn't speak," Raynauld said later.
"I was so angry I couldn't give my opinion in a rational
way. The worst of it was that we had a caucus meeting
on the eve of that and he didn't say a word about it, not
a word. " Raynauld had been forced to his knees by Ryan
over the matter of his seven conditions for entering the
leadership race in 1978. After that they never quite established the good working relationship you might expect
between a leader and his chief economic spokesman. Raynauld, a former chairman of the Economic Council of
Canada, found that Ryan treated him like a schoolboy.
In the referendum, "he wanted to orchestrate everything,"
Raynauld complained.

"He's a man who has the fault of his qualities," Raynauld observed after he left politics in 1980. "He has a
certain meanness of spirit with regard to others. He's a

man who has business relations with people. You play a role. I play a role. He's not the type to pat you on the back, but he's very cold, very businesslike. He's a very complex man."

The origins of the relationship between Ryan and Raynauld were typical of Quebec's emerging political and social elites after the Second World War. With few exceptions, like Pierre Trudeau and René Lévesque, they had their beginnings in Catholic Action, the lay movements of the Church Militant. Claude Ryan was only 20 years old in 1945 when he was named the first general secretary of L'Action Catholique Canadienne in Montreal, a post in which he remained for the next seventeen years. Along the way, he would meet the people who would become a virtual *Who's Who* of Jean Lesage's Quiet Revolution and, later, Pierre Trudeau's French Power in Ottawa.

To one eminent member of that pioneer generation, sociologist Guy Rocher, Catholic Action was nothing less than "the beachhead of the Quiet Revolution."

For André Raynauld, "the Quiet Revolution was not after 1960, it took place between 1945 and 1960. It was a revolution of the mind."

Typically, Raynauld worked for Ryan in the summer of 1951, in the university youth section along with another student named Marc Lalonde. Jeunesse Étudiante Catholique (JEC) was one of the mainspring movements whose activities were coordinated to a certain degree by Ryan, working out of an office in the Archbishop's Palace on Cathedral Street. This made him somewhat suspect among those activists who regarded him as the eyes of the bishops, and who resented any interference by the clergy in their affairs.

The *Jécistes* were one of the pioneer Catholic Action movements in Canada, founded by the Holy Cross Fathers on the campus of College St. Laurent, in 1932. But the Oblate order was first to organize Catholic Action with the Jeunesse Ouvrière Chrétienne (JOC), who helped ease Quebec's transition from a rural to an urban society in the recession-wracked 1930s.

The *Jocistes* grew very quickly. By the mid-1930s, JOC was operating nineteen federations in 172 parishes, with 6,000 members in four Canadian provinces. The *Jocistes* ran summer camps, provided temporary shelter, food, and clothing to young people down on their luck.

It was the *Jocistes* who founded the Ligue Ouvrière Catholique (LOC) in 1939. By the next year, they had formed some twenty-two chapters. By 1944, notes researcher Sandra Wheaton Dudley, some 15,000 militants attended a national convention where the LOC drew up a charter of the working-class family.

Other groups included the Jeuneusse Rurale Catholique (JRC) and the Jeunesse Indépendante Catholique (JIC), primarily for the bourgeoisie. Pierre Juneau, later a Trudeau mandarin before his nomination to the CBC presidency in 1982, recalled that the movements hadn't been inspired by the church hierarchy but "by the young priests in the newer orders. You had the Holy Cross with the students, the Oblates with the workers and the Clercs St. Viateur with the agricultural people. The Jesuits didn't want to be left out, but they didn't fit, as they stressed nationalist values more than spiritual and social values."

The origins and model of Catholic Action could be traced to a 1922 papal encyclical, *Ubi Arcano*, in which Pius XI urged laymen to take a more active role in the affairs of the church by spreading Christian values and principles to the people of their communities. By the mid-1920s, there were some 37,000 of Jeunesse Ouvrière Chrétienne in Belgium alone. By 1931, the movement had spread to North America with the founding, by an Oblate father named Henri Roy, of the first JOC chapter in the Montreal parish of St. Alphonse de Youville.

"The goal of Catholic Action," recalled Pierre Juneau, "was the dropping of moralistic and ritualistic concepts in favor of individual values within a spiritual framework."

Catholic Action would prove to be a political and social training ground for the men and women of Juneau's generation. It produced writers and theorists like Guy Rocher

and Fernand Dumont, provided a rational base for so-
ciologists like Maurice Pinard and Soucy Gagné. It encouraged people like the Breton brothers, Albert and
Raymond, to go off and study at Columbia and Chicago
universities.

On the clerical side in Montreal it produced Maurice
Lafond of the Holy Cross fathers, who performed the
kind of leadership role among the students in Montreal
that Père Georges-Henri Lévesque filled at the social sciences faculty at Laval.

And there were intellectual men of action like Fernand
Cadieux, the founder of the Social Research Group that
was the hothouse for Maurice Pinard, Soucy Gagné and
Yvan Corbeil, Quebec's three leading pollsters into the
1980s. "Cadieux was a prophet," Pinard said in 1980. "He
was enormously cultivated, an educator in the fullest sense
of the word. He had an enormous influence on an entire
generation by the sheer force of his intellect. He wasn't
a technician, he was a creator who ceded his place to
others." On Saturday afternoons in the 1950s, Cadieux
would spend hours at the Laurier Barbecue in Outremont
in the company of Marc Lalonde and Pierre Trudeau. He
would urge them, as Pinard later recalled, to take power
in the federal government from a base in Montreal. "We
have to pass to action," Cadieux would insist, and in
1965, they did. Till the end of his life in 1976, Cadieux
remained an important adviser to Trudeau. And a Cadieux
protegé, Albert Breton, by then an economist at the University of Toronto, would also be a sometime member of
the prime minister's court. (In the 1980s, Breton filled a
behind-the-scenes role with the Kent Commission on
newspapers before his appointment as a member of the
Macdonald Commission on the economy in 1982.)

And the Catholic Action movements produced an in-
ordinate number of career politicians, such as former federal
Liberal cabinet ministers Jeanne and Maurice Sauvé. Gérard
Pelletier, later a Trudeau minister and ambassador to France
and the United Nations, came to Montreal as a young
student in 1939 and served four years as the general secretary of the JEC. The student movement in Quebec was

a small and intimate place in those days. "It wasn't difficult to know everyone," Pelletier recalled. "When I arrived in Montreal with the student movement, the president of the Jeunesse Étudiante of Montreal was Jean Drapeau, and the next year it was Daniel Johnson. So if you were involved in the student movement, you knew those two guys. And I could say, all the others who were there, too. The universities were very small places at that time."

There were Catholic Action movements springing up all over the place. "The bishops of Quebec wanted to coordinate all these movements," said Jeanne Sauvé, herself a Catholic Action alumna, "and that's where Ryan came in."

Of Ryan's stewardship at Catholic Action, there were two very different perceptions. There were those, like Jeanne Sauvé, who perceived him as the intermediary between the bishops and the activists, and there were those who saw him even then as a champion of the individual, a defender of the workingman, a genuine reformer in the affairs of the church. On one point, there was later no disagreement: Ryan knew how to organize, and he knew how to foster a consensus.

The work of the lay Catholic activists was inspired by the motto of Thomas Aquinas, *Voir, Juger, Agir* (Observe, Judge, Act). More than a slogan, it was the basis for the intellectual and administrative organization of the movement. Every year, as Sandra Wheaton Dudley noted in her research paper on Catholic Action, the executive of the national body would suggest a theme for the year's activities. Then Ryan would send representatives to all the dioceses of French Canada to discuss the theme. This was the *Voir* part of the motto, the period of observation and analysis. In the *Juger* part, the chosen theme would be analyzed under Ryan's guidance. Having completed the analysis, the militants would be urged to act, *Agir*. In organizing all these themed activities, Ryan broadened his background beyond the East End of Montreal.

For he travelled a lot, not just in Quebec but across Canada. With his excellent English, he was in demand for seminars and panels. Even before his Catholic Action days, he was a student activist in the Commonwealth Cooperative Federation (CCF), and attended some of its national meetings in the 1940s. In the 1950s, Ryan further broadened his horizons as president of L'Institut Canadien d'Éducation des Adultes, which made him one of the leading figures in the field. Most of all, during the Catholic Action years, he was schooled in the toughest kind of politics, the ecclesiastical kind.

So in that formative period of his career, Ryan developed an outlook and a personal discipline. His vantage point, though very much rooted in Quebec, did not make him uninterested in the rest of Canada. That nationalist-federalist perspective would later shape his writing at *Le Devoir*, and mark his entry into politics at a time when the Liberal party was looking for that third option between separatism and the status quo. As for his working habits, once formed, they seldom varied. "He's doing in the Liberal party what he's done all his life," Pierre Juneau observed in 1980, noting that Ryan spent a lot of time travelling around the province, attending a numbing succession of boring meetings. "He even wrote a book on committees, and how they should meet." Indeed he did. Published by the adult education institute in 1962, it was called, *Les Comités : esprit et méthodes*. No mere pamphlet to picked out of a rack at the back of a church on a Sunday morning, it ran to 252 painstakingly constructed pages. In one chapter, titled "Difficult People in Meetings," Ryan characterized every type, down to drawing distinctions between the compromiser and the *bonne-ententist*, which he allowed were from the same family.

The mandarins might have laughed at this, but for adults who hadn't been to graduate school, and hadn't learned how to run a meeting, it doubtless served a real purpose. There was one final legacy from Ryan's Catholic Action period, the network of contacts, sources and friends that he would always fall back on, whether he was in journalism or politics.

They included clergymen and educators, credit union managers and mayors in every region of the province. They were the people Ryan had come to know in the thirty-five years of his public life before he became a public figure. They started turning up in his leadership campaign. He would fly into Val d'Or or drive over to Lévis, and there would be someone there to meet him.

"He knows the population and the instincts of the population better than most journalists," observed Pierre C. O'Neil, who worked for *Le Devoir* in Ottawa before becoming Pierre Trudeau's press secretary and, eventually, director of news and current affairs programming at Radio-Canada. "He has his ear on the track, he knows when the train is coming and at what time."

His fifteen years at *Le Devoir* may have provided the best clues to the personality and management style of the man.

It is interesting to note that only two years after his arrival there in 1962, Ryan had acceded to the publisher's chair at the Montreal daily, whose influence seemed to be in inverse proportion to its circulation. Other, more logical candidates, were somehow passed over in favor of Ryan. One of them was Jean-Marc Léger, a veteran of the Catholic Action movement and later René Lévesque's delegate general in Brussels. André Laurendeau, the paper's editor-in-chief, was away co-chairing the Royal Commission on Bilingualism and Biculturalism, a landmark work that took most of his energies for the remainder of his life. Besides, Ryan was an outsider, and as such conformed to the paper's tradition of reaching outside its ranks for a boss. Finally, he had the evident backing of Gérard Filion and of the Archdiocese, which in those days still had its word to say on the board of L'Imprimerie Populaire. Ryan fit the bill as a committed Christian activist, and a prudent but progressive-minded person who was well acquainted with the upheaval in the church.

When Ryan assumed control of the paper, it was struggling financially, as it always seemed to be in those days. One of his most lasting decisions was his determination to run the paper as a business that paid its own way. He had little use for a foundation known as Les Amis du *Devoir*, which more or less lapsed during his stewardship of the paper. He liked to point out to people that *Le Devoir* was not St. Joseph's Oratory, with its little collection box in corner stores around the city. The paper had to be rationalized as a business, had to show a profit. And before long, under Ryan's rigorous cost management, it did. Long before other major papers switched to cold type, Ryan junked *Le Devoir*'s ancient linotype press, paid off the printers and had the paper printed by a modern, outside shop. That single decision may have saved the paper.

Ryan became famous for being so close with a buck he practically squeaked. Reporters from all over Quebec soon became familiar with the stories of how he advised journalists going out of town on assignment to stay at the YMCA, as he sometimes did when on the road. Or how he once took a group of reporters to dinner as a reward for a job well done at a convention. They dined in style, at a St. Hubert Barbecue. But for all his legendary tight-fistedness, Ryan could be generous on important matters, especially with life's underdogs. When he bought out his printers at the end of the 1960s, he gave them six months'severance pay. "I found him rather generous," Filion said many years later. "It was more than I would have done." (Ryan never forgot Filion. After his election to the leadership, he took the time to go to Toronto in 1978 to testify as a character witness for Filion in the Marine Industries dredging trial, in which Filion was ultimately acquitted).

Early in the 1970s, Ryan moved the paper from its rundown offices on Notre Dame Street to a "new" old building of its own — *Le Devoir*'s present offices on St. Sacrement Street, in the Old City. Hence Ryan's sobriquet as the Pope of St. Sacrement Street. He paid for the building in cash, and had it fixed up with government re-issue furniture. Once when Michel Roy tried to convince him of the economies of industrial carpets for the office, Ryan replied: "there will be no wall-to-wall carpets at *Le Devoir*."

All in all, the Ryan years at *Le Devoir* were marked by a tendency to keep administrative authority for himself. He always signed the paychecks at the paper, a practice he continued at the Liberal party. In his dealings with a militant journalists' union, he could be ruthless. For him the welfare of the institution was always more important than the sensitivities of its employees. They could argue about monetary clauses, and he would show them the bottom line, and give where he could in the good years. But the one thing he guarded like a watchdog was the director's authority to run the paper, and as long as he was there, he never negotiated any of it away. On the ideas side of the paper, he was more inclined to generosity. His ideas might prevail in the end, but he would entertain lively discussions in editorial conferences. In the newsroom, he had a proven record for hiring, if not always keeping, talented reporters and writers, from Jean-V. Dufresne and Gérald Leblanc of one generation, to Claude Lemelin and Lise Bissonette of the next. Somehow, he managed to bring order out of the intellectual anarchy that prevailed at the paper in the 1970s. He weathered a serious challenge to *Le Devoir*'s well-being when the Parti Québécois, exasperated at its lack of support on St. Sacrement Street, launched its own paper in the mid-1970s. The experiment was a short-lived failure, but for a time, it cut deeply into *Le Devoir*'s earnings and Ryan never made the mistake of underestimating a rival daily that went after part of his clientele.

When he left *Le Devoir* at the beginning of 1978, it had never been on a sounder financial footing, with a reserve in excess of $1 million. Nor had its prestige ever stood any higher. The paper's founder, Henri Bourassa, had made his way from politics into journalism. The most illustrious of his successors was now making his way from journalism into politics.

Jean-V. Dufresne, while admiring the Liberals' capacity to accept this "transplant," also recognized the risks posed by Ryan's complex personality. "Ryan has always had a mystical side," Dufresne observed, "as if he was the recipient of a mandate. The fact that he won't share power is because it poses risks for the execution of his mandate.

"It's the Achilles' heel of Ryan, and that's where the whole future of Ryan and the party will be determined."

"I agree he doesn't delegate," said Ryan's ex-chief organizer, Jacques Lamoureux, "but it may not be a reluctance to delegate so much as a lack of confidence in people. " Yet those who had the closest working relationship with Ryan in his political years insisted that he was far from authoritarian, and even a good-humored boss. There was a time after the Iranian revolution in 1979 when Ryan was nicknamed the "Ayotollah. " Pierre Pettigrew, his executive assistant, remembered being buzzed by his boss. "The Ayotollah," Ryan said with a chuckle, "wants to see you."

"With the people around him," Pettigrew insisted, "he shares everything. When I went to work for him, he said, 'Nothing is closed to you. Every file in my office is open to you.' He wants the people around him to know everything he knows, so that when we come to advise him he's well informed."

Lina Allard, who organized his agenda in those days, saw Ryan "as a guy who is very sympathetic with people he has an affinity for, and to whom he confides important jobs. He's a bit paternalistic with us but not in the negative sense. He is not hard but he is demanding, and he respects a capacity to work."

But finally it was Pierre Pettigrew who posed the fundamental rhetorical question of Ryan's leadership: "Is he mean-minded and vindictive?" Pettigrew thought not, and could cite instances of Ryan's magnanimity and generosity of spirit. Political oracle Léon Dion, for one, had written unfavorably of Ryan during the leadership campaign. Yet Dion was one of the first people Ryan went to see the day after his victory, and almost immediately offered him the chairmanship of the party's constitutional commission. When Dion evidently declined on grounds of wanting to maintain his political objectivity, Ryan informed him he wouldn't be having time for long Saturday morning chats on the state of the constitution.

"He's not mean, no, but he does have a long memory," said Gerry Ryan of his brother. "But where do you draw the line between that and *mesquinerie*? His level of tolerance for opportunists is very low."

He was also known to have a low level of tolerance for those he considered his intellectual inferiors. "My concern," said Guy Saint-Pierre at a time when Ryan was still riding high, "is that like Trudeau he is so superior to others, and knows it, that he might develop a contempt for them." Gerry Ryan had a plausible explanation for that. "When he was a student he studied before he spoke," said the older brother. "And he has no patience for those who speak before studying."

He also had no time for flattery, unless he was the one being flattered. "He's very susceptible to flattery," said Lucette St. Amant. "When he says, 'that's a good guy,' it may be someone who has flattered him." For the rest, as Claude Forget observed, "Ryan is totally incapable of flattering the vanities of ordinary mortals. He will say nice things, but it's always less glittering somehow." For Thérèse Lavoie-Roux, it was just that Ryan was incapable of the hypocrisy of politics. "He's incapable," she said, "of saying things or behaving in a manner that does not correspond to what he believes. It's not meanness at all, it's just the fault of his qualities."

On one aspect of his personality there was general agreement: Claude Ryan was a bit of a gossip.

Michel Robert, who even after falling out with Ryan recognized his qualities as a man who was "authentically modest in his tastes," as well as one who had a meticulous devotion to duty, saw him as occasionally contemptuous. "He always has something bad to say about someone who's not there," Robert said. "He's a big gossip. He sees the bad side of people. The other thing I don't like is that he preoccupies himself with the personal side of people's lives, does so and so live with his wife, is he separated, that sort of thing." Lucette St. Amant, who was fairly close to Ryan in those pre-election days, acknowledged that "the gossipy, mean side of his personality is the side of him that people don't like."

But that was part of Ryan's file, going back some thirty years.

Ryan had been sued for slander by a social activist named Renée Morin. At the time, Ryan went around telling people she was a communist. The case dragged through the courts for years, with Ryan winning in the Superior Court in 1953 before losing in the Court of Appeal four years later. His defence had always been one of "qualified privilege," as to Miss Morin's suitability to be a UNESCO delegate in 1949. However, the plaintiff eventually demonstrated that Ryan was in a position to give an appraisal on only ten of the seventeen occasions on which he repeated the accusation. For the rest, Justice John McDougall found that it was malicious slander, repeated even after the original charge was brought against Ryan.

There was another side to Ryan that disturbed people, and that was his tendency to bring people to their knees.

But that was Ryan, and you took him as he was. He saw this side of himself, the streetfighter side, and he offered no apologies. As he said of his later arguments with Jean Chrétien over the organization of the No committee in the referendum campaign: "You have to go for the crotch, eh?"

9
NON MERCI!

For all the talk of Ryan's ascendancy and dominance of the party, the fact remained that six months after his accession to the leadership, he was still without a seat in the National Assembly, and still without interesting prospects of finding one. It reached the point in November of 1978 that Ryan had to guillotine discussion of the matter in his caucus. Everybody agreed he should be in the House, but no one was in a hurry to give up his seat for Ryan.

Finally, Zoël Saindon, a veteran member from Argenteuil, went to House leader Gérard D. Lévesque. "Everybody wants to go to heaven," he told Lévesque, "but nobody wants to die. I'm prepared to die."

Lévesque took this back to Ryan who said he thought Argenteuil, a mixed urban-rural riding of forty-five municipalities northwest of Montreal, would be "an interesting prospect." So Lévesque set up a meeting between Saindon and Ryan and there ensued a discussion which the leader characterized as "rather painful." Saindon decided that he wasn't ready to die politically after all. "If you want to keep the seat, it's yours," Ryan told him angrily. "I'm not asking for it, I never asked for anything."

By this time the affair of Ryan's seat, or his lack of one, assumed overtones of a comic opera. "On a single day," veteran Quebec correspondent Robert McKenzie reported in *The Toronto Star*, "two former cabinet ministers from Montreal ridings, Fernand Lalonde and Victor Goldbloom, issued press releases denying they might surrender their seats."

To compound Ryan's embarrassment, his vanquished leadership opponent, Raymond Garneau, was anxious to resign so that he could take up his second career as a business executive. Garneau was enough of a party man to wait for Ryan to find another seat, and thus be spared the embarrassment of running in Garneau's Quebec City fortress of Jean Talon, where the knives would almost certainly be out for him. But Garneau was not going to wait forever.

Finally, in the last week of the legislative session of 1978, the matter was satisfactorily resolved. Saindon would resign after all, Garneau could receive the tributes of the House and go off to his insurance and banking career.

Argenteuil turned out to be a good place for Ryan to hang his legislative hat.

In the best traditions of a candidate on the hustings, Ryan could even claim Argenteuil as his home riding, for it was here that his mother, Blandine Dorion Ryan, had been born at the turn of the century. Abandoned by her husband in 1928 when Claude Ryan was only three, she was left to raise her boys alone, and at the height of the Depression. The experience may have hardened her as well as her sons, who grew up in the mean streets of East-End Montreal. For them it was a treat to sneak into baseball games at De Lorimier Stadium after the fifth inning, or to be bussed to the Forum to sit in the "Millionaires Section" along Nosebleed Alley, in those years of the 1930s when they were practically giving away tickets for the Canadiens' games.

Half a century later, Blandine Ryan could take a special maternal pride in the attainments of her three sons, one a justice of the superior court, one a mayor of a large Montreal suburb, the other a prominent journalist turned politician.

It was not bad for a bunch of kids from Chambly Street. The oldest, Gerry, was a wounded naval serviceman who at Claude's urging went to McGill law school after the Second World War on the veterans' college plan. The youngest, Yves, had started out as a canned-goods salesman, and by his early thirties was mayor of fast-growing Montreal North, a city that he administered so well that during his stewardship it paid off the civic debt and built an imposing new city hall. And then there was the middle brother, whose whole career as a committed Christian activist and newspaper oracle seemed a preparation for what he was doing now in the home county of his mother.

For in those palmy days of 1979, Ryan was still very much the man the federalist forces were waiting for. And on April 30, a year and two weeks after his accession to the leadership, he finally arrived as the elected leader of the opposition in the National Assembly.

On the night of April 30, Ryan waited out the formality of the count for half an hour or so before Radio-Canada declared his election over the PQ's Dr. Charles Roy, an area dentist. The final margin was an impressive 9,000-plus majority. Ryan had 16,600 votes to Roy's 7,300. He won every municipality in the riding, from Thurso on the banks of the Ottawa River, down to Lachute. "Well, that's done," Ryan told his small circle of staff. "I knew we would would make it. " Madeleine Ryan came in, she cleaned his glasses and then they were off in one of those ridiculous motorcades, with shortwave radios linking several cars going four blocks in a small town, the town which then had every reason to think it was giving Quebec its next premier.

The voters in the country at large seemed to think so, too. Since Ryan arrived on the scene in 1978 as a full-blooded national figure, Pierre Trudeau's fortunes had been on the wane outside Quebec. There was a sense, and Joe Clark acknowledged "there might be some of that," that to the extent Ryan was perceived in English Canada as being able to win the referendum, Trudeau was no longer indispensable. Ryan himself did not make much of this suggestion, saying that national elections hinged on much more than the results of a by-election in a provincial legislature. But even as he was talking on his front lawn three days after Argenteuil, Ryan had just waved goodbye to Trudeau. And why had the prime minister come to lunch at 425 St. Joseph Boulevard? Just to congratulate Mr. Ryan, he said. In fact, the federal Liberals, desperate for a break in the home stretch of the 1979 campaign, arranged the meeting so that they could present the image of a common front between the two leaders. Ryan, for once, was more than obliging. He threw his arm around Trudeau, who looked distinctly uncomfortable, bade him farewell with a "good luck, Pierre," then turned to reporters and chided Clark for his apparent misunderstanding of the importance of self-determination as an underlying issue in the referendum debate. On that sunny May afternoon, Ryan had done everything the feds could have asked, and more.

Three weeks later, with the defeated Trudeau on his way out of office, Ryan was at the zenith of his political career. Suddenly he walked in the sunlight, clear of Trudeau's long shadow. Ryan had become, in the real as well as the legal sense of the term, the undisputed leader of the federalist forces.

As for the Lévesque administration, it was experiencing its own problems. With the referendum just around the corner, the government was having to negotiate with the province's quarter of a million public-sector employees, members of teachers', hospital workers' and civil servants' unions who could be expected to be sympathetic to the government's cause. But in the negotiations, they held the referendum as a hostage, with the gun pointed directly at Lévesque's head. Despite Lévesque's sincere protestations that the referendum must be above such sordid business, he caved in to most of the union demands in a contract that both sides might have regretted when it came to be renegotiated in 1982. In the midst of the the worst economic downturn in half a century, the government simply decreed a settlement that included temporary wage rollbacks of twenty percent, and reductions in union strength.

In mid-1979, Lévesque was also experiencing the difficulties of a founding father with his political party. It came to Quebec for a June convention mostly to do his bidding in the matter of defining sovereignty-association, but the government still had to spell out what it meant by it in a long-delayed white paper. As for Ryan's performance in the National Assembly, he was proving to be surprisingly adept. In question period, he relied on his own instincts and the advice of seatmate Gérard D. Lévesque, who in his nearly quarter of a century in the place, had seen just about everything.

In the fall of 1979, Ryan appeared to be doing just what he had been hired for, defending the federalist option and demolishing the PQ thesis. When the government finally came through with its white paper in November, Ryan picked it to pieces in the space of an hour in his office, and then said the whole thing was a "house of cards."

From Ottawa, Prime Minister Joe Clark was staying out of it, denying Lévesque a target and doing his best to remove what he called "irritants" between Ottawa and Quebec.

But before many months had passed, the Clark government was out of business, essentially because of poor inventory control—they forgot to count. The fall of the Clark government on December 13, and Pierre Trudeau's subsequent five-day performance as Hamlet, caused a certain amount of consternation in the Bunker, as the concrete pill-box of a building which housed the premier's office on the Grande-Allée was derisively known in Quebec. Trudeau did not fit into René Lévesque's referendum plans. He had delayed eveything about the referendum— the white paper, the question, the vote — in the hope the voters of Canada would get rid of Trudeau for him. When they finally obliged on May 22, it appeared all Lévesque's temporizing had paid off. When the white paper came out in November, it was Opposition Leader Trudeau, in something resembling high dudgeon, who walked out of two French-language interviews because of technical foul-ups. "*Merde*," he said, giving up the second time. Those who knew him suspected that what was really bothering him was that the moment had arrived, and it had missed him. Six weeks later, by some seemingly supernatural kind of luck, he was walking into an election campaign with an insurmountable lead of twenty Gallup points. Once again, there was a confluence of events between Ottawa and Quebec, between Trudeau and Lévesque.

Two days after Trudeau ended his retirement, Lévesque finally published his mandate question. He had apparently written the final version only the night before.

"*Non, merci*," Ryan said in the Assembly on the afternoon of December 20. "No thanks, we do not want it."

It was one of his more memorable performances. And with characteristic logic, he tore the question to pieces. "Our conclusion," Ryan said, "is that the question falls far short of meeting the expectations which had been nourished by the government themselves in the statements of the past few months. The question goes beyond the true meaning of the option of the government. It centers upon the means which is proposed by the government, that is to say the negotiation of a new understanding with the rest of Canada. It has no clear explicit reference to the fundamental objectives of the government, which is sovereignty-association, that is to say political independence or separation on one hand, and economic association, if possible, on the other."

Ryan had his own proposals to make in what would be known as the "Beige Paper," the constitutional option of his own party. For most of the time, Ryan had taken little part in the work of his constitutional committee, except when the work bogged down. Finally, over the Christmas holidays, he took control of it and wrote the opening and closing chapters himself.

Of all the constitutional documents published during the referendum era, the "Beige Paper" was the most comprehensive and coherent. The "Beige Paper" was introduced by Ryan and committee chairman Raynold Langlois at a tumultuous news conference in the Queen Elizabeth Hotel on January 10, 1980, two years to the day after Ryan announced his candidacy for the Liberal leadership. Some 200 reporters filled a salon in the biggest gathering of the media hordes in Montreal since René Lévesque's momentuous press conference on the morrow of his 1976 victory. While everyone assumed that Ryan had approved the general parameters of the document, nobody suspected that he had done a furious rewrite job and personally written the important statement of principles at the beginning. "They must have produced seven, eight or ten blueprints," Ryan later recalled. "None was acceptable. They were too theoretical. They were dry, they were not *engagé* at all. I insisted with them that they should stop trying to write an introduction and they should go into the work of writing the substance of chapters on sharing powers, on institutions. And as soon as they started adopting that approach, the work went very well. I said, 'Let's reserve that part for the end when we know what kind of blueprint we have in mind.'

"When it came to that," he continued, "they began again attempting to write something. One day they came to me and they said, 'You will have to do something.' I took the opening pages and began writing myself, so I must have written a couple of drafts. We had a lot of redrafting to do on other chapters as well. I was here with three or four colleagues and we worked night and day during the Christmas season."

The "Beige Paper" was a tremendous piece of work, a literary achievement as well as a draft proposal for constitutional realignment. As superficial as the PQ's white paper had been, the "Beige Paper" was, in Ryan's own appraisal, "a beautifully conceived paper, a very fine document, a model of balance, of equilibrium."

The party's commitment to Canada was unequivocal, although the paper also proposed a certain realignment of federal-provincial powers, but in conventional ways that had been essentially proposed in other precincts. Reforming the Senate, for example, as a Federal Council with nominees coming from the provinces, was an idea that had been kicked around by the Conservative party in a position paper proposing a House of the Provinces, by the Task Force on Canadian Unity in its proposal for a House of the Federation, by some of the provinces, and even by the Trudeau government in its 1978 paper, "A Time for Action." So Ryan was really not venturing onto dangerous territory.

But there were definite risks involved in publishing the "Beige Paper" before rather than after the referendum.

He felt he had to offer something, to give the people a reason for voting No, for turning a No into a Yes for renewed federalism. In fact, renewed federalism wasn't on the program, wasn't part of the mandate question. Instead of being on the defensive for their own option, the PQ now appeared to be in a position to attack Ryan's as not going far enough in proposing additional powers for the provinces. "It's a gift for us," said Claude Morin, the father of the referendum, when he ran into Ryan's executive assistant Pierre Pettigrew in a hotel elevator.

As careful as Ryan had been to avoid any claims of special status, he was running nominal risks with some of the other provinces, if some of the premiers didn't keep their counsel until the referendum. Peter Lougheed, for example, was dead set against the Victoria amending formula, which was endorsed by Ryan as the best achievable means of retaining Quebec's veto, along with Ontario and any two Atlantic or Western provinces. It was well known that Lougheed was adamantly opposed to veto powers for any province, especially Ontario. Even then, he was an advocate of what would later become known as the Vancouver Formula, requiring the consent of any seven provinces adding up to half the population. But Lougheed had the good political sense to stay out of the debate.

For the next two months, Ryan took the "Beige Paper" on the road with him. In every region of the province, Liberal activists gathered to discuss it in the run-up to the party's policy convention February 29 to March 2 in Montreal. In hindsight, it would later be said that the Liberals wasted their energies on the hypothetical question of the "Beige Paper," while the PQ was preparing for the decisive debate on the real question, which would begin on March 4 with the first of thirty-five hours of debate.

The PQ braintrusters had been laying low over the long winter recess, gathering arguments and preparing speeches for government members. When the session opened, they were more than ready. What began as a debate soon became a rout.

"Look, with hindsight," Ryan said later, "I will admit we made one mistake during that debate. We had prepared our own constitutional position. It was well prepared. We had decided it was not going to be the object of debate in the House or in the referendum campaign for reasons which I think were justified.

"But," he continued, "we had not really prepared for that debate in the House. We thought it would be a debate on the question, and it was a debate on the issues. And we were shorthanded at that time, in the way of arguments. We did not have all the documents to defend the federalist thesis."

Ryan appeared to be the only leading member of his own team who was fully up to the challenge. He was also on the receiving end of some of the intellectual intolerance which seemed to be a specialty of the PQ. One Péquiste referred to him as the Lord Durham of the 1980s, in effect an assimilationist. "I expected that from them," Ryan said later. "And frankly, I thought to myself, that's going to be good stuff for us to use during the campaign. That was good stuff for us. But personally, I was used to it. I was being branded a traitor at *Le Devoir*, I couldn't care less."

By Week Two of the debate, there was the beginning of concern in the federalist camp, and by Week Three, after the publication of the first unfavorable poll for the No side, it became something approaching panic. Despite the unfavorable omens of the poll and the disastrous course the debate was following, Ryan remained curiously unperturbed. In fact, as he later admitted, he was hoarding a lot of his themes and arguments for the real campaign. "I had a lot of documentation myself," he said. "I had not the time to share it with people. I was not disposed to throw it to the wolves at that early stage. I kept telling our people we have to reserve that material for the campaign itself."

But he readily admitted that the PQ had a big inning in the debate on the question.

"The PQ succeeded for a while in creating the impression that they had dominated the debate," Ryan admitted later on, "because they let loose all their ammunition at that premature stage. And I think that in the long run, we were wiser than they were."

If so, it was not apparent at the time.

10
YVETTE

The secretary at the Montreal Forum neatly summarized the general opinion of the idea. "I think you're nuts," she told the woman at the other end of the line. Nothing daunted, Diane Fortier wanted to know the cost of renting the Forum. She didn't want it for a rock concert, or a prayer meeting of Holy Rollers, but for a rally of women supporting the No option, the Yvettes.

"It wasn't organized by crazy ladies," Louise Robic would say much later, after she had become president of the Quebec Liberals. And they were certainly aware of the risks of trying to fill the Forum, one of the most dangerous high-wire acts in Canadian politics. "We were told," Robic recalled, "that if we bombed out, it would be the end, the referendum would be lost. But we knew we could get between ten and fifteen thousand people, and the Forum told us that at 10,000, it would look full."

So quite on their own, an ad hoc committee of four women took what turned out to be the most momentous decision of the 1980 referendum. They would go to the Forum, on April 7, Easter Monday, symbolically the day after the Resurrection, which is what the Yvette rally proved to be for the No campaign.

It was that rarest of political events, a spontaneous demonstration. It was all in reaction to some comments by Lise Payette, minister responsible for the status of women in the Lévesque government. She was a former talk-show personality at Radio-Canada and was considered the PQ's star recruit of the 1976 campaign. She could help the PQ where it was weakest, among married women of a certain age. In the Lévesque administration, she proved to be a temperamental but talented minister. As consumer affairs minister, she was able to steer an auto insurance bill from controversy at the outset to general acclaim at the time of its adoption. When she would occasionally be caught thinking out loud, notably voicing her low opinion of parliamentary institutions and their inhabitants, she always managed to escape the censure of René Lévesque and his advisers. The operative assumption was that he needed her for the referendum, especially with women.

She was expected to play a starring role, second only to Lévesque himself. At one of the PQ's pre-referendum rallies, it was Payette who led the singing of the Yes campaign's jingle. Before many weeks had passed, it would become clear that the Yes forces were going nowhere, due in no small measure to Payette's condescending remarks about stereotyped women she called Yvettes, after a character in a schoolbook reader. She was exhorting women to get out of the kitchen, to break free of their confining roles. The women on the other side were a bunch of Yvettes, she said. Claude Ryan had married one.

Payette said this on Sunday March 9, and at the time hardly anyone noticed. The only journalist who picked up on her remarks was from *Le Devoir*, and this was how it came to the attention of Lise Bissonette, then an associate editor of the paper and later to become its editor-in-chief. She wrote a savage commentary in the edition of March 11, castigating Payette for her intellectual intolerance.

By the next day, the matter had reached the floor of the National Assembly, then beginning the second week of the debate on the referendum question. Rising on a point of privilege Payette tried to explain away her remark by quoting from the grade-two reader in question. Yvette, she read, "always finds a way to please her parents. Yesterday at mealtime, she sliced the bread, poured hot water on the tea in the teapot, carried the sugar bowl, the butter dish and the milk pitcher; she also helped serve the roast chicken. After the meal, she happily dried the dishes and swept the carpet. Little Yvette is a very obliging girl."

Payette put down the reader and went on to say that Quebec women deserved a lot of credit, "having been raised as Yvette, to have become something other than Yvette."

And she concluded: "If I hurt anyone by this remark, including the wife of the leader of the opposition, I apologize publicly, because that wasn't my intention. My intention was to continue, as I have been doing for twenty years, to help the women of Quebec rid themselves of encumbering stereotypes."

For the women and men on the No side, it was a pretty morbid time. Ryan's Liberals were getting their clock cleaned in the referendum debate. By the close of the three-week debate on March 21, the No side was thoroughly demoralized. In Quebec City, a woman named Andrée Richard decided to do something about it. She rented the ballroom of the Château Frontenac for a brunch on Sunday, March 30. Only women would attend. Only women would speak. It was one of those things that give other people ideas. By the time Louise Robic got back to the party's office in Montreal the next day, it was decided that they would do something there. In no time at all, they sold 2,000 tickets to a coffee and tea party to be held the following Monday evening at the Queen Elizabeth Hotel. By Wednesday, Robic's people had sold 7,000 tickets when the largest convention hotel in the city had room for only 4,000 people. Clearly, they had to go somewhere else. The question, as Robic said later, was what was available and what was advisable. There were four women in the Gilford Street office on Holy Thursday: Robic, Diane Fortier, Renée Desmarais and Annie Pelletier. They told no one of what they were up to, certainly no men, least of all Ryan and chief organizer Pierre Bibeau.

Finally, they came to the conclusion that they had to try for the Forum, that every other place was too small. "We analyzed what it would take to fill the Forum," Robic said later. Because they were selling tickets at five dollars a head, rather than giving them away, they could be sure that everyone would show up. And because they never sent out more than fifty tickets at one time to one riding, they kept a close count of things. Finally, they decided to go for it. "We thought," Robic said, "that the impact would be fantastic. Just the name of the Forum would make it a big event."

What nobody then realized was how big.

Pierre Bibeau, finally informed of what the women were up to, practically fell on his head. "Who did you consult? " he asked them.

"We consulted ourselves," Diane Fortier replied. Bibeau's senior staff, regional organizers such as Georges Boudreault and Jim McCann, men with long experience in the packing of halls, politely voiced their doubts. Bibeau had one overriding concern as to the difference between 7,000 people at the Queen Elizabeth and 14,000 at the Forum. "Do you think you can fill it? " he asked.

They would fill it all right, without giving anything away. By Easter Monday, Diane Fortier was at the Forum with a certified check for $21,000. By early evening, there was a line-up of women stretching four-deep around the Forum. In a building that had seen everything from the Rolling Stones to the Maurice Richard riot, it was probably the most genteel crowd in Forum history. As the women made their way into the building, each was given a long-stemmed red carnation. The Forum was transformed into a huge bed of flowers swaying in the breeze. The twenty-one-piece orchestra of Paul Capelli, the type of band that plays black-tie and graduation balls, serenaded the crowd.

At centre ice, a knot of journalists simply stood and gaped at the crowd. "It's my fault," said *Le Devoir*'s Lise Bissonette, only half in jest. Long afterwards, serious journalists would try to quantify the social as well as the political significance of the Yvette movement, which pushed in a ripple effect from Montreal to practically every village and town in the province. In Sept-Iles, a fortress of the Péquiste option, there were over 1,000 women for lunch. In Bonaventure county, down on the Gaspé peninsula, there were 1,200. In Sherbrooke, where the armed forces people were reluctant to rent out an armory for a political event, they found that Robic's people were not shy about picking up the phone and calling the defence minister, Gilles Lamontagne, to get what they wanted. Another 5,000 women turned up there in the

Eastern Townships. Before long, there was a Ryan tour and an Yvette tour crisscrossing the province. In all, the Yvette organizers calculated that they brought out some 50,000 women over the course of the spring campaign, most of whom had never attended a political meeting in their lives. "Because they were invited to a meeting where there were just women," Madeleine Ryan suggested later, "because there were no conditions of admission, they sensed that they weren't at an ordinary political meeting where they could be held up to scrutiny. They went there, and it became for them a way of assuring themselves that they were far from being alone in their opinions. Some women told me afterwards that where they had been afraid to put on their No buttons, they were no longer shy."

Afterward, much was written about the nature of the Yvette movement, some of it purely speculative and some of it highly nonsensical. But the organizers themselves tried to get a handle on this by conducting an attitudinal survey of some 300 women who had been signed up to the Yvette movement. The result, as Lysiane Gagnon was able to inform the readers of her political column in *La Presse*, was that the Yvettes had a progressive rather than a conservative social outlook. "Many commentators have presumed rather rashly," she wrote, "that it was the outraged housewives against the career women, that they were social reactionaries, who were totally dissociated from the feminist movement . . . . What makes this all the more interesting is that these respondents express very progressive ideas."

As the women polled measured the important things in their lives, their married life came first, children and family second and third, with work in fourth place, and religion arriving in ninth place, after vacations and sporting activities. As the women measured their socio-political priorities, they were in favor of aid to the handicapped and aged at home, they were against sexist advertising, in favor of services to rape victims and so on.

But in April of 1980, Louise Robic said "They felt a danger to their country." For in the weeks leading up to the Easter Monday rally at the Forum, there had been a tremendous amount of social pressure building for the Yes option. An IQOP survey published on March 16 in *Dimanche-Matin* indicated the Yes option had taken a slight lead among decided voters. For four years now, at every family reunion since the accession of the PQ, women had experienced these political divisions in their homes. The Yvette rallies offered them the chance to express their own opinions. "We probably helped a lot of women come out of their homes," Diane Fortier observed later, "and a lot of women to come out of themselves."

At the Forum, as at later meetings, women were the only speakers. There were twenty of them onstage that night, from Ryan's appointments secretary Lina Allard to Commons Speaker Jeanne Sauvé. "If you had told me a week before there would be 15,000 people at the Forum I wouldn't have believed it," Allard said later. "If you had told me I would have spoken, I wouldn't have been there." For her, there was some element of women and housewives, who had been degraded by some of the more aggressive elements of the feminist movement, getting an opportunity to renew their self-esteem. "A lot of people were revolted by what Payette said," Allard observed. "For me, emancipation is going to work if you want it to."

For Jeanne Sauvé, a veteran of the political stump, it was another kind of meeting. "When I got out of there," she said later, "I would never have known that there could exist such a thing as a very feminine meeting. You know, it was beyond my conception, what would a feminine meeting be? A meeting with a lot of women there, or what, what is it? But it was a meeting with a lot of women, which made it a very feminine meeting. But it was sweet, it was soft, there was no hostility, no aggressiveness, they all came there to say, listen, we've got an idea, we've got an opinion, this was it. We're just telling you."

And there was one living link with the pioneer feminists in the person of 84-year-old Thérèse Casgrain, who had been in the battle forty years before to obtain the right for women to vote in Quebec. She told the crowd they might not be important in the eyes of Mme. Payette, but René Lévesque would learn "that even the little cricket's voice can be heard across the meadow."

And so it went, for nearly three hours, the most extraordinary soirée in the recent history of Canadian politics. "There hasn't been since the time women got the right to vote an event that was so important," suggested Andrée Dontigny, a housewife and mother of two from the Montreal suburb of Laval. "For many women, it was their first experience at really expressing themselves. Payette, when she said that, she said it not to put women down, but to wake them up. She did, involuntarily, exactly what she set out to do."

Looking around the Forum that night as he stood under an exit, senior Liberal organizer Jim McCann looked as if a great burden had been lifted from his shoulders. "It's a boost," he said, with a glance at the great arena, filled to its farthest corner. "And to be frank, we needed that."

Did they ever.

The Ryan Liberals had sailed confidently out to their policy convention on the first Sunday of March, only to go aground a few days later on the shoals of the National Assembly debate on the referendum question. For a while there in mid-March, it looked like they might be shipwrecked.

In fact, there were those who maintained that Ryan had set off on the wrong course by unveiling his party's constitutional option, the so-called "Beige Paper," when he did in January of 1980. After all, it wasn't his question that was being answered in the referendum, and as much as he tried to define his option of renewed federalism, there would be needless controversy. For some of the feds, it would go too far in decentralizing and redistributing powers as between the two senior levels of government. For the Péquistes, it obviously wouldn't go far enough. Moreover, it would take the heat off the PQ for the obvious shallowness, logical gaps and plain wishful thinking apparent in the government's white paper on sovereignty-association, *La Nouvelle Entente*, rather grandly dubbed "A New Deal," in English, which inspired some digs about Franklin Delano Lévesque.

Walking out of Ryan's news conference, his former *Le Devoir* colleague Michel Roy foresaw the dangers that lay down the road. "Maybe," Roy suggested in a passing remark to one reporter, "he doesn't want to win by too much."

The problem with the "Beige Paper," in retrospect, was that it consumed too much of the party's time when it should have been gearing up for the referendum debate. All through January and February, when the public and a good many of their own activists were preoccupied with the surprise winter federal election campaign, Ryan's people orchestrated an exhaustive series of regional and riding-by-riding consultations on the "Beige Paper," leading into the full policy convention in Montreal. All the while, the PQ braintrust was preparing for the three-week debate, an event that was widely anticipated to be of a crucial nature. What the PQ had prepared, through the office of its brilliant House leader, Claude Charron, was a color-coordinated television spectacular. Every speech other than Lévesque's, with the single exception of Jacques Parizeau's, had been vetted by Charron's office. Every last one of them had an appeal to some emotional chord, excoriated some federal devil, appealed to some sectional or sectorial interest, or as with Charron's own contribution, tried to assuage the doubts and fears of a group of voters like Quebec's senior citizens, who had the usual concerns about losing their pensions if they changed countries. Apart from their strategic advantage, they had a 2 to 1 numerical advantage in the House, giving them a huge advantage in television time, as the rules were finally adopted.

On the Liberal side, Ryan, so often accused of intellectual high-handedness, left his members free, as he told them, to speak from their own minds and hearts. For three weeks, it went on before a huge audience of Radio-

Quebec and Radio-Canada viewers. For the Ryan forces, it was an acknowledged disaster. "We lost the first inning," he admitted later, "but what counts is the final score."

The parliamentary rout, and the publication of the first IQOP referendum poll, indicating the Yes forces had taken a 38 to 35 lead among decided voters, did not exactly inspire confidence in Ryan as manager of the federalist team. With Easter fast approaching, with the 35-day referendum campaign expected soon after, the Ryan people acknowledged that they had some catching up to do. "The assault was badly planned," admitted his appointments and policy secretary, Lina Allard, "the mood was never lower."

And never lower than in the late afternoon of Thursday March 27, when the Ryan team, supplemented by a couple of feds, met in the Hampstead room of the Bonaventure Hotel.

Looking around the table, chief organizer Pierre Bibeau noticed the people who would play key roles in the coming weeks. They were: chief fundraiser Gilles Hébert, policy adviser Yvan Allaire, Lina Allard and Louise Robic, the ineffable Lucette St. Amant, advertising man Jacques Dussault, Liberal party president Larry Wilson, Léonce Mercier, director-general of the federal Liberals in Quebec, and Eddie Goldenberg, the diminutive and indispensable right-hand man of Jean Chrétien. The meeting would last for more than eight hours. "The debate and the polls have created a climate of concern," Bibeau began, "and that's why we're meeting today."

Afterward, everyone who was there remembered a comical moment that said everything about the predicament the No forces found themselves in. Bibeau held up a big white organization chart, filled out in pencil. Nobody could read it. One of the advertising brainwaves put forward was a print campaign of thirty-six reasons why people should vote no. As if anyone would wade through that much ad copy. For the rest, Dussault said his campaign, when it began in April, would understandably be aimed at the undecided voter. They would waste no time reassuring their nervous supporters about their presence. Yvan Allaire made a scholarly presentation as to the relative strengths and weaknesses of the two sides.

Everyone agreed they had to find a way to stop the social pressure and momentum building for the *Oui*, but no one could agree on an approach.

The first of the Yvette meetings was coming up that Sunday in Quebec, and Bibeau thought that might make a good beginning. Someone else suggested they needed some prestigious people on the 300-member national committee of Quebecers for the No. "We need people like Guy Lafleur and Gilles Villeneuve," someone said, "we don't need any goddamn writers." Ryan, who had joined the meeting, turned red as a beet, and then burst out laughing. All this time, they were talking their way around the edges of the question that was on everyone's mind: how to make the most effective but discreet use of Pierre Trudeau.

Ryan's executive assistant, Pierre Pettigrew, suggested that Trudeau must "show his confidence" in the No forces. What they couldn't agree on was how. At this point, Trudeau was being urged in some quarters to make an address to the country before the writs were issued in Quebec. Others wanted him invited into the campaign full time, as Larry Wilson noted, because "you don't keep Guy Lafleur on the bench during the Stanley Cup playoffs." Round and round the discussion went, to no resolution. Finally Chretien's man, Eddie Goldenberg, piped up. "I'm going back to Ottawa," he said. "What do I tell them? " He would not tell them much of anything, since it would be left to Trudeau and Ryan to work out the details at their Good Friday meeting in Ottawa the following week. But there was a developing sense not to overplay the Trudeau card. They broke up after midnight without really having settled anything.

Ryan had pleaded for a little more self-confidence in their cause and patience to strike at the right time. "We can't," he said, "launch the ship before it's built."

Ten days later, well into the month of April, they were still trying to get people aboard. Ryan's ship, built according to the blueprints of the enabling legislation, was duly christened *Les Québécois pour le Non*, at a press launching on April 8, the day after the success of the Yvette rally at the Forum. Jean Chrétien called it a "committee of 400 that never met." Actually, it did meet once, that afternoon in a salon of the Meridien Hotel. From A to Z, there were some impressive names on Ryan's list of *prominenti*, none more so than Father Georges-Henri Lévesque, the Dominican monk who had founded the Laval University School of Social Sciences. In many ways, Georges-Henri Lévesque was considered the true father of the Quiet Revolution, in that he turned out the men who came to power in Quebec in the 1960s. By 1980, still the good-humored monk, the much-honored Father Lévesque was aligned with Ryan. So were most of the business and professional elites, as well as the leadership of the English-speaking minority and ethnic communities. The committee tended however to be a little short on talent from the popular and performing arts, most of whom were on the other side. When asked why No committee member Claude Valade was asked to sing the national anthem at a big campaign rally, a Ryan staffer responded only half in jest: "She's our artist."

This was the honorary committee that Quebec Federation of Labor president Louis Laberge, from his perspective with the Yes, would scornfully dismiss as a reactionary coalition. Ryan met with them for what seemed like the longest period of time, delaying the start of his news conference by fully an hour, while TV reporters fighting supper hour deadlines simply stood around and stewed. Instead of having the committee's manifesto adopted as tabled, Ryan insisted on reading it all the way through. Meanwhile the representatives of the news media who would be with him for the coming six weeks were left to stand outside and make wisecracks about the grotesque buffet motifs that had been designed by the Meridien Hotel. One was a beaver and the other, presumably a representation of a Quebec tourist, had on a Mexican hat. Meanwhile, secretaries scurried about with photocopies of the committee list, which was still being put together.

In terms of care for the media and organization of the campaign, it was not a very promising beginning. As someone suggested, maybe "they should turn the whole thing over to the Yvettes."

11
LE OUI ET LE NON

I t was, as René Lévesque said, "as if we had decided to start our campaign in Westmount."

There was Claude Ryan, sitting up front in a chartered DC-9, winging in for a landing in the countryside of the Kingdom of the Saguenay, which on Sunday, April 13, was still covered in snow. Back in the zoo section of the aircraft, reporters wondered why Ryan had chosen to kick off his campaign in Chicoutimi, the regional centre of "le Royaume," which was the PQ's strongest region in the province. The justice minister, Marc-André Bédard, had been a member of the PQ pioneer class of 1970, and had survived the Bourassa landslide of 1973. Not only was Ryan going into the area first, he was inaugurating his campaign in the Georges Vezina arena, capacity 6,000. It had all the possibilities of a disaster, which is exactly what it proved to be. The No organizers had managed to turn out a very respectable crowd of about 3,000, which would have made the event a huge success in a place like the Hotel Chicoutimi. In the drafty old arena, the press corps had hardly got their coats off before they began counting the empty spaces. In their very first rally of the referendum campaign, the No organizers had broken the cardinal rule of advance work: always make sure the hall is too small for your crowd.

And then there was the manner in which the meeting unfolded, which established the pattern for the entire campaign. Ryan was about the fifteenth and last speaker, after the area councilmen, mayors, MNAs, down to the Union Nationale leader Michel LeMoignan, and federal justice minister Jean Chrétien. Chrétien had flown in on a government JetStar on the pretext that he was opening a federal tax centre in nearby Roberval before linking up with Ryan again that evening in Val d'Or on the other side of the province. By the time it came his turn to speak, Chrétien was furious at the way the afternoon had gone. Half the crowd seemed to have drifted out, and he tried to bring them back with a stemwinder.

To the suggestion that the feds had no role to play in the campaign, Chrétien riposted that "no SOB" was going to stop him from speaking in his native province. Finally, nearly three hours after the meeting had begun, it was Ryan's turn. He promptly committed the first unforced error of the campaign when, for no good reason, he made a disparaging remark about Marc-André Bédard. It made no sense to launch a gratuitous attack on the justice minister, who was something of a hero in the region.

But then, Quebecers were discovering that Ryan could be a man of back-alley, down and dirty rhetoric. Only the previous Wednesday, at a warmup rally in Kamouraska, he had suggested that intergovernmental affairs minister Claude Morin had "gone down on all fours, sucking" for an endorsement from a prominent French socialist leader. When even the parliamentary press crowd thought the metaphor was somewhat explicit, a rather chagrined Ryan told his assistant Pierre Pettigrew that he had another image in mind. "I was thinking more of a mother-child relationship," he explained, "You know, stop sucking at the mother's breast. " It would not be the last time Ryan's rhetoric would get away from him. When a No committee room was vandalized later in the campaign, he accused the Yes forces of resorting to "fascist" tactics, in the textbook sense of the word. And when he referred to the nationalist's profoundly pessimistic interpretation of Quebec's history in Canada, he compared the Péquiste intellectuals to the "revisionist historians in the Kremlin." But that was Ryan, you took him pretty well as he was, and before long it was clear the fundamental issues of the campaign were much more important than any of the players, or anything they might say.

The issue, in its simplest and most eloquent terms, was defined by a filling-station operator in the Eastern Townships city of Sherbrooke. One side, the Yes, was

offering Quebec. The other side, the No, was offering
Quebec and Canada. For him, when he thought about
it, the choice was easy. The No was offering more. In
terms of constructing the necessary majority, it was a
question of building blocks. Or rather, voting blocs. "We
were starting with a base of 40 percent," said Ryan's chief
organizer, Pierre Bibeau. "The PQ was starting with 30
percent. So we had to pick up only 10 percent of the
remainder."

Roughly speaking, the No forces began with all of the
20 percent non-*francophone* vote. They had another rock
solid 20 percent of the *francophone* vote, among the elderly,
the bourgeoisie, and the professional and management
class. The PQ began with the 20 percent of the population
who were supporters of outright independence, and began
building on that by the softness of their option. All the
polls had indicated that roughly 30 percent of the voters
supported sovereignty, even if it amounted to the same
thing as independence. From there, to sovereignty-association, to a mandate to negotiate sovereignty-association, the PQ built to around 40 percent. But in order to
take it from there to a majority, Lévesque needed to put
still more water in his wine. He began this process with
the text of the referendum question itself, which made it
clear that any results from the process of what one journalist
dubbed "sovereignty-negotiation," would be submitted
to the voters in a second plebiscite. The second referendum
was only one of four arguments in the PQ's soft sell to
the soft federalist vote.

The others were the argument of le *bargaining power*,
for a mandate to seek more powers for Quebec in some
kind of revamped Canadian federation. Then would come
the second referendum. Then if the voters still wanted
to pull back from sovereignty-association, they could still
change the government at the next election which had
to be held within a year. And after the Trudeau restoration
of February 18, the Yes side had another argument: anyway, Trudeau will say no. Therefore, you have nothing
to lose by voting yes, and everything to gain in affirming

la fierté, the pride, of Quebecers. It was with these arguments with swing voters that the PQ began building toward a majority during the three-week televised debate in March. They had another argument going for them. In a word: solidarity.

Afterwards, when the recriminations set in, many of René Lévesque's supporters reproached him for the ambiguous referendum question cloaked in the gradualist strategies of Claude Morin. But the tribute came from a tested adversary. "Morin," said Jean Chrétien, "tried it the only way it might have worked, inch by inch."

It was conveniently overlooked by the critics that without Lévesque the independence movement wouldn't have been respectable in Quebec. And that without Morin, the *indépendantistes* wouldn't have been in power. Lévesque, with his middle-class instincts and his vote-pulling appeal, made the separatist option appear less radical and less risky. He took an idea that had been dressed in jeans and sweatshirts and put it in a grey flannel suit.

From the 11 percent of the vote gathered by Pierre Bourgault and the Rassemblement pour L'Indépendance Nationale in 1966, Lévesque took the Parti Québécois to 23 percent of the vote its first time out in 1970, and to 30 percent in the 1973 election. This is where opinions diverged within the PQ as to the nature and packaging of their option.

After the 1973 election, the PQ formed the official opposition in the National Assembly. The Péquistes then had to decide as between two schools of thought: those who argued it was just a matter of time before they took power, and those who thought they had come as far as they could with an undiluted program of independence. Before the voters would take this first step into the unknown of electing the PQ, they would want a safety net below. This is where Claude Morin came in. He had been the principal constitutional adviser to four premiers, from Jean Lesage to Robert Bourassa. After he left government service in the early 1970s, he made his way into the PQ, where he was regarded as a closet federalist just as much as he was viewed as a closet separatist in Liberal circles. It was Morin who devised the referendum strategy that Lévesque sold to a PQ convention in 1974. It was the beginning of *étapism*, Morin's reversal of the old Chinese proverb: that a journey of a single mile began with a thousand steps.

Once Lévesque and Morin had attained power in 1976, it remained for them to put more water in the wine of independence, and then explain what they meant by it. The first task was Lévesque's. The second fell to Morin.

For Lévesque, the option had always been something he felt. He never defined the parameters of it very well. If you asked him to define independence or sovereignty in constitutional or institutional terms, he would refer to that as the "plumbing" that would come later. The things he knew, he knew as a politician, and what could be sold to the voters. He knew they would never go for a Quebec dollar, and so he packaged a monetary union between Quebec and Canada. In the name of pride, he would be asking Quebecers to vote for a country in which they would still have the likeness of the Queen of England on their currency. The man who was asked to sell this pre- posterous notion, finance minister Jacques Parizeau, knew perfectly well that it was nonsense. He knew perfectly well that a country which did not control its own money supply, or set its own monetary policy, was no country at all. The interest rate crunch in the Great Recession of 1981-82 offered an interesting hypothetical case study of the kind of predicament an independent Quebec might have experienced in a monetary union with Canada.

Monetary policy was not Morin's area of expertise. He was a constitutionalist, a man whose idea of heaven, as the joke went along the Grande Allée, would be a permanent first ministers' conference on the constitution. Once Morin's referendum idea could be put into practice, it remained for him to define what the government meant by a mandate to negotiate sovereignty-association. This he finally did in the long-awaited white paper of November, 1979, *La Nouvelle Entente* or the New Deal mentioned earlier. Actually, it was notable mostly for its intellectual poverty, and for a rather dangerous amount of political daydreaming. Morin supposed that in the political association to be negotiated with Canada, Quebec, with one-quarter of the people, would have half the power and half the shares in jointly administered crown corporations like Air Canada. To be sure, it was only an opening position, but Morin was never able to explain to anyone's satisfaction why English-speaking Canada should go for such a bad deal, and at a price of breaking up the country rather than keeping it together.

This was the sort of thing Lévesque called the plumbing, the details of which he knew few voters would concern themselves with until they were presented with the bill. He was more concerned with safety nets and insurance policies, and giving people a good feeling, rather than a sense of trepidation about what he was asking them to do. In this sense, the mandate question itself was much more important to Lévesque than Morin's white paper. The mandate question, Lévesque's Christmas gift to the voters in December of 1979, ran to 114 words in French and 107 words in the English version. The essence of it was that the Quebec government was seeking exclusive powers to make laws, levy taxes and establish foreign relations, "in other words, sovereignty." All this, including the economic association with Canada, would be negotiated. And here was Lévesque's safety net. "No change in political status resulting from these negotiations," the question continued, "will be effected without approval by the people through another referendum." To change metaphors, it was part of a double-indemnity insurance policy Lévesque was offering the voters.

They could vote Yes now and No later.

And then the premier wanted a contagious good feeling about his option, a sense of solidarity. In nearly every speech, the word was on his lips. The meaning of sovereignty-association might be as elusive as the blue smoke rising from Claude Morin's ever-present pipe. But Lévesque knew what he meant by solidarity. It meant Quebecers, mostly francophone Quebecers, making an historic affirmation of pride in themselves as a people. He was asking them for "bargaining power," so that for once a Quebec premier could go to Ottawa on his feet rather than on his knees. "Quebec, like all societies, is necessarily divided into all kinds of compartments," he said in a church basement in North-End Montreal on April 22, 1980. "It's perfectly normal, but there are moments in our history, and they don't come too often, when we have to find solidarity out of those divisions."

Lévesque had more than The Speech going for him. He also had certificates of good conduct, good citizenship that were passed out to any little "Regroupement" that wanted one, whether it was a block in a suburb of Quebec, a bunch of bus drivers on Montreal's South Shore, or, for all anyone knew, a bunch of bartenders on Rue St. Denis Street. It was a deliberate strategy of raising the social pressure, to create a bandwagon effect in the workplace to bring undecided voters on board. The only problem with this was that many voters had suffered the divisions of the referendum era around the privacy of their family table. Now Lévesque and his organizers were bringing it onto the job. Yes supporters, in faithfully carrying out their instructions to be contagious, were effectively shutting up supporters of the other side. But the adherents of the Yes, with their unremitting pressure, were also putting a lot of people off. By early April, the social pressure had been broken by the big Yvette rallies of women in Quebec and Montreal, which gave birth to a series of meetings around the province. Lévesque's big mistake, and that of his handlers, was not to recognize that with their little certificates, they had overplayed their hand. Claude Ryan, often vilified as a failed cleric, effectively scorned Lévesque as some kind "Brother Superior," handing out certificates of good conduct. Still, Lévesque started his campaign with the certificates and the solidarity pitch on April 17, and stayed with it even when he knew it wasn't working. A couple of weeks later, when it was clear that the Yes strategy was backfiring, Lévesque was confronted in Hull by reporters who wanted to know why he was not adjusting to the realities of the campaign. "When you see your strategy isn't working," he said privately, "there's no point changing in midstream. It just serves to confuse your own people and to tell your opponents you're losing. "Even a week into the campaign, when Lévesque was supposed to be carried along by the momentum of the March 1980 debate, it was clear from the premier's mood that something was wrong. He is nothing if not a man of transparent moods. When things are going poorly for him backstage, he suddenly becomes a little man with a very big chip on his shoulder. Less than a week into his campaign of serenity and solidarity, Lévesque was taking cheap shots at the owners of the English-language media as "the number one profiteers in Quebec." Later on he began to take out his frustrations even on his own audiences. At a big rally in Quebec City, where the crowd was psyched up and welcomed him with a monstrous ovation, Lévesque would have none of it. "All right," he told the crowd, "that's enough."

Lévesque's worst moment of the entire campaign came when he went up to the James Bay construction site, 1000 kilometres north of Montreal. Here was the New Quebec, the very symbol of the Quebecer's capacity to go it alone, the symbol of hydroelectricity synonymous with the pride of Quebecers. Lévesque never had a chance to get wound up on his spiel. The men at the remote LG-3 worksite loudly demanded more beer rations and mixed dormitory privileges, taking the wind completely out of his sails. Instead of listening to the mens' demands with tolerance and amusement, Lévesque, as noted by radio reporter Bernard St. Laurent, "lectured them about attaching more importance to their beer than their futures."

It quickly turned into that kind of campaign for Lévesque, one in which practically everything that could go wrong, did.

There were two other problems for the Yes campaign. It was built entirely around the personality and persona of the premier. More fundamentally, they had less to offer the voters than the other side.

The difference in the two campaigns was startlingly clear. The Yes side had Lévesque bumping around the province in an old F-27 leased from Québecair, because it simply wouldn't do to be chartering from Air Canada. The Ryan campaign, when it was airborne, whisked around the province in his *"DC-Non."* But there were several other components of the No campaign. If Ryan was travelling around with the "A" team, the Yvettes formed the "B" team. There was also a "C" team, composed of the likes of Robert Bourassa and others, who spoke to regional meetings around the province.

The Lévesque campaign was not without its moments. There was a meeting in an Old Montreal restaurant where he told a group of lawyers backing his option that he was comforted by their support. This was a man who was the son of one lawyer and the father of another. He had been deeply influenced by his father, Gabriel Lévesque, and was immensely proud of his son, one of the outstanding young attorneys of Montreal. And it showed in the way Lévesque spoke that day, in simple, moving terms, with none of the gratuitous attacks that marred so many of his speeches. But even the success of that meeting indicated the divisions Lévesque's team had created by raising the social pressure. A few days later, Ryan and justice minister Jean Chrétien spoke to a huge cocktail-hour gathering of lawyers for the No, who filled to capacity the main ballroom of the Queen Elizabeth Hotel.

The countermovement spread throughout the professions. Soon there were doctors and engineers who had organized for the No, and were staging meetings of their own. None of this would have happened if the Yes forces hadn't decided to raise the social pressure that was broken by the Yvettes, the lawyers and other groups of ordinary citizens who effectively shattered the illusion of solidarity that Lévesque had tried to foster. With a week to go before the vote, it was pretty clear that Lévesque had lost. Even the crowds were staying away, and if there was one thing the PQ had always been able to turn out, it was an audience. On May 14, the night of Pierre Trudeau's dramatic speech in Montreal, Lévesque was 100 kilometres down the road in Drummondville, making a listless speech in a half-empty arena. On the bus out of town afterwards, reporters struck off a chorus of *C'est fini*

pour le Oui, their version of *C'est parti pour le Oui*, the
song with which the Yes forces had launched their campaign only a few weeks before. Even Lévesque's press
secretary, Gratia O'Leary, joined in the chorus. A year
later in the spring of 1981, near the end of an election
campaign with a different outcome, a reporter observed
to Lévesque's chief of staff that the PQ had kept its momentum going this time. Jean-Roch Boivin's rather revealing reply was the "last time, we never had any
momentum."

If the issue of the referendum was as clear-cut as that,
it was not entirely evident when Boivin and Lévesque
climbed into the back of a blue government limousine to
begin the referendum campaign on Thursday, April 17.
But it was clear to insiders on both sides that the momentum
was shifting back to the No forces. As Lévesque and
Boivin pulled out of the Bunker, Ryan was just finishing
up a news conference down the street at the Château
Frontenac with Bourassa, Jean Lesage and Gérard D. Lévesque. It was an important expression of solidarity within
the Liberal family, but it had not been easily arranged.
Lesage had been in Miami Beach, staying at the Beekman
Towers and playing golf at La Gorce, a course with a
heavy French-Canadian membership. He was in no hurry
to interrupt his spring holiday for Claude Ryan, for whom
he had no reservoir of affection. Moreover, Ryan wasn't
even asking—Bourassa was—on Ryan's behalf. Finally,
Lesage was prevailed upon to fly north for the press
conference of Liberal leaders past and present. And before
they met the press, they met for lunch up the street in a
quiet salon of the old Garrison Club, a symbol for generations of the Quebec political establishment.

As every conversation did in Quebec in those days,
the table talk soon got around to percentage predictions
of how the vote would come out. Given the morbid state
of morale among No organizers in mid-April, the bullish
predictions of the Garrison Club were rather surprising.
Bourassa thought that if things came together as they
should in the next month, they should win "a good 58
to 42." Lesage called it within a half a point, at 60 to 40

for the No. Former interim leader Gérard D. Lévesque
went along with Lesage at 60 to 40. It was Ryan who was
the most optimistic of all, calling it at 62 to 38. It had been
his prediction from the beginning and would remain so
until the end, and he was a bit disappointed on May 20
when the No vote couldn't achieve that final push over
60 percent. (Bitterly disappointed as René Lévesque was,
the result may have saved enough legitimacy for the government and enough face for its leader to put off an early
election and keep the premier in office. He had told an
interviewer from a French newsmagazine that he "wouldn't
be very interested" in continuing as premier if the Yes
forces obtained less than 40 percent. At 40.44 percent, he
scraped in just over his own bottom line.)

The press conference of past and present Liberal chiefs
was an important event for the No forces. For it conveyed
the notion of solidarity that Lévesque was trying to co-
opt exclusively for the other side. Also, the joint appearance
of Bourassa and Lesage with Ryan might have served as
a subtle reminder to some undecided voters that Liberal
times were, by and large, good times. To the extent that
the Quebec Liberal party felt comfortable with the nationalist outlook, it was on the economic themes of the
Lesage and Bourassa years. It was Lesage who had run
in 1962 on the slogan of *maîtres chez-nous* for the nationalization of the hydroelectric companies. It was Bourassa
who had promised 100,000 jobs in the 1970 election, and
proceeded to fulfill that pledge, at least partially, with
the construction of the "project of the century," at James
Bay. In a way, Lesage and Bourassa reminded voters that
they could be good Quebecers and good Canadians at
the same time. And more prosperous for it.

Lesage brought something more to the referendum
race—the moral authority of an elder statesman. This was
a sufficient cause of concern to Lévesque that he met the
National Assembly press corps at noon on the same day.
"You're going to see my ex-boss," Lévesque said light-
heartedly. But the presence of Lesage, even a decade after
he renounced politics forever, was not something to be

taken lightly. He still had the elegant manners of a great actor, he still had the voice that you would recognize anywhere. And with his blond hair turned a silvery grey, he looked more distinguished than ever. At the Liberal leaders' joint news conference, the first question came from Normand Girard, dean of the press corps and a veteran of the Lesage era. "Mr. Premier," he began, and everyone in the room knew to whom he was referring. The salutation brought a smile to Lesage's face. "Ah, Normand," he said, "I told them the first question would come from you."

Lesage would also have some kind of impact in the Quebec City area, where he was held in special regard, and not just in the salons of the Grande Allée, but on the balconies of Lowertown as well.

More than one woman would answer her door in the month of May and find the patron of the Quiet Revolution introducing himself. *"Bonjour, Madame,"* he would say. *"Mon nom est Jean Lesage."*

Altogether, Lesage made quite an impression on the campaign, but never more so than on the evening of May 7 in the Quebec convention centre. It was, in every sense, the best meeting of the campaign. In the space of three weeks, the mood of the No supporters had turned from one of fighting a grim battle to a joyous air of victory. The crowd of some 6,000 people filled the hall two hours before the meeting began. Ryan and the other members of his road show were on stage, but the real stars of the evening would be Pierre Trudeau and Jean Lesage. Trudeau, who had flown in from Vancouver, gave an emotional address of the kind he delivered only in Quebec, a city that seemed to bring out the best in him. But for sentimental value and local impact, the evening belonged to Lesage. Following Trudeau to a podium was no enviable task, but Lesage stole the show. He had not spoken in public in ten years, but that made what he had to say all the more interesting. He may have been a bit rusty, but he called on the reserves of a great and gifted orator, and the crowd cheered him on. He could never see the logic of the Yes option, he said. Moreover he was emotionally incapable of supporting it, for to do so would be to "betray not only my conscience, but the country of my birth."

As for the argument that Trudeau was a centralizing devil, Lesage noted that when he had gone to Ottawa in 1945, the central government spent 70 cents on every dollar expended by the two senior levels of government, and today the figures were reversed. How much did Trudeau have left? As if on cue, Trudeau turned out the empty pockets of his trousers.

But the news in Lesage's speech, the 30 seconds that would run on local radio stations all the next day, was his reference to the resignation of his former minister, Eric Kierans, from the board of the Caisse de Dépôt et Placement, the huge provincial pension fund, because it was being forced by the government to lend money to crown corporations at a slightly preferred rate. The timing of Kierans' resignation, in the crunch of the referendum campaign, looked rather suspicious to his old friend and former colleague René Lévesque. But the point was that the government was playing around with the voters' pension money. "Mr. Kierans was right," Lesage thundered. "They're siphoning off money that belongs to you. You've been robbed." For some in the audience, it seemed Lesage was finally settling accounts for the grief Lévesque caused him in the last couple of years before he finally quit the Liberal party in 1967. It seemed a kind of catharsis for the former premier—he was getting it out at last. Lesage apologized for going on so long, but said the warmth and generosity of the crowd had carried him back to a former time. And then he sat down. It was the last major speech of his life. On that very morning, he had evidently been informed that he had cancer. Seven months later he was dead. Pierre Trudeau walked in the winter cold behind his coffin. René Lévesque, who owed everything to Lesage, stayed in Europe on official business.

Claude Ryan was the last speaker that night, as he always was during the campaign. It was a position he liked, for it permitted him to summarize the arguments and the situation, something he had been doing all his life.

"It was a well established pattern, which suits me," Ryan said later, "because I'm good at summing things up at the end of a meeting. I've done that all my life." And he noted that he would often have to "redress things that were said by other speakers," who would become excessive in their attacks on the other side. The problem was, there was no one left to redress the things that were sometimes said by Claude Ryan, who never worked with a text, only from handwritten notes that he would often jot down on his lap during the course of an evening. And sometimes, when he wanted to say the right and generous thing, it came out all wrong. In Quebec, thinking that the debate should be marked by a climate of serenity in the final days, looking ahead to the time when all Quebecers would have to live together again, Ryan invited René Lévesque to accept the inevitable defeat. At this point, there were two weeks left in the campaign. It was an absurd statement, making Ryan look at once naive and arrogant, when his intent had been something else.

There was another problem with Ryan's speaking last: by the time he finished, and more often than not even by the time he started, the television reporters had missed their deadlines. This was not the case with Trudeau's two prime-time interventions in Quebec and Montreal. Practically as a condition of his appearance, his people insisted that he get on by eight o'clock at those two meetings, so that the French-language TV networks would have their stories prepared and edited by the time they went on the air at 10:30 with Radio-Canada's "Téléjournal" and the private network's TVA newscast.

No so with Ryan. Day after day, television reporters missed their deadlines, either because Ryan went on too late, or the evening meeting was in a remote location where they could neither feed their stories, nor fly them out in time to get them on the air. Their complaints fell on deaf ears. Eventually, many reporters suspected that the No organizers wanted to keep Ryan off the news, since he was already being perceived as a bit of a drag

on their potential vote. Actually, it was nothing that systematic. It was just Ryan being Ryan, setting the agenda
for his audiences rather than for the news media.

"I had to make a choice," Ryan would recall, "whether
I was holding the meeting for the people who were there
or using them as a pretext to address the entire province.
I made the first choice without any hesitation.

"I remember at the stategy meetings of the executive,"
he continued. "They came up repeatedly in the first two
or three weeks with suggestions that we must modify
the order of speakers so that I would be accorded time
on TV. I would listen to their arguments and at the end
I would conclude we're not going to change the order of
speakers for this or that reason."

Morever, Ryan knew that the rules of balance and
fair play would require the television people to put something on their supper hour and late evening newscasts,
even if it was footage from earlier in the day. And generally,
it was the kind of image Ryan wanted to present, of
himself meeting and greeting people, mainstreeting all
over the province.

He took this to rather extreme lengths on May 6 when
he decided to do a bit of door-to-door canvassing in a
trailer town at the LG-2 site in James Bay. Off he went
to the first house, where there was no one home. At the
second house, the woman did not come out, but invited
him in. All the time the cameras were rolling, and Ryan's
aides rolled their eyes in despair. But he was unconcerned,
perhaps thinking that the normal TV viewer would not
find it unusual that there would be no one home in the
middle of the afternoon. Besides, the message was getting
through. And the message was the non-message, meeting
the voters rather than the media. It was the image of the
citizen politician, who was above the normal political
packaging. Ryan was in fact turning his lack of charisma
to his advantage, as he had all his adult life.

From start to finish in the referendum campaign, he
ran the equivalent of a whistlestop tour in the jet age.
What's more, it worked, not so much because of the Ryan
style, but because of the cause he had going for him.

Night after night, the meetings would run on too long, but the crowds would stay. The speeches would be interminable, but they would listen, assimilating arguments they could take away with them. And always, without any prompting, the audience would break into O *Canada*. It would start with some timid voices at the back of the hall, as if it wasn't done, and then it would carry over to the stage, where the speakers would shuffle hastily to their feet.

Fundamentally, whatever he said or did in the spring of 1980, Ryan had a cause going for him. Also, he was not alone. The cousins were with him.

12

THE COUSINS

In the afternoon of Wednesday, May 7, Claude Ryan presided over a meeting of his executive committee. Jean Chrétien was also there. In a few hours, they would both be going to the giant Quebec City rally with Pierre Trudeau and Jean Lesage. The reports Ryan received that afternoon, at the No committee office overlooking the Grande Allée in Quebec, were all positively glowing. The *pointage*, or canvassing, was unbelievably good, pointing to a victory in a range as high as 65 percent. Chrétien, the federal delegate on the No committee, agreed things were looking good everywhere but in the Saguenay-Lac St. Jean region and along the North Shore. Ryan was in a relaxed and philosophical mood, showing none of the aggressive traits and insecurity that put so many people off. That afternoon, he was inclined to be generous to everyone. "You make friends as you go along," Ryan observed with a nod in the direction of the federal justice minister. "I think Mr. Chrétien and I have learned that."

It was not always so. As Chrétien acknowledged in something of an understatement: "There were some very difficult meetings at the beginning."

The first time Chrétien came to see Ryan after the Trudeau restoration, the meeting was bitterly acrimonious on both sides. They met in Ryan's Montreal office on Gilford Street at the end of the afternoon on March 7. It was just four days after the swearing in of the born-again prime minister and his cabinet. There were extravagant sensitivities on both sides. As generous as Ryan had been to Trudeau after his defeat in 1979, as much as Ryan acknowledged that Trudeau was a better man than Joe Clark for prime minister even though the prospect of his return would complicate his own life, Ryan now had to live with the reality of the federal Liberals' return to office. It meant Ryan had to defend himself from the charge that the feds would be running the show in the referendum, and that his party was only a branch plant of the federal Liberal head office in Ottawa. For his part, Chrétien was anxious to assure a meaningful role for the feds, and for himself, in the coming campaign.

As Ryan recalled one of their early discussions, Chrétien suggested the two sides work on an equal basis, *égal à égal* as it were. Ryan replied that there would be no sovereignty-association in his organization, and he later took up the point with Trudeau at their Good Friday luncheon at 24 Sussex Drive. "He said," Ryan recalled, "'I agree you must lead that organization. Your party must be in charge.'"

Though the composition of the No committee later proved to be inconsequential, Ryan and Chrétien had a blazing row over the position of the federal Liberals on the sixteen-member executive. Ryan would be president and the leaders of all the parties represented in the National Assembly, including Camil Samson of the Democratic Créditistes, would be vice-presidents. Chrétien would be a simple member, along with Conservative representative Claude Dupras (later co-chairman of the 1983 Tory leadership convention).

"Chrétien wanted to be on a special level," Ryan said later. "He said I'm the federal minister of justice and I can't be on the same level as these people."

For his part, Chrétien later replied that "being a vice-president of the No committee was not something I needed for my curriculum vitae . . . but we the federal Liberals had twelve ministers, including the prime minister, from Quebec, and we passed for the Christian Democrat Créditistes of Quebec."

That, Ryan said, was when he told Chrétien, "You take it or you don't." Chrétien, according to Ryan's recollection, actually got on his feet and started toward the door before coming back to resume the discussion around

Ryan's small conference table. Chrétien bit his tongue, but he didn't soon forget the rough nature of the meeting. "I can understand Jimmy Carter a lot better now," Chrétien told a group of aides in Ottawa a few days later. "He has to deal with the Ayotollah Khomeini and I have to talk to the Ayotollah Ryenni. Everybody has his own burden to carry."

That first meeting between Ryan and Chrétien was entirely unsatisfactory and inconclusive. "It was," said Chrétien aide and confidant Eddie Goldenberg, "like negotiating the shape of the table at the Paris peace talks."

One week later, on March 14, they had another meeting in Ryan's office. "The atmosphere," as Goldenberg later noted, "was completely different from one week to the next."

For one thing, there was a raging blizzard in progress, and Chrétien was unable to land his JetStar at Dorval. He flew into the air base at South Shore St. Hubert, had a military driver take him as far as Longueuil, and took the subway the rest of the way to Ryan's office on the Laurier Métro stop. For another thing, both Chrétien and Ryan had advance word of the IQOP poll that would run in the following Sunday edition of *Dimanche-Matin*, that put the Yes side in front for the first time, 38 to 35. It was enough for Ryan to put aside his concerns about the federal presence in the campaign. Where only the previous week, Ryan had been saying that the issue was between Quebecers and that the Quebec Liberal party was fully capable of acquitting its responsibilities, he was now looking for fuller participation by Ottawa. It was night from day as compared with the previous week, and the only explanation for it was the poll. "Now," Chrétien told Goldenberg as they walked back across the street to the Laurier Métro, "you know what responsibility is."

At noon on St. Patrick's Day, Eddie Goldenberg reported back to the first and by far the gloomiest of the Monday luncheon meetings of senior federal aides and officials. Goldenberg called it a "strategy planning group." More than that, it was the core referendum group of the

Trudeau mandarinate which would set the tone in the capital in the next two months.

There was Roger Tassé, the deputy minister of justice; Paul Tellier, the former head of the Canadian Unity Information Office that was set up after the accession of the PQ to power in 1976 and virtually disbanded by the Clark government in 1979. Tellier, who had been shunted off as deputy minister of Indian and northern affairs, was brought back into the referendum picture by Chrétien (and would later become Chrétien's deputy minister of energy). There was Gérard Veilleux, then the assistant deputy minister of finance, later head of the Federal Provincial Relations Office, and considered a coming man in the federal bureaucracy. There was Claude Lemelin, also with the finance ministry and later Veilleux's deputy at FPRO. Lemelin, a former journalist at Le Devoir under Ryan, was a kind of short Robert Redford, who could dictate a stream of witty and incisive memoranda while pacing back and forth in his finance ministry office in Place Bell Canada. There was Bob Rabinovitch, later deputy communications minister, a Lachine boy who had worked his way up in life into the Privy Council Office, effectively the prime minister's department and the central control of the federal bureaucracy. There was George Anderson from External Affairs and Tommy Shoyama, the former deputy finance minister under Chrétien, who by 1980 had retired to the academic life at University of Victoria. "They wanted him around," said Goldenberg, "just for the quality of his advice." With the exception of Shoyama and Anderson, all the men around the table at the justice department on Wellington Street were Quebecers who had a keen awareness not only of the issues in play, but of the touchy sensibilities involved. And all of them had been attracted to the federal public service by Pierre Trudeau and his notions of Quebecers taking their rightful place in the federal administration.

"Last Friday," Goldenberg reported on the second of Chrétien's two meetings with Ryan, "I saw a changed man. The arrogance was gone. He acknowledged the situation was serious," and invited full federal participation, but felt that it would be best "outside the umbrella" of the No committee.

Ryan was concerned, Goldenberg reported, that Trudeau's victory in the February 18 election would send the anti-Liberal vote in Quebec into the Yes camp as a form of backlash. Ryan said the PQ's appeal to "bargaining power" was proving to be a very effective argument. Implicitly, the federalists needed to counter that argument with an argument of their own, and the best person to make it would be the only person who could answer it, the prime minister. And there was some discussion of whether Trudeau should make an address to the country before the issuing of the writs, so that the TV time would not count against the No forces allotment, and the networks would not be obliged to offer Lévesque equal time.

"Ryan indicated," Goldenberg reported, "without saying so directly, that the PM should play a central role because of his credibility in Quebec."

Nor, Goldenberg said, was Ryan inclined to minimize the consequences of a Yes vote. He thought, Goldenberg reported, that in the event of a Yes, there was "a 50 percent chance," the federalists "would lose control of events."

Goldenberg then reported on the touchy discussions of the federal particpation in the No committee, on whether the federal Liberals should join as party members or individuals, on whether they should have a joint caucus of the federal and provincial members (this was agreed upon and took place on Holy Thursday, at the Ramada Inn on Sherbrooke Street East in Montreal next door to the Sambo restaurant and across the street from the pyramids of the Olympic Village). There was even a discussion as to whether it would be appropriate for the Speakers of the House and the Senate, Jeanne Sauvé and Jean Marchand, to participate in the campaign, as they were clearly itching to do.

"Frankly," Ryan was reported by Goldenberg to have said, "I'm asking myself if the federal parties should be on the committee." There was no acrimony in this, Ryan insisted, it was merely a question of strategy. And, he might have added, of perception.

The federal and provincial Liberal parties had gone their own way back in 1964. On April 26 of that year, the governing general council of the Quebec Liberal Federation decided it would be best all around if they formed a fully autonomous Liberal party; best for appearances' sake, best in organizational terms, and the best way of sparing the Liberal family nasty quarrels over the different constitutional perspectives developing in Ottawa and Quebec.

Premier Lesage, present at the general council, concurred in the recommendation. And on July 5, at a general meeting of the Quebec Liberals, the provincial party decided to withdraw from the National Liberal Federation. (At the time, the provincial party's initials in French were FLQ, for Féderation Libéral du Québec, which had a rather unfortunate connotation in terms of the activities of the Front de Liberation du Québec, the ragtag terrorist outfit that was then blowing up mailboxes in the Montreal area. In any event, the Quebec Liberals soon became the PLQ, Parti Libéral du Québec.) As Bob Giguère, the chief organizer in Quebec for the federal Liberals, noted in a memo to Prime Minister Lester Pearson: "The separation was official."

It was probably just as well for both sides, as Giguère ventured in his memorandum to the PM, to "help resolve the conflict of interest that existed between the two wings of the party, many of which were the natural outgrowth of holding office at both the federal and provincial levels." Moreover, as Giguère noted in that prescient 1964 memo, "A distinct federal organization will allow us to devote our time and resources to federal policies, being no longer inhibited by an organization which devoted its entire energy and money solely to provincial matters." Looking back on the separation of the two parties, it was an important preliminary in the recruiting by Giguère's organization of Pierre Trudeau, Jean Marchand and Gérard Pelletier as Liberal candidates in the federal election of November, 1965. They were in no way beholden to the

Lesage Liberals, and were free to develop their own Quebec policy perspectives in Ottawa.

There was the appearance of things as between the federal and Quebec Liberals in organizational and attitudinal terms, and there was the reality of things at the grass roots level, where the organizers and members were essentially the same people. In 1980, the federal Liberals counted some 100,000 members and the Quebec Liberals, gearing up for the referendum, had boosted their membership over 200,000. If you called up the two membership lists from the computers, officials of both parties acknowledged, you would get about an 80 per cent overlap of federal Liberals who belonged to the Quebec party. And in the rural ridings of Quebec, this tendency was even more pronounced. A *rouge* was a *rouge*, and neither the old time *bleus* nor the new *bleus*, the Péquistes, made any distinction between the two.

Neither, for that matter, did many Liberals, especially when the cousins were in power in Ottawa and the Quebec Liberals found themselves out of office in Quebec.

So the federal Liberals, restored to power in the late winter of 1980, were not in the same predicament with respect to the referendum as they had been only a couple of months before, obliged to march to Ryan's tune. Ryan might have been leader of the No forces, but he was still only leader of the opposition in the legislature. Pierre Trudeau was the prime minister, Jean Chrétien was his referendum minister, with all the resources, brains and machinery of the federal government at his command. And he had every intention of using them.

The Goldenberg group was but one example. Part of their function, each Monday at noon, was to put together the various federal scenarios in the event of a Yes or No victory. At that first meeting on March 17, Goldenberg reported that if "yesterday's IQOP is accurate, Lévesque is likely to win a narrow victory." For the feds, it was a chilling prospect, and the Wellington Street group discussed all the implications of it. "For example," as Goldenberg later noted, "the currency markets the next day would have been in terrible shape. It wouldn't take a genius to figure that out. But it would take a genius to figure out what to do about it."

Not long after this first meeting, Goldenberg ran into Bank of Canada governor Gerald Bouey, and discussed the problem at some length with him.

"There are lots of options," said the laconic Bouey. "My recommendation is that you'd better win and win big."

From the time of the government's swearing in on March 3, Chrétien worked full-time on the referendum problem. After hearing from the weekly meeting of his officials, Chrétien would meet at the end of every Monday afternoon with a committee of the Quebec caucus: Dennis Dawson, a Quebec City youngblood; Jean-Claude Malépart, a street-smart operator from the East End of Montreal; Rémi Bujold, a former Trudeau aide and freshman MP from the Gaspé region; André Maltais from Sept-Iles on the North Shore; Irenée Pelletier from Sherbrooke; Maurice Dupras from the southern Laurentians; Marcel Ostiguy from Ste. Hyacinthe; and Raymond Dupont from the riding of Chambly in the provincial PQ stronghold of South-Shore Montreal. There was one other member of the caucus group, Senator Maurice Lamontagne, the economist, who had been one of the precursors of the Quiet Revolution in the days when he was teaching political science at Laval University in Quebec. Lamontagne was bringing out a book for the referendum, summarizing a lifetime of arguments of how separatism made no economic sense for Quebec. When he died in 1983, he did not receive the credit he deserved for his role in both the Quiet Revolution and making a place for francophones in Ottawa during the Pearson and Trudeau eras.

Chrétien would meet with this caucus group to receive a grass-roots update from every region of Quebec, and to receive advice for his Tuesday morning meetings with the Quebec ministers.

The referendum committee of Quebec ministers generally met over breakfast at 8 o'clock in the cabinet committee room of the Langevin Block, which housed the

Privy Council officials and most of the aides in the Prime Minister's Office. In the early going, they had two primordial preoccupations, the role that Trudeau would play, and the need to unblock politically sensitive files concerning Quebec.

In the beginning, there was earnest advice from some cabinet quarters that Trudeau should go whole-hog in his participation in the campaign, with an early address to the country and extensive participation in the campaign. Trudeau himself argued against massive intervention by himself. "I'll do it," he told Chrétien, "but I don't want to overshadow Ryan." And fundamentally, as one senior federal official put it, "Trudeau realized that one speech by the PM was worth a thousand speeches by a minister."

Then there were the sensitive files, notably Ottawa's looming choice of a fighter plane and its prospective loan guarantees to Chrysler Corporation of Windsor, Ontario.

On the long delayed choice of a fighter plane, the defence department leaned strongly in favor of the McDonnell Douglas F-18A rather than the F-16 from General Dynamics. What made the choice so touchy was the timing of it, and the fact that the F-16 builder had promised an industrial-benefits package of more than $1.5 billion for Quebec. The Quebec caucus argued convincingly that if the F-18 were indeed chosen, then Quebec would have to receive an enriched benefits package that would be the equivalent of that promised for the F-16. By borrowing here and adding there, the feds were able to bring the F-18 Quebec package up to speed with the F-16.

They did so by practically cooking the numbers, as an angry René Lévesque noted, "by federal functionaries who can't be very proud of their work." On the $200 million federal loan guarantees to Chrysler, Lévesque was able to ask rhetorically, at a meeting of nightshift workers in the United Auto Workers union hall near the General Motors plant at Ste. Thérèse, why it was always Ontario that received the industrial and financial benefits of Confederation.

The feds did what they could to fast-track public works and construction projects, as a means of accentuating the federal presence. Chrétien himself flew into Jonquière on April 13, between No rallies in Chicoutimi and Val D'Or, to inaugurate a new tax centre. It was the modern-day equivalent of the bulldozer along the side of a country road during an election. But Chrétien, aware of the tight spending rules governing the referendum campaign, warned his colleagues not to be too loose in their use of government JetStars during the coming weeks. "Make sure," he said, "that you have a damn good reason to use a government plane."

At the meeting of Quebec ministers on April 8, the day after the Yvette rally in Montreal, there was a discussion as to whether there should be a national unity debate in the Commons, either early or later in the referendum campaign. Still concerned to counter the effects of the color-coordinated Oui debate in Quebec's National Assembly, the feds decided that if they were going to have a debate at all, they should do it sooner rather than later.

They decided to turn the Throne Speech into a debate on the referendum. They would have six days of televised proceedings, with Trudeau leading off the following Tuesday afternoon, the same day Lévesque set May 20 as the day of the vote. In the House, the seating arrangements on the government side were such that Trudeau was surrounded by his Quebec ministers, Chrétien alongside in the front row, Francis Fox and Pierre de Bané off to one side, Pierre Bussières and Charles Lapointe also within easy camera range, along with Yvon Pinard, Marc Lalonde, André Ouellet and Monique Bégin. It was a conspicuous, rather too obvious, display of French Power.

So far as that went, Ryan agreed that Ottawa had every right to stage its own little debate since, as he had told Chrétien at their weekly meeting on March 28, the federal government had been tried and convicted in *absentia* in the National Assembly. Beginning with Trudeau's remarkable speech of April 15, in which he refuted the arguments for bargaining power, saying No to a Yes, the feds fought back with a vengeance. As in the case of the PQ's strategy, the speakers' material was put together and vetted in one place and by one person: the Canadian

Unity Information Office and its director general, Pierre Lefebvre. There was one notable and rather unfortunate exception—André Ouellet.

In the House on April 15, Trudeau's chief Quebec organizer spoke in the evening, a few hours after the prime minister. Because Ouellet was following an historic address, because reporters had a plateful with the PM's statement, because it was frankly late in the day, nobody paid much attention to what Ouellet said until the transcripts came up the next day, and then the Ouellet speech became the video tape replay of the referendum campaign. It was a blunt, savage, even crude speech. In short, it was what a lot of people expected from André Ouellet, a man of fine intelligence and generally sound political instincts which he sometimes did his best to conceal.

"We have made a martyr of Quebec and a villain of Canada," he said. "And I think that joke has lasted long enough of having us believe that Canada is a dirty word and we must always talk about Quebec. I suggest that this invading propaganda has been the systematic work, of course, of convinced separatists, who have infiltrated everywhere in Quebec. . . those separatists have striven hard to spread their philosophy."

So far Ouellet was staying within the bounds of partisan but acceptable rhetoric. Even his reference to Quebec teachers, "who have set young Quebecers against Canada," was not altogether a distortion of reality. It was also known, as Ouellet stated, that many reporters had separatist sympathies that sometimes influenced their work. But then Ouellet got carried away, as all the stored up grievances of the feds, all the accumulated resentment at being scorned by the Quebec intelligentsia, came pouring forth in a stream of bitter invective.

"Those artists overpaid by Radio-Canada," he said, "who have been whining about this country for years, those union leaders and politicians have enjoyed total freedom in their work of torpedoing Canada unity. There is no doubt that if these people had tried to do this in any other country around the world, they would have been socked, they would have been clubbed, they would have been jailed. More still, in a number of countries, they would have been shot for doing less than they could do in Canada."

Altogether, that was quite a mouthful. The reaction was predictable and immediate. *The Globe and Mail's* Ottawa columnist, Geoffrey Stevens, wrote an indignant column that his desk in Toronto summed up with a one-word heading: "Disgusting. " In *La Presse*, columnist Lysiane Gagnon wrote a scathing open letter to Ouellet.

Months later, when the incident had blown over, Ouellet still made no apologies. "My career was strongly influenced by Jean Marchand," he said in his office one afternoon in the fall of 1980." And Marchand had a political style that was very *débardeur*, very roughneck. It's obvious not everyone on the team can be a statesman. On a well-balanced team you have to have someone who can go on the ice and into the corners and give a few shots.

"A well-balanced team," he continued, "must be able to address itself to a different clientele." His clientele, he acknowledged, was the rural milieu and the old Créditiste counties. "My speech," he said, "was an echo of many opinions within a large segment of Quebec society."

Oddly enough, it was Ryan who stood by Ouellet, appearing on the same platform with him twice afterwards, and going out of his way to say that Ouellet had expressed sincerely held sentiments, even if the choice of words might not have been his own.

At the operations level of the federal bureaucracy, there were two key players in the referendum, Pierre Lefebvre of the Canadian Unity Information Office and Richard Dicerni, a brilliant young Montrealer whose strength was translating policy into concepts easily explained and assimilated.

Lefebvre, 37 years old in the spring of 1980, was from the inner-city of Montreal, one of those neighborhoods where, as he recalled, he had to fight his way past the English into school. A graduate of Laval's psychology faculty, he looked more like a mail-order Péquiste than a federalist. He was a lanky former college basketball player, who had the face of a Gérald Godin and the beard of a Denis Lazure.

He had arrived at the Unity Info Office under Paul Tellier and Claude Lemelin at the height of the separatist panic in 1977, and stayed on after Tellier was transferred out by the Clark government in 1979.

By then, Lefebvre himself was in charge, but he didn't have much left to run. The Conservative government wanted to emphasize the Canada-wide mandate of the unity shop, rather than concentrating almost exclusively on Quebec as Tellier had done under the Liberals. "But they gave us no mandate," complained one official of the Unity Office. Within Clark's Office of the Prime Minister, Senator Arthur Tremblay was given the constitutional and unity dossier, but never really got going on it. Tremblay also had a different approach from the Liberals. A former deputy minister of intergovernmental affairs in Quebec, he understood the Péquistes well enough to ignore them. He counselled Clark on a policy of benign neglect of Quebec, of avoiding provocation, giving the PQ no federal targets and leaving the field in Quebec to Ryan. Clark followed the advice to the letter, and in the fall of 1979, it was clearly working. The Lévesque administration was never so unpopular, or never so at sea, as when it was denied its familiar Liberal devils in Ottawa.

All this changed with the election of February 18 and the Trudeau restoration. "Chrétien said, in effect: I'm in charge of the referendum, make me a presentation," Lefebvre later recalled. Lefebvre and his officials worked up an audio-visual show on three levels of intensity. Immediately Chrétien went for the third-level package, the all-dressed federal pizza. And he told Lefebvre and his people what he had told officials in other departments. "I'll handle the politics," he said, "you do the rest."

Which they did.

Altogether, by the estimate of their own knowledgeable officials, the feds spent five million dollars on a blaze of radio, television, and newspaper advertising. And that wasn't counting the cost of the material and human resources.

For a start, Lefebvre and Dicerni had a an attitudinal poll of Quebecers conducted in the fall of 1979 by Allan Gregg's Decima Research, the Conservative party's polling house. The Gregg data confirmed that Canada, the word itself, was magical in the minds of Quebecers, along with their *appartenance Canadienne* and their sense of the North.

"The Gregg data confirmed the overall impression to use, number one, Canada," Dicerni said later; "two, to stress the usefulness and presence of the federal government, and three, the benefits of federalism.

"But Canada was the strong selling point, we knew that if we could make the focus of a yes or a no, for or against Canada, then we would win. Our surveys showed that loud and clear. If we could just reinforce the importance of Canada to Quebecers."

If Dicerni and Lefebvre didn't exactly raid the federal treasury, they had no hesitation in putting their hands in practically every cookie jar in the federal capital. They drew on every departmental budget that could be useful to them. In their advertising campaign, they played on every intellectual argument, and played without hesitation on every emotional chord, every *corde sensible*, that they perceived in the electorate. They packaged a series of television ads that ran before newscasts, during talk shows and between periods of hockey games. In one six-week period alone, in April and May of 1980, the feds spent, by one highly informed estimate, nearly $3 million in television spots, most of it aimed at the undecided French-speaking voter in Quebec.

If you wanted arguments as to the presence of the federal government in Montreal, why you just had to turn on the television between periods of the Stanley Cup playoffs and look at the Good Works of Transport Canada, which had built and paid for half the cost of the Trans-Canada Highway, not to mention thirty-three airports, forty-four ports and the St. Lawrence Seaway. All of which was brought to you courtesy of Canada, in letters that lit up the screen. As for the proprietary sense of the North, they arranged, in the year of the Arctic Centennial, for a teenager in the North West Territories to write a pen pal in Quebec, describing the life of the territory. "I'm a Canadian of the North," the letter concluded, "and I love my country." That was not all, the Department of Health and Welfare reminded viewers that they meant pension checks and family allowances checks and New Horizons programs. And the Secretary of State merely went on the air and played the National Anthem, a shorter version of the 84-second hymn produced by the National Film Board that ends with a couple of blond kids kissing. It was evidence of how hard the feds were prepared to fight. Altogether, it was pretty powerful stuff.

All of this was quite systematic, and the federal propaganda blitz got under the skin of the Yes forces, who with all the powers and spending limitations of their enabling legislation, were quite helpless to stop the spending of one red cent outside the referendum umbrella. But finally what got under René Lévesque's skin, as evidence of the diabolical works of the feds, was almost an accident along the way.

Near the end of March, at the regular meeting of Quebec ministers, Health Minister Monique Bégin casually mentioned that her department would be sending around a householder preaching against the excesses of alcohol. In fact, Health and Welfare intended to repeat the slogan it had used the previous year: "*Non merci*, that says it well."

"Does anybody have any problem with that?" she asked around the table.

"It was discussed for about thirty seconds," Chrétien aide Eddie Goldenberg said later, "and then everybody said go ahead."

By early May, when the householder was to be mailed out with family-allowance and old-age security payments, there was definitely a problem. In the meantime, "*Non, merci*" had emerged as the principal slogan of the No campaign. The feds appeared to be blundering into the situation. "We tried to stop the goddamn inserts from going out with the checks, which were being sent two weeks early because of the threat of a postal strike," Goldenberg recalled; "it was too late to stop them." Chrétien himself later admitted to having "some reservations about that." Nevertheless, even if it was too late to stop the mailers, Bégin's department went ahead with a billboard campaign utilizing the same slogan.

For René Lévesque, beside himself over the federal interventions, it was simply too much. You can always tell when Lévesque is about to go berserk in a speech by the way he rushes out on stage and waves a newspaper clipping or a piece of paper, as he did on May 8 in the Montreal North arena, where he brandished a copy of his pending legal action against the federal government, its advertising agency, the billboard company, and anyone else involved in this dubious affair. As it happened, Lévesque was to lose the case, in which he alleged the feds had violated the umbrella rules of the game.

Nevertheless, the incident created a serious difference of opinion within the federalist forces. Solange Chaput-Rolland, never one to understate a problem, said the situation was indecent and accused the feds of staging an "orgy" of publicity. Ryan's chief organizer Pierre Bibeau bit his tongue in public, but was privately furious about the unnecessarily negative impact of the *Non, merci* affair at a time when the No forces were on a roll. The last thing they needed was this kind of overkill. "I think Bibeau warned us it wouldn't help," said Goldenberg. "I don't blame him for being angry about that."

But on the whole, the Ryan group and the cousins worked together with a remarkable degree of harmony. Dicerni, for example, was thrown in with Jacques DuSault to coordinate the advertising and publicity campaign. It was DuSault who came up with the slogan of the campaign, the one aimed at critical undecided voters: *Plus j'y pense, plus c'est Non.* The more I think about it, the more it's No. DuSault may have deserved a special medal just for working for Ryan, who was always suspicious of admen and all their works. "It must have been difficult," as Dicerni observed, "to work in an area where your skills are not appreciated."

Dicerni himself worked anonymously, but was considered a hero of the referendum campaign in Ottawa.

The federal blitz was basically his design, right down to the "lazy speakers," the kits of facts and figures, on each of the nine regions of the province, prepared by the Unity Office. Each one indicated how many federal jobs there were in the area, each one answered "affirmations," by the other side. And the affirmation strategy was filled out by a series of 20 to 60-second radio spots that tackled the fifteen worst criticisms of the federal system. "There was tremendous feedback to this," Dicerni said later, "much more than to the TV spots, which were basically soft."

But Dicerni, then a 31-year-old Lachine native who had been educated at College Ste. Marie, was not without his own problems of living the referendum. "I knew that the more effective I was in my job," he said later, "the more I would be contributing to divisions within my home province." By the fall, he would go on a previously arranged sabbatical at the Kennedy School of Government at Harvard University.

But in the months of April and May, he also played a critical role as a liaison person between the cousins and the hypersensitive Ryan. By the end of March, the cousins had also placed Léonce Mercier, the director general of their Quebec wing, in the No campaign. That meant that the whole federal organization, which had just ridden Trudeau's coattails to win 74 of 75 federal seats in Quebec, was thrown into the fray.

"We're ready to play second fiddle," Chrétien had told Ryan at their March 14 meeting, "but not the triangle in the rear."

There remained serious differences of style and approach between Chrétien and Ryan. As much as Chrétien was the professional politician who enjoyed delegating and being treated as the client of his civil servants, Ryan insisted on seeing and approving everything, and everything had to be written down. It was as if, after his years at Catholic Action and *Le Devoir*, nothing existed unless it was on paper. The differences of style and substance between the two men were illustrated at their Friday meeting on March 28. Ryan asked Chrétien if he had any objections if he read the draft manifesto of *Les Québécois pour le Non*. At this point, Richard Dicerni kicked Eddie Goldenberg under the table.

Despite their difficulties in working together, there would come a time when Ryan would be grateful to Chrétien. Absent from the terrain, fretful about the way the campaign was unfolding in April, Pierre Trudeau sent a letter to his Quebec caucus colleagues urging them to stress the aspects of the pride of being Canadian. Chrétien not only corrected the prime minister's impression in a private huddle in the Commons, he did so in public. "Ryan was very embarrassed by what Trudeau said," Chrétien later observed, "but then he was very happy with what I said. I think he appreciated it."

Chrétien also noted that "Ryan never panicked in the bad moments of the campaign, and neither did I. We didn't believe we were in trouble, although public opinion did. We knew that once the polarization set in, we would be all right, not based on polls but on political experience."

For his part, Ryan later had no complaints about the role of the cousins in the referendum. And as for Trudeau, he went out of his way to heap extravagant praise on the born-again prime minister.

But it did not cut both ways. Ryan was deeply wounded when he attended Trudeau's Chamber of Commerce speech in Montreal, where the prime minister didn't even acknowledge his presence at the head table. "He didn't even mention my name," Ryan later told aides.

But it wasn't, as Trudeau press secretary Patrick Gossage noted, "as if he hasn't been told."

13

RYAN AND TRUDEAU: TWO HARDHEADS

Perhaps they were never meant to be friends. They were too alike in some respects, too unlike in most others. They had known one another from young adulthood until late in their careers. Occasionally, as in the Quebec referendum of 1980, they had made common cause. More often, as in the constitutional debates that followed, there was a decisive clash of opinions. In the end, all that should have united them divided them, these two hardheads named Pierre Trudeau and Claude Ryan.

For they had in common a deep commitment to individual freedoms, and for much of their careers were devoted to constitutional reform, although they espoused different ideas of Canada and Quebec's place in it. "These are two strong personalities," observed André Raynauld, a Trudeau appointee to the chairmanship of the Economic Council of Canada and later, as a member of the National Assembly, an early member of the Draft Ryan movement. "Ryan is a provincialist in the good sense of the word. Trudeau is an internationalist, open to the rest of the world." Later, after he left politics, Raynauld suggested that "Ryan has always detested strong people."

There are definite similarities of character and experience, as both were marked by the absence of their fathers. Trudeau's mother was widowed when he was 14, Ryan's mother was abandoned by her husband when Claude was still a toddler. Both, as boys, had serious complexion problems that left them pockmarked. Both married late, Ryan at age 33, Trudeau at 50. Both apparently felt things more deeply than either cared to let on. "Ryan is exactly like Trudeau," suggested Pierre C. O'Neil, who was a reporter at *Le Devoir* before becoming Trudeau's press secretary from 1972 to 1974. "Deep down they're very emotive, and they have that much in common."

Such men are perhaps not meant to get along. Francis Fox, who had worked as a Trudeau aide before entering politics and had more than a passing acquaintance with Ryan, had an uncomplicated version of what stood between them. "It is," Fox said, "the war of the intellectuals."

They grew up, worlds apart, in the same city. Trudeau was sheltered by the gentle trees of Outremont, studied at his leisure at the best universities, came and went as he pleased for many years afterwards. Ryan grew up on the hot pavements of Montreal, left university before completing his degree and worked, as most people did, for a living. Trudeau's sense of public service was derived from his *noblesse oblige*, Ryan's from his sense of duty.

In short, Trudeau was rich. Ryan was poor.

Pierre Trudeau, 33 years old when he called on Ryan in Rome in 1952, was much the more wordly of the two. Ryan, though he was then only 27, was much more experienced in the ways of the world. While Trudeau studied at Harvard, LSE, and Paris in the late 1940s, while he dabbled in the occasional cause like the Asbestos strike, Ryan was already a full-fledged man of action. He was not yet 21 years of age when he was named general secretary of Catholic Action. All his youthful energies were devoted to mobilizing adherents in the service of ideas. Along the way, he learned a good deal about the rough and tumble of ecclesiastical politics, an admirable apprenticeship for the tests that awaited him in the secular world. As for the rounding off of Ryan's education, he now found himself, for the first time in his life, outside the tiny parish of Quebec and the minor basilica that was Canada. He was in the great cathedral that was Rome, studying church history for two years at the Gregorian College.

It was here that Trudeau called on Ryan, at the house in which he was staying. They had lunch and afterwards went for a long walk through the streets of the Eternal

City. Trudeau evidently struck Ryan as troubled about
his faith and worried about his future.

"You remind me of the wealthy young man in the
gospel," Ryan said as they walked. "You know what the
Lord told him. He should throw away his riches and start
living like the rest of us. That's the only difficulty that
stands between you and us. You have this big pile of
money you don't know what to do with. You should get
rid of it."

Trudeau said nothing and they continued on their
way.

They had been introduced in Montreal in 1948 by a
mutual friend named Guy Beaugrand-Champagne. He
knew Ryan through Catholic Action and, later, was a
colleague at the Canadian Institute of Adult Education.

Ryan saw Beaugrand-Champagne not as "a man of
action, but he was very fond of action and he liked to
look at the prospects for the future. He would say, 'there
are five or six guys who are going to influence the future
of this society,' and among them he would mention Trudeau and myself. He mentioned Gérard Pelletier and
Charles Lussier. He said, 'I don't know what the future
holds in store for you, but I feel you will have a lot to
say.' He had told me repeatedly that he wanted me to
get acquainted with Trudeau. And I went to his mother's
house one afternoon."

And there, in the rambling brick house on McCulloch
Avenue, the two young men talked for hours. "It was a
discovery for me," Ryan would say more than thirty years
later. "I had never met the man before. He had a very
broad culture. He spoke in very broad terms."

Practically from their first meeting, Ryan said he "tried
to enlist him in Catholic Action as I would do with anyone
at the time." But Trudeau was never much of a joiner,
especially in those days. "He felt," Ryan said, "he must
not be bound by ties to any particular organization. He
declined the invitation to join with us. He wanted to
pursue his solitary destiny."

Though none of them really knew it at the time, the Catholic Action movements became the training ground for a new generation which would oppose Duplessis in the 1950s and take over the Liberal establishment in the 1960s, ruling into the 1980s. By contemporary standards, they would be considered social workers. In those days, they were Catholic activists who made up a social movement as they went along, a movement reaching into every corner of Quebec society, from the universities to the trade unions. As Catholic Action was neither controlled by the government nor under the thumb of the bishops, it was free of reactionary influences, open to the expression of new ideas. Naturally, most of the best and the brightest of Ryan's generation flocked to Catholic Action.

But Trudeau did not. Nor did Ryan become a part of Trudeau's small group that launched *Cité Libre*, the little magazine that became an important intellectual forum in the 1950s. Ryan never wrote in *Cité Libre*, Pierre Juneau noted many years later. "They wouldn't have thought of inviting him and he wouldn't have thought of going there. Ryan always had a suspicion of the kind of Outremont, educated, elegant type of people whom you might call sophisticated."

So it would be fair to call them friendly acquaintances in the 1950s, each more or less aware of the other's activities, but each in his own orbit. From time to time, during his periodic travels, Trudeau would be in touch with Ryan by mail. "Beautiful letters," Ryan recalled. "I remember one in which he told me he was going around the world looking at the condition of liberty." Occasionally, their paths would cross at one of those *colloques* that were a cottage industry in Quebec even in those days. Ryan recalled a meeting of the Canadian Institute of Adult Education, in which he was deeply involved, where Trudeau turned up to give a keynote speech on individual liberties. "It was a beautiful speech," Ryan said, "but I had to oppose him on that occasion. To him everything stemmed from the authority of the state. I think the theme of the seminar was the role of voluntary organizations in the promotion of freedom. Trudeau said all those voluntary organizations are pressure groups, creatures of the law-maker. If the lawmaker doesn't want them to exist, they do not exist. And I remember saying to him, even if the lawmaker doesn't want them to exist, they do exist prior to any decision by the authority, because they spring from the free will of the people. And by giving them a legal status, the lawmaker only confirms what they have already decided. And we had a profound difference of opinion there.

"I represented the popular stream," Ryan continued. "I had done all my work without the lawmakers or governors having anything to do with it. We had done our work in Catholic Action during the Duplessis era. And we could not care less about Duplessis in those days. We felt we were developing freedom at levels that were unattainable, completely out of reach of M'sieu Duplessis."

Even in those days, then, there were some profound differences between Trudeau and Ryan in their approach to public policy. "They have common convictions with different temperaments," suggested André Burelle, a soft-spoken former philosophy professor who became Trudeau's principal speech writer, and the man who drafted the notes which the prime minister committed to memory for his celebrated speeches in the Quebec referendum. "They have a community of thought, but different means of expressing them."

From the early days, Gérard Pelletier knew Trudeau and Ryan better than most, and had always been struck by their common intellectual sources. Pelletier was in Catholic Action and journalism with Ryan, being editor of *La Presse* when Ryan became publisher of *Le Devoir*, as he was in public life with Trudeau.

"It's very, very curious," Pelletier observed. "They are two guys who have the same favorite authors. And rather curiously in literature, one thing that isn't very known is the English Catholicism of Cardinal Newman and Lord Acton, and rather curiously among all the people I know, the only two guys for whom they were the intellectual masters were Ryan and Trudeau. They were the only two guys who spoke to me of them. It was

Trudeau who had me read Cardinal Newman and spoke of that with Ryan, who had also read him. So they have common sources.

"One thing that has always seemed important to me in the relations between the two men," Ambassador Pelletier continued, "was that Ryan would like to have been a scholar, and he wasn't able to because he had no money, and Trudeau had, and I've often thought that bothered Ryan a lot. Trudeau was the guy who could do what he couldn't. And Trudeau has an independent spirit, and Ryan likes very much to dominate the people with whom he works."

So while they may have been nourished by the same intellectual sources, their ways had been set by upbringing and disposition. The street conversation in Rome in 1952 indicates how very far apart they already were. Trudeau might follow the way of the gospel, but he would never renounce his wealth, for it gave him the freedom to be what he was, and do what he did, then as later in life.

But it was not until twelve years later that Ryan found himself in a position where he was required to make some comment on Trudeau's views. In May of 1964, a group of seven Montrealers published what, in English, they rather immodestly called "A Canadian Manifesto." The French version of the text had the less ringing title of *"Pour Une Politique Fonctionnelle."* The French title was much closer to the utilitarian spirit and rather dry tone of the text, which had been drafted by a group of seven Montreal intellectuals. What was interesting, and rather daring, about their concept was that amidst the full euphoria of the Quiet Revolution, they decided to press for a renewed emphasis on the Canadian link.

The seven co-authors went on to more practical pursuits. Lawyer Claude Bruneau became an executive of Power Corporation, and in 1983 was named chairman of its insurance company, Imperial Life. Economist Albert Breton, later a professor at the University of Toronto, would become an adviser to the prime minister. His brother Raymond Breton was a sociologist, who also gravitated to the University of Toronto. They were an interesting

pair, being Francsaskois, French Canadians from Sas-
katchewan. Maurice Pinard, later a McGill sociologist,
became Quebec's most respected pollster. In the 1976
election, he predicted the Parti Quebecois would win 70
seats; The PQ took 71. In the 1980 referendum, he predicted
the No side would win between 57 and 60 percent of the
vote, but probably closer to 60; the result was 59.56 percent
for the No. In the 1981 election, he forecast a PQ comeback
in the range of 75 to 84 seats; the PQ won 80.

Yvon Gauthier was a psychoanalyst who was attached
at the time to St. Justine's children's hospital in Montreal.
In political terms, he was to remain the most anonymous
of the group.

The last two would become the most famous. Marc
Lalonde would become the prime minister's principal secretary in the 1960s, health minister and justice minister
in the 1970s, energy minister and finance minister in the
1980s. All this time Lalonde was doing the bidding of the
seventh member of that obscure group, the most obscure
of the obscure, who became the fifteenth prime minister
of Canada, law professor Pierre Elliott Trudeau.

There were seven members of the group, but as Breton
put it, "There was one writer, Pierre."

The manifesto created an immediate sensation, and
in the week of its publication in the Montreal papers, it
was the subject of a lead editorial in *Le Devoir* by its
recently appointed director, 39-year-old Claude Ryan. At
that point, he had been in the newspaper business all of
two years, having quit Catholic Action after seventeen
years to become an editorialist with the more or less implicit
understanding that he could become publisher when the
incumbent, Gérard Filion, moved on. Filion kept his
promise and, early in 1964, Ryan was installed in the
publisher's chair of *Le Devoir*, keeping up the tradition
that the paper be put in the hands of an outsider to
journalism, a tradition that was upheld in 1981 with the
long-delayed appointment of Ryan's own successor, Jean-
Louis Roy of McGill's French Canada Studies Program.

Though the "Canadian Manifesto" was written by a committee, Ryan's critique noted that it "was signed by Pierre-Elliott Trudeau and six other Montreal intellectuals."

And why should Ryan not have suspected that Trudeau was the driving force of the group, since he had stated many of the same arguments in other forums such as *Cité Libre*? Trudeau was known, for example, to be a scourge of Quebec nationalism, which the Manifesto asserted "distorts one's vision of reality, prevents one from seeing problems in their true perspective, falsifies solutions and constitutes a classic diversionary tactic for politicians caught by facts."

And then there were the authors' stated reasons for their attachment to Canada.

"We refuse to let ourselves be locked into a constitutional frame smaller than Canada," wrote the seven-member Committee for Political Realism. "First, there is the juridical and geographical fact called Canada. . . . To take it apart would require an enormous expenditure of energy and gain no proven advantage." They went on to assert that "the most valid trends today are toward more enlightened humanism, towards various forms of political, social and economic universalism." Canada, they concluded, "is a reproduction on a smaller and simpler scale of this universal phenomenon." It was Trudeau, all right. Ryan was sure enough that he called it "the Trudeau group," in a generally warm and approving editorial. On the reproach of the Seven to the nationalists, Ryan observed that "the Trudeau group stands up vigorously to this deformation of patriotism. The group reminds us of three elementary truths of good will; first, that politics must be based on the individual, not on a race; second, that politics must be the work of logic and reason, not only facile sentiment; and third, that the most respected modern schools of thought incline towards an open, humanistic view of the world rather than a falling back on frontiers."

"I wrote well in those days," Ryan said with a laugh when he was shown the clipping many years later. But in 1964, as in later years, Ryan found the Trudeau group "dealt too coldly with the national and cultural realities," and were "too abstract" in their approach to other policy areas. This would become a running sore between Ryan and Trudeau after his entry into politics the following year.

It was at a late Friday afternoon news conference on September 10, 1965, that Trudeau, Pelletier and Jean Marchand confirmed their rumored entry into federal politics at the side of Lester Pearson's Liberals. While they were reading their statement, Claude Ryan was somewhere in the room, perhaps alone with his thoughts. Ryan would not have been the sort to keep a political rendez-vous of his own as a member of a team. But he did acknowledge that "I was on good terms with Pearson in those years, and Pearson had made approaches to me to see if I was interested in running. But I said at the time there was no prospect of that." It was not only the prime minister who had been after Ryan to enter federal politics, but one of the most significant if lesser known figures of the era, Fernand Cadieux.

Cadieux was a comrade-in-arms for the newspaper editor. When Ryan was general secretary of Catholic Action, Cadieux was national president of the youth wing, Jeunesse Etudiante Catholique. Later on, Cadieux became the intellectual's intellectual, one of the inspiring forces behind Maurice Pinard's Social Research Group, which sought to put sociological studies in Quebec on a sound methodological base. Cadieux was also involved behind the scenes with the Manifesto group, urging them on to action. Everyone of Ryan's and Trudeau's generation who knew Cadieux spoke of him with a special awe. Ryan remembered him as "a very close friend of all of us. He was a real light, you know." Until the end of his life, Cadieux remained a special adviser to Trudeau in the Privy Council Office. When he died, in February of 1976, Ryan phoned in his obituary to *Le Devoir* from Ottawa, where he was attending the Conservative leadership convention. Cadieux's funeral passed unnoticed by the national press, which had other errands that weekend. Among the mourners, the elite of a generation, were the prime minister of Canada and the director of *Le Devoir*.

Afterwards, Trudeau gave Ryan a lift, and for a few minutes they talked as old acquaintances.

Back in 1965, Cadieux was pushing all the bright people of that generation in the direction of Ottawa. He leaned very hard on Ryan, telling him Ottawa needed men of action like himself. "I said to Fernand," Ryan recalled, "he was a very close friend of mine, I said, 'No, sorry, I have more important work to do here. Nothing will distract me from that work, so you go and work with your friends if you want to.' "

So while there is no doubt that Ryan could have been one of Pearson's bright new boys from Quebec in the class of '65, he had his own priorities. Besides, he wasn't the type to go along as a member of a group. Watching Trudeau and the others that day in 1965, it evidently occurred to Ryan that they had made quite a leap from their leanings towards the NDP, to the more pragmatic world of the governing Liberals. It was Trudeau, after all, who had written a scathing essay about Nobel laureate Pearson being the defrocked prince of peace for his acceptance of nuclear weapons on Canadian soil; it was Trudeau who referred to men of his generation who had been seduced by the "rouged face of power." It was Trudeau who had worked actively in the 1963 campaign of the NDP's Charles Taylor in the Mount Royal riding where he would run against the same man barely two and a half years later.

Ryan thought it was neither impertinent nor irrelevant to point out that the new Liberal triumvirate had missed a rendez-vous with the NDP. "This rendez-vous," Ryan observed, "would have given hope, without crying from the rooftops, to the NDP's Quebec leader, Robert Cliche. At the moment the socialist idea is taking hold here, at the moment it is finding powerful support among the intellectuals and trade unionists, three men who could have contributed a great deal to preparing the way have renounced this idea to join the ranks of the Liberals."

Nor was Ryan persuaded by their rationale for going over to the Liberals. "These three men invoked, the other day, to justify their choice, their desire to save Canada.

This argument doesn't impress me very much. There are a hundred different ways of working for the intelligent achievement of the Canadian hypothesis."

Ryan was quite prescient in sounding the death knell of the NDP's hopes in Quebec. Cliche was himself buried in the Trudeau landslide of 1968, and in the mid-1980s the party was still waiting to win its first seat in Quebec. "At the time," Ryan said later, "I still entertained the notion that perhaps the NDP could offer a new way to Canadians. These people had been very close to the NDP. And I thought their decision was a real watershed for the NDP. It meant the end of the road for many, many years to come. And I was a bit sad because of that."

But it was just the beginning for Trudeau and his colleagues, who went up to the capital after their elections of November 8, 1965. Within a year, Trudeau was parliamentary secretary to the prime minister. Within two years he was justice minister, and it was in this capacity that he ran afoul of Le Devoir for the first time. In Quebec to address the Canadian Bar Association in September of 1967, the justice minister met the press at a rather tumultuous news conference where he gave his unqualfied opinion of Premier Daniel Johnson's constitutional position, which was summed up by the slogan Egalité ou Indépendance. Trudeau dismissed it as a "huge intellectual joke" and a connerie, a rather rude anatomical reference. For his flippant and rather vulgar remarks, Trudeau wasn't long in hearing from the director of Le Devoir. "The Pierre Trudeau of the '50s," Ryan wrote, "would at least have made the effort to study the same propositions with care. He would not necessarily have espoused them. He would at least have analyzed them and dissected them, in good faith. His conclusion could have been negative: at least it would have been based on a semblance of reason."

In the same editorial, entitled "The Deplorable Attitude of Pierre Elliott Trudeau," Ryan also referred to his "arrogant intransigence," and his "detestable tendency to judge from on high and afar problems which he does not understand." It was about the roughest Ryan ever was on Trudeau, and years later the former editorialist made no apology for it. "That criticism would still apply today," Ryan said before his defeat in the 1981 election. "I think that's one of the weaknesses in Trudeau. I think that is one flaw in his temperament, that he's so prone to logic and he distorts his opponent's argument and presents it in a way that makes it very easy to dismiss it. But he misses some essential elements of the argument."

By the end of 1967, it was quite apparent that Ryan and Trudeau were not getting on at all. In the early days of the race to succeed Pearson as Liberal leader, Ryan evinced little enthusiasm for the prospect of Trudeau's candidacy. In *Le Devoir*'s appraisal of the candidates, Trudeau barely made it to the finals. In the second of three editorials on April 3, 1968, Ryan eliminated eight names from consideration for the paper's endorsement. That left him with Paul Hellyer, Mitchell Sharp and Trudeau. Ryan was all set to endorse Sharp the next day, but in the meantime the finance minister suddenly and unexpectedly withdrew, throwing his support to Trudeau. Ryan would not do the same. Though he acknowledged that "on an intellectual level, Mr. Trudeau is superior to Mr. Hellyer," Ryan could not overcome his reservations about Trudeau's constitutional posture and his adamant opposition to the notion that Quebec constituted a distinct society within the Canadian framework. Ryan put it bluntly: "We believe that, on this problem, the rigid and all too frequently negative attitude that Mr. Trudeau espouses reflects badly the thinking of a great number of his fellow Quebecers."

So Ryan went with Hellyer. "I did not feel at the time that Trudeau was ripe to become prime minister. He was not the man to deal with the Quebec problem; I thought we had to throw what little weight we had behind Hellyer's campaign."

Trudeau may have claimed in later years that he never read *Le Devoir*, but he was certainly reading it in those days and his close associates acknowledged that he never forgave Ryan for not supporting his favorite son candidacy at the Liberal convention of April 4 to 6, 1968. "I think Trudeau never forgot that," said André Ouellet, later chief Liberal organizer for Quebec.

But Ryan was not finished with Trudeau in 1968. In the Trudeaumania election of June 25, with Ryan's own brother, Yves, standing for the Conservatives in a Montreal seat, the publisher supported Robert Stanfield's Conservatives. "That never surprised me," said Gérard Pelletier, "because Ryan always struck me as a closet Conservative, and he often wrote articles saying it was too bad there wasn't a Conservative party of Quebec, because there's a Conservative point of view that has no means of expressing itself. He had a natural sympathy for Stanfield. Ryan had sympathy for the man and for his Conservatism."

And for the *Deux Nations* proposition put forward by the Tories after their Montmorency think-in of 1967, as opposed to the One Nation product that Trudeau was selling around the country that spring, when the campaign was over, and the inevitable Trudeau sweep was complete, Ryan took a rather more conciliatory view. In a piece entitled "The Beginning of a New Era," Ryan acknowledged the decisive nature of Trudeau's mandate and offered his "sincere congratulations" to the victor. "The head of government, without prejudice to the right of dissent which everyone holds in a democracy, has the right to the collaboration of everyone who would make Canada a great country. It would be contemptuous to refuse him that on the morrow of a result like yesterday."

It was an olive branch held out in the direction of Ottawa, an invitation for Trudeau to pick up the phone and come calling. But Trudeau was not about to come calling, for which Ryan, in his turn, never forgave the prime minister.

"One day he made a disclosure to me," said Pelletier, "I was often in contact with him, as I was in politics then. He wrote one or two articles on Trudeau that seemed to me to be really stupid. He had the right to disagree, but I found him really mean. And I said to him, why do you become so mean on the subject of Trudeau? He was director of *Le Devoir* and he said to me, 'Everyone has come to sit in this office to ask my advice and Trudeau has never come.' It revealed a few things to me. But Trudeau has never gone to any editorial office to ask advice."

Least of all after the events of October, 1970.

14

THE HEIRS
OF LORD ACTON

Long afterwards, everyone agreed that the October
Crisis was the worst time between Trudeau and Ryan,
the low point of their relationship over thirty-five years.
The falling out concerned the famous provisional government plot, and whether Ryan was behind it, and
whether Trudeau believed it.

It began, innocently enough, around a table in the
director's office of *Le Devoir*, which was then on Notre
Dame Street before it moved to Saint Sacrement. It was
October 11, 1970, the day after the kidnapping of Pierre
Laporte, a one-time labor reporter at *Le Devoir* and then
labor minister in the Bourassa government. Ryan called
an extraordinary Sunday meeting of his editorial board
to discuss the escalation of the crisis which had begun
the previous Monday with the kidnapping of the British
trade representative in Montreal, James Cross, by another
cell of the Front de Liberation du Québec.

Besides Ryan, the meeting was attended by writers
Michel Roy, Jean-Claude Leclerc, Vincent Prince and
Claude Lemelin.

"Laporte's kidnapping of the previous day had been
an abrupt aggravation of the crisis," Roy recalled a decade
later. "Ryan thought it created a grave political situation.
One of the things that worried him was that the government of Quebec would be put in trusteeship by the government in Ottawa. One of the other aspects was that
maybe Bourassa should reinforce his government
somehow."

It was, as Roy, the paper's future editor-in-chief recalled
it, a free-wheeling discussion of the kind that occurs all

the time in editorial meetings, in which all hypotheses are examined in the formulation of editorial policy. Then of course, Ryan always saw himself playing a larger role than that of a newspaper publisher. He saw himself as an intermediary. From his almost daily contacts with Bourassa, Ryan was concerned that the premier was not able to manage the situation. From other sources, the *Le Devoir* board had indications that Ottawa was preparing a hard line, and from their point of view, the thought of the feds moving in and taking over the management of the crisis was unthinkable in that Quebec would become the marionette of Ottawa.

Ryan was fairly intrigued by the idea of Bourassa accepting a few prominent figures into a government of unity. One of the prospective candidates in this hypothetical discussion was Lucien Saulnier, then in his final days as chairman of Montreal's executive committee. He was Mayor Jean Drapeau's administrative right-hand man, and he was Ryan's contact man at City Hall, since even in those days Ryan and Drapeau were hardly on speaking terms. After the meeting, Ryan drove out to Saulnier's home on suburban Ile Bizard and discussed the idea with him. Saulnier, under a great deal of stress in those early days of the Crisis, reacted very negatively. And that should, or could, have been the end of it. But almost immediately, Saulnier informed the superior authorities of his conversation with Ryan.

"It was Saulnier," said Robert Bourassa, "who informed me, in emotional terms, there's someone who is betraying you, trying to stab you in the back."

Nor did Saulnier stop there. He also informed Marc Lalonde, then Trudeau's principal secretary and one of the chief crisis managers in the prime minister's office.

A decade later, Lalonde acknowledged that he had been informed "very rapidly" by Saulnier of his conversation. After that, Lalonde said, it became "an affair that developed a momentum of its own."

Even if it was just a talking point, he maintained, "it was a crazy idea. It wasn't even imaginable as an option. Maybe it was just an error, but it was a double error, a grave error in judgment, to have seriously considered this matter and, secondly, to have discussed it with a politician in place. What if he had said, yes. What next?"

Lalonde shortly informed Trudeau, who was discussing it with Bourassa, as the former premier recalled it, "by Tuesday or Wednesday at the latest.

"Trudeau was furious on the telephone," Bourassa said. "He believed it. He thought Ryan was capable of doing that."

Trudeau discussed the so-called plot with Bourassa in the presence of Drapeau the following week in the premier's office. But by then, Laporte was dead, left in a car trunk on Saturday the 17th, after Trudeau had invoked the War Measures Act in the early hours of the 16th. One of the key events leading up to the imposition of War Measures was a communiqué put out by Ryan and several other public figures, including René Lévesque and labor leaders Louis Laberge and Marcel Pépin, urging the Bourassa government to negotiate for the release of "political prisoners," as demanded by the FLQ. As Ryan later informed his readers, he had received a telephone call from Lévesque at the end of the afternoon on October 14, asking if he would join in the statement. When published the following day, it may have contributed to the appearance that the will to resist the FLQ demands was collapsing among the intellectual and political leadership of Montreal. Trudeau and his advisers had that to think about in addition to the incomplete reports they were receiving about spreading campus protests.

Years later Marc Lalonde acknowledged that the statement put out by Ryan, Lévesque and the others "could have been a factor" in Trudeau invoking War Measures in the sense that "it was a sign of decay of political legitimacy in Quebec. I never believed in the possibility of a *putsch*. It's just that it demonstrated a difficult situation. Faced with that situation, with a lack of information, it was a question of not knowing the enemy. Nobody knew, and there was a certain deterioration of the political situation."

As Lalonde said, the provisional government affair developed a momentum of its own. Trudeau evidently believed it, and from there it got whispered around the cocktail circuit in Ottawa. By this time, the distinctions had been blurred between Ryan's original conversation with Saulnier, and the communiqué put out by the leading public figures.

What really blew it up was an unsigned article on the front page of the *Toronto Star* on Monday, October 26. The story, attributed to "top-level sources," asserted that "the factor that finally drove the Trudeau government into action was that they became convinced a plan existed to replace the Quebec government of Robert Bourassa."

Neither the sources nor the plotters were named. Nor was the story signed, though it was always attributed to Peter C. Newman, then editor of the paper's editorial page, who kept up his Ottawa contacts from his days as the paper's columnist in the capital.

"There was a lot of misunderstanding about the thing," Newman said. "One of the things, one of the misunderstandings was over who wrote it, or why my name wasn't on it. My name wasn't on it because I didn't write it. And it was the usual thing when more than one person writes it." Newman maintained that at least two other *Star* reporters checked the story and that "it was written basically at the desk. The other misunderstanding was that I believed it. And I never said I believed it. Anyway, the point is that they believed it. What I was reporting was what they believed. And it was true, as it came out later, that they believed it, and that's all one can say of it." Asked if Trudeau was his source, Newman said, "No." Here he may have been protecting his source, since one colleague later claimed that Newman got the story from the prime minister.

But that wasn't the end of it. Three days later, on October 29, *The Montreal Star* picked up the provisional government plot and ran it under the byline of its respected Quebec editor, Dominique Clift:

> Federal officials firmly believe that Claude Ryan, editor of *Le Devoir*, proposed forming a provisional govern-

ment of public safety to replace a faltering Bourassa government and restore the shattered unity of French Canadians in Quebec.

In spite of the denials which he printed in *Le Devoir* this week, Ryan approached several prominent personalities at the time suggesting that the Bourassa government was in danger of imminent collapse and that various citizens of note should step forward to pick up the pieces and ensure stable government in the province.

Ryan was absolutely livid, and he had every right to be. Clift had not checked the story with him, and here was *The Montreal Star* running rumors as fact. Ryan was forced to write a detailed narrative explaining the whole story in the next day's edition of his paper. "Neither with Mr. Lévesque," he wrote, "nor with Mr. Pépin, nor with Louis Laberge nor with any of the others who signed the joint declaration, at any time have I discussed a plan for a provisional government. Furthermore, none of them mentioned this possibility to me."

Confronted by a scrum of reporters later that day in Ottawa, Trudeau insisted he had "solid information" about a plan to set up a provisional government. Referring to Ryan's editorial, the prime minister said he understood the director had "made a clean breast of it," when of course Ryan had done nothing of the sort. Finally, Trudeau paraphrased the celebrated dictum of Lord Acton, that power corrupts and absolute power corrupts absolutely. "What was it that Acton said?," Trudeau said at the stairwell below his Centre Block office. "Lack of power corrupts and absolute lack of power corrupts absolutely." It was a cruel, unkind cut. He was quoting, or paraphrasing, one of the two favorite authors of himself and Claude Ryan.

Nothing more ever came of the affair, and years later Trudeau's closest friend, Gérard Pelletier, admitted that "Trudeau jumped much too quickly on the story of the parallel cabinet. And when he quoted Lord Acton, there he was really. . . but there was a guy in a difficult situation."

I understood his impatience, but he went too far because there wasn't too much to it."

In the October Crisis, Pelletier had come home to live in Montreal and keep his ear to the ground, "because from Ottawa you had a deformed image." From the moment Pelletier heard the story of the parallel government, he said he dismissed it. While he thought "it wasn't brilliant of Ryan" to be suggesting that so-and-so be taken into the government, it was a long leap from there "to talk of a parallel government, which I found far-fetched."

The whole problem with that "damn October crisis," observed Albert Breton years later, "is that Trudeau was too damn close to it." A few weeks later, in January of 1971, Trudeau received a group of eight intellectuals, Ryan, Guy Rocher and half a dozen others, who had previously called on Premier Bourassa.

"It was an icy conversation," Ryan remembered. "It lasted two hours and I think he wanted to spend as much time with us as Bourassa had two weeks before. It was as if he was resolved we could not say we had been treated lightly."

After that, nearly three years passed before Ryan saw Trudeau again, alone or in a group. Finally, at the end of 1973, the people around Trudeau prevailed upon him to have Ryan for dinner at 24 Sussex. It was obviously an effort, for as Lalonde observed, "you always had to twist Trudeau's arm to get him to sit down with Ryan." Finally in the 1974 election, Ryan relented and endorsed Trudeau for the first time. But Trudeau's opinion of him did not greatly improve. After Bourassa's defeat in the 1976 election, in which Ryan had endorsed the PQ, the outgoing premier received a call from Trudeau who remarked early in the conversation that "Ryan dropped you" in his post-election address to the Montreal Chamber of Commerce.

But the succession to Bourassa was another matter. When Ryan's name began to come up, Trudeau did not express any opposition to the idea. Even though it was unthinkable for the feds to endorse one candidate or another, they could still swing a pretty big stick in the campaign, since the federal and provincial Liberals were essentially the same people at the grass roots level. In this regard, nobody had more clout than Marc Lalonde, Trudeau's Quebec lieutenant. The feds never intervened against Ryan, and there is a good deal of evidence to support the view that they were backing him, from the establishment crowd in Outremont to the organizers at the grass roots.

"Before the '78 leadership," Pelletier recalled, Trudeau said to someone who asked, in my presence, 'Yes, I think Ryan's a guy who could beat Lévesque.'"

Whatever their personal reservations, Ryan and Trudeau realized in the spring of 1978 that they were both on the same side. There was some doubt as to who was the captain of the team. Until the referendum, they knew, they would have to gloss over their differences on the constitutional question. It was the touchstone of both their careers, the one thing they really cared about. It jibed with their ideas of the country, and of Quebec's place in it. When Ryan published his "Beige Paper" on constitutional revision in January of 1980, Trudeau had to dodge questions as to what he thought of it. This was barely a month before the election that returned him to power. Ryan, for his part, had to keep his peace when

May 3, 1978: On the eve of a scheduled visit to Trudeau at 24 Sussex, Ryan receives Tory leader Joe Clark at his home in Montreal. Brian Mulroney, who arranged the meeting, tells reporters that "I'm just the driver." To a furious Trudeau, Ryan will reply that "my door is always open." Exactly a year later, Trudeau will take him up on it. (Staff Photo by Chuck Stoody, *Canadian Press*)

Trudeau went rushing off to make constitutional history after the referendum.

Those episodes were still to be written when they met at 24 Sussex for a long and much-publicized lunch on a cold May afternoon about a month after Ryan's accession to the leadership. Trudeau, looking at the possibility of an election in mid-1978, was angry that Ryan had received Conservative Leader Joe Clark for dinner at his house in Montreal only the night before. The dinner had been arranged by Ryan's friend, Brian Mulroney, as a favor to Clark. When it was over, they walked into the spring evening and the national newscasts, smiles and handshakes all round. It dissipated the impression the feds hoped to create of a common front between Trudeau and Ryan. And it reminded voters in Ontario that with Ryan now in place in Quebec, Trudeau was somewhat less indispensable for the national unity debate. For Ryan was himself a national figure, with national stature, and at the time he was at the peak of his popularity, the preferred leader over Lévesque by a 2 to 1 margin, a rather disconcerting statistic in view of what happened later on. In any event Trudeau was angry with Ryan.

"When Clark wants to see you, you invite him to your house," Trudeau said. "When I want to see you I have to issue an official invitation to come and see me at Sussex."

"Pierre," Ryan replied. "My house has always been an open house. You're invited there any time, you don't even have to let me know. You're always welcome. I thought you knew that."

Trudeau would avail himself of the invitation the following spring, when he was nearing the end of a losing campaign.

It was everything Trudeau's people could have hoped for. Ryan was becoming a politician: he was doing his friends a favor. And he genuinely thought that Trudeau was the better man to lead the country. Though he remained scrupulously neutral in the campaign, he told his executive assistant, Pierre Pettigrew, that the country needed a man of experience with some credentials in the Western world. "We need a man of international stature,"

Ryan told his assistant, "so that Canada can play its full role."

After Trudeau's defeat on May 22, Ryan appeared to stand as the unchallenged leader of the federalist cause. Not only was he the leader in law, according to the enabling legislation for the referendum. But there was now a power vacuum with the defeat of the cousins in Ottawa, and Ryan quickly filled it. Trudeau was relegated to whatever role Ryan would deem appropriate. As for Joe Clark, the youngest-ever prime minister decided to hold himself above the fray, partly out of strategy and partly out of necessity. By taking some of the irritants out of the Ottawa-Quebec relationship, he wisely denied Lévesque a target.

So Ryan could afford to be generous when Trudeau announced his retirement on the morning of November 21. In the National Assembly that afternoon, Ryan rose to propose a motion of thanks to Trudeau for his services to the country. Ryan then launched into a generous and even extravagant tribute to Trudeau, and lashed out at the former prime minister's critics, including by implication, himself. "There are even those who would sometimes have you believe," Ryan said, "that Mr. Trudeau's attachment for Canada translated itself into an unrealistic conception of the future of Quebec and its destiny. If Mr. Trudeau is attached to Canada, it's because he considers that Canada offers the greatest challenge." Ryan concluded by expressing the hope that "the qualities of courage, high-mindedness and intelligence that characterize Mr. Trudeau will long be available to his fellow Quebecers and all of Canada."

It was too much for René Lévesque, who in his reply was constrained to remind Ryan that he had endorsed Robert Stanfield in 1968. When he got back to his office, Ryan had a call from Trudeau, and they had a good laugh about the PQ being in the position of endorsing a motion praising their sworn adversary, "Lord Elliott." They agreed to meet a few days later in Montreal, where Ryan was anxious to ascertain how Trudeau planned to carry on as a lame duck leader.

"I'm going to stay on until the convention," Trudeau said.

"Then I want it to be very clear," Ryan replied, "that my dealings will be with you until the end, and no one else, and you can count on me not to be a party to any intrigue."

Ryan later said this was the basis of their continuing relationship. "And I could not have been more pleased at what I did, in view of what happened later."

What happened later was of course the fall of the Clark government in December, and Trudeau's announcement that he would, after all, run again. For Ryan, it was not a wholly welcome development. For the prospect of a Trudeau restoration would cast a shadow over himself. There was also the possibility that with Trudeau back in office after the February 18 election, Quebecers would feel free to vote for the Yes side in the referendum, since they would have the security of Trudeau in Ottawa to say No to the mandate they would have given Lévesque. It was a kind of system of checks and balances which, lacking in the constitution, Quebecers had built into the ballot box. It was not for nothing that Quebecers were fond of recalling the old saying, *Bleu à Québec, rouge à Ottawa.*

Still, Ryan told one of his Liberal members, Herbert Marx, in January, that Trudeau was much the better man to be prime minister. And in his Montreal office on election night, he struck his campaign director, Pierre Bibeau, as being "very happy for Trudeau."

But within a matter of weeks, there was a new set of tensions between the Trudeau and the Ryan Liberals as to the management of the referendum campaign. In the National Assembly over a three-week period in March, Ryan's Liberals took a beating. With the first polls indicating the PQ might pull it off, something approaching panic set in in Ottawa. Trudeau was being urged to make an address to the country, to make a full commitment to the campaign. On Good Friday, he had Ryan up for lunch at 24 Sussex. "Some of the guys are nervous that the campaign is not going well," Trudeau said. "Well, Claude, is it going well? "

Ryan insisted that everything would be all right in the end. Trudeau said he was available and would go where Ryan asked. In the end, the prime minister made only four referendum speeches, one in the House of Commons on April 15, and three in Quebec in the month of May. At two rallies in Quebec and Montreal, they sat beside one another, as comrades-in-arms, at last.

But it was to be a short-lived alliance. On referendum day, May 20, Trudeau called on Ryan at his house, and informed him that he was going to move quickly on patriation of the constitution. Ryan said there were a few conditions that had to be met. The very next day, flush with the referendum victory, Trudeau told the Commons that he was going ahead with all deliberate speed. The justice minister, Jean Chrétien, would go across the country and visit the premiers before a first ministers' meeting at 24 Sussex in early June. This was as Ryan was calling for new elections in Quebec to clarify who was to be the province's bargaining agent. He was afraid that Trudeau was in a terrible hurry to make history, and equally concerned that he was conferring a new legitimacy upon the Lévesque government.

When the September Summit of first ministers failed to strike a constitutional bargain, Trudeau moved ahead in October with a unilateral patriation package, with an entrenched charter of rights. Privately, Ryan was appalled, telling his aides it was "immoral."

Lévesque now had the perfect pretext to put off his election until the spring of 1981, to buy time and hope for the depolarization of Quebec voters. It was not a big gamble. At that point, it was the only chance Lévesque had.

As Ryan said himself privately of Trudeau: "He screwed me royally."

After that, and especially after Ryan's defeat, it was inevitable that the old bitterness would come into their relationship. No one was very surprised at the end of 1982 when Ryan, by now the former Liberal leader, wrote a long piece for his old paper, levelling Trudeau and looking forward to the day when the prime minister would retire. "And the sooner the better," Ryan concluded, "for Quebec and the country as a whole." And when Trudeau finally announced his retirement on Leap Year Day, February 29, 1984, Ryan had some parting words in another guest column in his old newspaper.

Calling Trudeau's decision "wise," Ryan was nonetheless prepared to acknowledge that Trudeau had exercised "exceptional leadership," but reproached him for his "intransigent vision of Canadian unity" which often found him "opposed to Quebec, when he should have searched by all means to establish meaningful collaboration with Quebec."

Ryan cited the October Crisis and the constitutional struggle as evidence of "the kind of country to which Mr. Trudeau's conception might logically lead. This kind of country will always be inacceptable to thousands of Quebecers, including many federalists."

Still, Ryan said he would remember Trudeau as a man "of great frankness, exquisite courtesy, and remarkable simplicity." He had always found Trudeau more agreeable in private than in public, Ryan concluded, "but that doesn't

May 3, 1979: Pierre Trudeau, no longer viewed as the indispensable leader of federalist forces, visits Ryan at home on St. Joseph Boulevard in Montreal. Trudeau, in the middle of losing an election, needs Ryan's help. A year and a half later, when the shoe is on the other foot, the born-again prime minister will not return the favor by postponing his plan to patriate the Constitution. "He screwed me royally," Ryan would later acknowledge. They had known each other for thirty-five years, but were never friends. They were too alike in some ways, too unlike in others. (The Gazette photo)

mean we can't acknowledge that the public Mr. Trudeau
has dominated the Canadian political scene for the last
twenty years."

If nothing else, Ryan had the last word between them,
and ended on a grace note.

15
ELLIOTT:
THE FAVORITE SON

The man in the light wool grey suit stood third in line to register his name on the voters' list for the Quebec referendum.

The scrutineers, two Liberal ladies named Delphine Flavelle and Lois Conlon, and a young Péquiste named Christin Côté, failed to take any notice of him.

"Your name?" one of them asked without bothering to look up as he came to the head of the line.

"Pierre Trudeau," he replied. One of the startled women asked if he really was who he made himself out to be. Once that was established to everyone's satisfaction, it was agreed that his occupation should be put down as prime minister of Canada. He then gave his address as 1255 Laird Boulevard, a building where he kept his Mount Royal riding office.

"But you don't live in the riding," protested the young scrutineer for the Yes campaign.

"That's true," said Michel Robert, stepping forward as the prime minister's lawyer. "But he has a domicile here." While Robert went into the legal niceties, Trudeau amused himself by playing ping-pong for a few minutes with the young Péquiste there in the basement of St. Joseph's church in the Town of Mount Royal, across the street from his riding office, where they had gone to the trouble of installing a cot in case anyone should care to test his claim of being domiciled in the district. In the end, the case of Trudeau, Pierre, prime minister of Canada, 1255 Laird Boulevard, was decided in his favor by a three-member panel in the riding, two Liberals voting to have his name on the list, and a Péquiste abstaining.

It was the afternoon of May 2, 1980, and Trudeau had just come, without fanfare or outriders, from a speech downtown at the Chambre de Commerce. It was the second of four interventions he would make in the debate, each of them carefully observed and beautifully crafted. Someday Trudeau's referendum texts would define the texture of the times. What was rather extraordinary, that sunny first Friday in May, was that Trudeau should have come home to Montreal as the born-again prime minister. He had said his farewells to the city in that capacity the previous May 21, when he had gone to the Forum with a relative to watch the Canadiens' defeat the New York Rangers and win the Stanley Cup. It was the night before the 1979 election, and Trudeau, who would normally have sat in full view of the television cameras behind the Canadiens' bench, was declared out of bounds to the television producers who were under strict instructions not to give him any free television time in front of as many as fifteen million viewers only twelve hours or so before the polls opened. But Trudeau, as his luck would have it, caught a puck that flew over over the boards near the end of the third period. There was a tremendous ovation in his corner of the building and the television director had a camera look in to see what all the fuss was about. And there, flashing a souvenir puck, was the man who was not supposed to be shown on television that night. Afterwards, his friend and admirer Serge Savard, the Canadiens' captain, saw to it that he was invited into the victors' dressing room for a quick television interview and a dousing of champagne. In Quebec, there is a maxim that as the Canadiens go, so goes the Liberal party. It's nonsense, of course, except in the sense that campaign workers feel better about a spring election when the Canadiens are going well. For the people around Trudeau that night, the events of the evening seemed like a promising omen.

But there was no good fortune for Trudeau on the morrow. Twenty-four hours later, he stood in the old Château Laurier in Ottawa, conceding defeat for the first time in his life. In Quebec, where there was a great pride in the favorite son, there was no rejoicing. And there was a momentary sense of dread that the rest of the country had determined to remove him from office at the very time his moral authority was most needed in Quebec during the run-up to the referendum.

Those apprehensions proved to be ill-founded. With Trudeau's defeat, the debate between him and Lévesque became depersonalized and quickly evolved into a discussion of the issue—sovereignty-association versus renewed federalism, or Quebec versus Quebec and Canada. It soon developed that with Trudeau and his Quebec ministers out of the way, the characteristically aggressive Lévesque was deprived of his usual targets. And in his government's long awaited white paper on sovereignty-association, he would have to come up with some answers of his own. As prime minister, Joe Clark seemed determined not to provoke the Lévesque administration, and was concerned to remove "irritants," as he put it, from the federal-provincial process. Over the objections of some members of his own party in Quebec, he put Arthur Tremblay in the Senate. Tremblay, the former deputy minister of education and intergovernmental affairs in Quebec, knew the nuances of politics along the Grande Allée. It was a daring appointment by Clark, and Tremblay soon emerged as his principal constitutional adviser whose advice, for the moment, was to do nothing.

It seemed to be working. On November 14, the PQ lost another two by-elections, this time in ridings it had previously held. One was the swing riding of Prévost in the Laurentian foothills north of Montreal, where the Liberals swept one community college poll by an antonishing 2 to 1 margin. The other, even more astonishing, result came in from the PQ fortress of Maisonneuve in East-End Montreal, where Robert Burns had previously won easily for the PQ, even in the wilderness years of 1970 and 1973. It seemed that as long as the Liberals cared to make independence the issue, they could not lose.

While Ryan was savoring this latest triumph, Trudeau was stuggling to adapt as leader of the opposition. As if there weren't enough indignities to be suffered, it looked

as if the referendum would be won without him. To the
extent that he would come into the coming campaign, it
would be at Ryan's beck and call. As Trudeau flew back
from Toronto to Ottawa after a convention of Ontario
Liberals, he stared out the window for what seemed like
the longest time. Some of his staff people who were with
him that Tuesday morning were convinced that was when
he decided to quit. The next day, November 21, he made
it official. The Trudeau era was over.

Two days after that, Trudeau came home to Montreal
to keep a couple of previous engagements. At l'École des
Hautes Etudes Commerciales, the business school affiliated
with the University of Montreal, Trudeau kept an appointment with a new generation of Quebec students.
This was not the kind of campus crowd for which Quebec
had been noted during the Bourassa years, and it was
not the same Trudeau who had occasionally appeared on
campus during his prime ministerial years. He did not
feel constrained to defend his stewardship, nor was he
asked to. He was asked instead for his ideas, on the
referendum, on the PQ's white paper and its assumptions
of negotiating "between equals," and whether, with the
passing of "French Power," young Quebecers should feel
any attachment to the federal system. As he answered
questions for more than an hour, he sounded like a free
man. "One of the great things about federalism," he said,
"is the creative tension between the two levels of government. Sometimes it's a little inconvenient, sometimes
it results in little spats you'd prefer to avoid, but there's
always this tension, this negotiation between the two
powers . . . by nature, there will always be disagreements."
He thought the recommendation of the Pépin-Robarts
commission, for a system of partial proportional representation, would ease the regional disparities of party
representation in Ottawa, where the Liberals had nothing
to show for their 25 percent of the votes in the West, and
the Conservatives were chronically weak in Quebec. There
might even be some merit, he thought, in looking at the
French system and there, he said, "no one can accuse

me of trying to replace the Queen by President Trudeau because there's no more question of that."

Indeed, at that point, there was no more question of Prime Minister Trudeau.

The thought that he would no longer be around seemed anguishing for the audience who jammed a place called the Buffet Rizzo near the predominantly Italian suburb of St. Léonard in the northeast end of Montreal. Trudeau sat at a table on the edge of the dance floor, and was mobbed by successive waves of mothers and daughters, who wanted to touch him, talk to him, and have their pictures taken with him. For many of them, he was the only prime minister they had known as Canadians. For some of them, he was the man who had let them or some close relatives into the country. Trudeau always had a special affinity with minority ethnic audiences, for when he spoke of Canada as a privileged corner of the world, they knew from experience what he was talking about. Whenever he might have muttered about Canadians being a country of bitchers, he never meant them. So when he spoke to them for a few minutes, he seemed to sense their sadness at his leaving. He asked them to please remember that he would always be with them. But when he left, bound for Ottawa in the back seat of his newly leased Pontiac, it seemed he was gone for good.

Not three weeks later, fate or fortune intervened to give Trudeau another chance to make history. With the defeat of the Clark government's macho budget, with the country plunged into a winter campaign in mid-December, Trudeau returned again to Montreal, this time to the seclusion in which to consider his options. He saw mostly friends and family that weekend at the Outremont home of his sister, Suzette Rouleau. To one old friend who asked what he would do, Trudeau said that if he came back, he would win, stay on two or three years as prime minister and then, "do what I want to do."

What he wanted for himself then, after he and his party had thought it over a few days, was another kick at the electoral can. He knew that, going in with a twenty-point lead, it would be difficult for him to lose, since a five-point swing is considered the most movement that usually occurs in a campaign. He knew he had the issue in the Tory budget and its 18-cent gasoline excise tax, which cut across all regions and all income groups. He had another, unspoken issue, in Joe Clark and what the country thought of him, which wasn't much. So for two months he flew around the country pretending to be interested in gasoline prices and saying next to nothing about the constitution and the referendum, the two things that truly mattered to him then. After his election night welcome to the 1980s, after the restoration, there would time to talk of those things.

But time was on the move after the February 18 election. The day after the Trudeau cabinet was sworn in at Government House, the National Assembly was convened in Quebec to begin the long-awaited 35-hour debate on the referendum question.

There was no doubt that Trudeau was presenting a "referendum cabinet." Jean Chrétien was named justice minister, with particular responsibility for the coming campaign in Quebec. Former Quebec mayor Gilles Lamontagne was made defence minister, and given the touchy assignment of choosing a fighter plane that would not only fly for the Armed Forces, but produce the most industrial benefits for Quebec's aircraft industry. André Ouellet was back as consumer affairs minister and postmaster-general. The combative Marc Lalonde was in the energy portfolio. Monique Bégin was back as health minister. Francis Fox was named to the cultural hardware and software portfolio of communications and secretary of state. Pierre de Bané from the Lower St. Lawrence, Pierre Bussières and Charles Lapointe from the Quebec region, Don Johnston from English-speaking Montreal, rounded out Trudeau's Quebec team. In all, there were eleven Quebec ministers, including Trudeau himself. But as events would soon demonstrate, they had little time to enjoy the honors of their victory.

The three-week debate in the National Assembly soon became a rout. Even before the debate was concluded, the first poll of the campaign published in Montreal's

Dimanche-Matin on March 16 indicated a pronounced swing to the Yes option. It wasn't long before the Ryan forces were wondering how to recoup, before the feds were wondering how they could usefully be of assistance without appearing to take over the No campaign. They had one big ace in the hole: the Trudeau card. The question was how, and when, to play it.

"We wanted to maximize his impact," Chrétien said later. "At the same time we did not want to overshadow Ryan too much. I think we managed." That was how it came out in the end.

It became a question of what he would say and when he would say it. From Paris came his closest intellectual confidant, Gérard Pelletier, for "one long conversation," as the ambassador put it, in which they went over the touchnotes of what Trudeau would say. He would belittle the PQ for its lack of courage in posing such an ambiguous question. As to the vaunted "bargaining power" of the Yes, he would state from the outset the impossibility of negotiations. Then he would ask René Lévesque what he would do in the event of a No. Finally, there would be the pride of Canada, the pride of *les Canadiens*, and the pride of Quebecers in Trudeau, which would be stated by the simple fact of his showing up.

In the prime minister's office, Trudeau drew to himself a close circle of four advisers. There was Patrick McDonald, originally one of Pelletier's recruits. There was DeMontigny Marchand, a former Trudeau aide who had gone on briefly to work in the Pelletier embassy in Paris during the Clark administration but was now back as undersecretary of state. There was Claude Morin, not to be confused with the other Claude Morin, a 35-year-old former executive assistant to Francis Fox. Morin was the systems man of the group, in charge of pulling together clippings and documentation and overseeing the details of Trudeau's referendum appearances. And there was the wordsmith, André Burelle, the person who put down on paper the words and ideas that Trudeau put into his head. Later, it was generally acknowledged that Burelle was the most important member of the group, although he missed Trudeau's two key speeches in Montreal. "It was a bit," he said, "like raising a baby and not being there to present him to the world."

For those to whom Trudeau has seemed out of touch with audiences in English Canada, even out of touch with himself, those referendum speeches would have been a revelation. There were no insults, no rude gestures, and not a single gaffe. As a senior staffer once observed: "He can be brilliant for thirty minutes and screw everything up in thirty seconds." In the referendum period, though he was working largely from material committed to memory, there were no slipups. He was sure of himself, sure of his material, sure of how he wanted to deliver it. Each of his four speeches struck a higher note than the last one. He had also taken the full measure of his adversaries.

In a hushed House of Commons on April 15, with members on both sides sensing it was a little bit of history, Trudeau summarized his ideas of the country and Quebec's place in it. "After all," he said, "what is the feeling of belonging to a country, which we call citizenship? And what is the feeling of loving a country, which we call patriotism? Part of the answer lies in our debates, in the policies, laws and the constitution of this country. Part of the answer can be found in the geography and the history of this country, which in a sense are collective notions, history being the recital of things that we have done together in the past." After a bit more of this highroad stuff, Trudeau zeroed in on the PQ. "I had hoped the Parti Québécois would show more sincerity and conviction in this historical moment," he said. "As far back as January, 1977, I expressed the hope that the referendum question would be clear, that it would come soon, and that it would be definitive, so that we could leave the issue aside for a generation at least . . . . It is not definitive, since it is obvious in the very wording of the question that there will be a second referendum; and it certainly is not clear, since it is based on a deliberate ambiguity on the part of the Parti Québécois."

And then Trudeau gave the answer to a hypothetical question that only the prime minister could give, as to what he would do in the event of a Yes vote on Lévesque's mandate question for sovereignty-association. "Mr. Lévesque," said Trudeau, "will have to begin by recognizing that his mandate to negotiate sovereignty-association is a very ambiguous one. He must first recognize that, to associate, one must associate with someone." And since the prime minister and all the premiers had rejected association, they would have nothing to discuss.

"Perhaps Mr. Lévesque will then say: 'Well, since we cannot discuss association, let us talk purely and simply about sovereignty.' Obviously the reply will be: 'Mr. Lévesque, you . . . have no mandate to discuss sovereignty. As Canadian prime minister, I do not myself have a mandate to discuss this with you, since your concept of sovereignty is in fact defined in your question as the exclusive power to make your own laws, to collect your own taxes, and to establish your own external relations. Not even two months ago, the people in Quebec, together with the rest of the country, unequivocally elected a government to sit in Ottawa precisely to make laws for the entire country, to collect taxes and redistribute them throughout the entire country and to look after external relations. We have therefore just received from the people in Quebec a mandate to exercise sovereignty for the entire country.' "

Clearly, Trudeau's answer was a No to a Yes. The next question for Trudeau to ask would be whether Lévesque might answer Yes to a No.

"What will he do if the No vote wins?" Trudeau asked as he neared the end of his speech to the Chambre de Commerce on May 2. "Do you know? Does Mr. Lévesque know? And if he does, will he tell us?

"I wish," Trudeau concluded, "that every one of us would ask the leader of the government of Quebec, Mr. Lévesque, this question: What will you do if Quebec votes No? We are entitled to know, we want to know; and if you do not dare reply we shall then know that your referendum is a trap . . . ."

As a member of the Trudeau referendum circle noted later, Trudeau had left Lévesque with only two options: "One, he could avoid the question, in which case we were on our issue. Or answer the question, as he did, in which case we could come back on him."

Trudeau had thrown out the line like an expert fly fisherman in the swollen streams of Labrador. And Lévesque, like a big fat trout, had taken it.

Scarcely two hours after the Trudeau speech, Lévesque called a press conference to give the prime minister his answer. "We'll continue to go around in circles," Lévesque said. But he allowed as to how governments would do their duty, one to another. They would talk. So he answered the question, and at the same time he could not answer it, for it presumed the defeat of his option, "a hypothesis in which I refuse to believe."

What was occurring in the campaign was something that could be called the Trudeau effect. It was obvious that the prime minister was distracting the premier, whose serenity of the earlier days of the campaign was being sorely tested as new and less favorable polling results became available to him. Then there were the statements Trudeau was making, about the impossibility of negotiating in the event of a Yes, and the questions he was asking about what Lévesque would do in the event of a No. Canvassers for the No forces picked these up and took them back to the doorsteps of undecided voters.

Most of all, there was the pride in Trudeau's presence, a factor that was most tangible in his later appearances at mass meetings in Quebec and Montreal.

In the minds of most Quebecers, whatever their political affiliations, there was a certain pride in Trudeau for the place he occupied on the international stage. Like other Canadians, they might not think much about foreign policy, or Canada's place in the world, but they could relate to Trudeau addressing the United States Congress, or standing on the White House lawn with Jimmy Carter, or attending a Big Seven economic summit or Commonwealth Conference. In a poll conducted for the Montreal weekly *Dimanche-Matin* at the time of his retirement in 1979, his approval rating shot up to an incredible 84 percent in Quebec. So in Quebec City on May 7, he would play the role of *chef d'état* and favorite son. He flew into Quebec from Vancouver, where he had been meeting the Japanese prime minister Masayoshi Ohira, and he was skipping Marshall Tito's funeral in Yugoslavia. As he flew east in the government JetStar, Trudeau suggested to Burelle that maybe they could work that in somehow. On the ground in the Quebec convention center that night, Trudeau said he told Ohira that he wouldn't be going to Yugoslavia, that he would be going home instead to Quebec, "not because I felt you needed a hand, but because I myself needed to be among family."

By this time, Trudeau was occupying considerable space in the campaign, bolstering one side and bothering the other. Lévesque then made two serious mistakes. The first was to invite Trudeau to a televised debate, a sure sign the Yes camp was in hot water.

Trudeau went to the extraordinary trouble of personally preparing a press release refusing the invitation, reminding Lévesque that according to his own referendum law, he should be dealing with the head of the No committee, Claude Ryan. "Contrary to the spirit and letter of his own referendum law," Trudeau said in his May 13 communiqué, "he is asking me to short-circuit the No committee and its leader Claude Ryan by debating the referendum question with him. My answer to him is an unequivocal *Non, merci!*" It was an elegant little thrust that nicked Lévesque on the arm. But Lévesque's second error would lead to Trudeau smiting him the next evening at a climactic meeting in Montreal.

Over the weekend following Trudeau's Quebec speech, Lévesque explained that Trudeau was also named Elliott, an English name, that he wasn't a full-fledged Quebecer. Lévesque's remarks went virtually unreported, except for a small article under a single paragraph heading in *The Globe and Mail*. It did not, however, escape the attention of Claude Morin of Trudeau's core group. When they met on Monday, May 12, it was among the clippings put in front of the prime minister. "Some of the people didn't think it was too important," Morin said later. "But it was clear he wanted to discuss it." Speechwriter Burelle, who described Lévesque's denigrating reference to Elliott as an "extraordinary gift," set to work on looking "for Péquistes with English names."

As he prepared for the Wednesday night appearance in Montreal, there was also a fair amount of pressure growing on Trudeau to make some firm commitment that a No vote would not simply be taken as a vote for the constitutional status quo.

Chrétien went to see him for lunch at 24 Sussex on the day of the speech. "I told him it was an historic occasion," Chrétien said, "and that the speech would have to be meaningful." Chrétien said he urged Trudeau to go for broke on a promise of constitutional reform. Chrétien also said he raised the Elliott business with Trudeau, and had the impression the prime minister was hearing about it for the first time. What Trudeau really wanted to know was what Chrétien thought. "Give it to them, Pierre," he said.

And so Trudeau rode to Montreal that afternoon to make the speech of his career, the one that would later be referred to by both sides. The scene in the Paul Sauvé arena that evening resembled a rock concert more than a political meeting. There was a sweating, surging crowd,

May 14, 1980: Trudeau receives the acclaim of the thousands at the Paul Sauvé arena in East-End Montreal. Justice Minister Jean Chretien, who has had many difficult conversations with Ryan in the two months since the federal Liberals returned to power, introduces Trudeau as "the pride of Quebec and the pride of Canada." In what many consider the greatest speech of his career Trudeau makes the fateful promise to put his party's seats on the line for constitutional reform. The end result was far from what many people had in mind. (Photo by Tedd Church)

in full-throated cry of Trudeau's name. They claimed him
for their own, and a few minutes into the speech he made
the fateful promise of constitutional reform, of the Quebec
MPs putting their seats on the line for it, and promising
not to stop until the work was done.

But the heart and soul of the speech was the two
minutes of Elliott.

"Of course my name is Pierre *Elliott* Trudeau," he
cried. "Elliott was my mother's name. It was the name
borne by the Elliotts who came to Canada more than 200
years ago. It is the name of the Elliotts who, more than
100 years ago, settled in Saint-Gabriel-de-Brandon, where
you can still see their names in the cemetery. That is what
the Elliotts are.

"*Mon nom est Québécois*, but my name is a Canadian
name also, and that's the story of my name.

"Since Mr. Lévesque has chosen to analyze my name,
let me show you how ridiculous it is to use that kind of
contemptuous argument. Mr. Pierre-Marc Johnson is a
minister. Now I ask you, is Johnson an English name or
a French name? And Louis O'Neill, a former minister of
Mr. Lévesque, and Robert Burns and Daniel Johnson, I
ask you, are they Quebecers yes or no?

"And if we are looking at names, I saw in yesterday's
newspaper that the leader of Quebec's Inuit, the Eskimos,
they are going to vote No. Do you know what that leader's
name is? His name is Charlie Watt. Is Charlie Watt not
a Quebecer? These people have lived in Quebec since the
stone age; they have been here since time immemorial.
And Mr. Watt is not a Quebecer?"

It was the emotional and intellectual coup de grâce
of the referendum campaign. For here Trudeau spoke to
the history and experience of his people as a family unit,
in which most everyone claimed a drop of assimilated
English or Irish blood somewhere on the family tree.
There were O'Connells and O'Keefes and O'Neills in
Quebec who didn't speak a word of English. For that
matter, René Lévesque's own senior press aides were
called Gratia O'Leary and Robert Mackay. The crowd

sensed it, too; by this time their chants of "Trudeau, Trudeau", had changed to "Elliott, Elliott."

Afterward, Commons Speaker Jeanne Sauvé told him she had been on the verge of tears, and Trudeau admitted that he was a bit choked up himself. But he did not linger long to receive congratulations. At the back door, a sedan was waiting to take him to a drop point under Montreal's elevated Metropolitan Boulevard, where his limousine was waiting to take him the rest of the way home to Ottawa.

"Is anybody coming with me?" Trudeau asked no one in particular as he left the arena. Nobody was. His staff was remaining behind in Montreal to celebrate his triumph. Long afterward, they wondered what kind of man could make a speech like that and then ride home alone, as if nothing out of the ordinary had happened.

16
THE BIG VILLAGE: MAY 20, 1980

Claude Ryan's duplex on St. Joseph Boulevard, off the hill in Outremont, says something about what a small place Quebec is, really nothing more than a big village. Before Ryan bought it in the mid-1960s, the downstairs had been the headquarters of the Social Research Group, where pollster Maurice Pinard and the others had met to put sociological studies of Quebec on a sounder methodological footing. When Ryan moved in, the upstairs tenant was none other than Marc Lalonde, like Pinard a member of the Group of Seven that included Pierre Trudeau in the drafting of the "Canadian Manifesto" of 1964. For years afterwards, Ryan liked to refer to Lalonde as "my former tenant."

It was to this modest brick house that Trudeau came on the bright Tuesday morning of May 20, 1980, Referendum Day, a day in which a generation of Quebecers would have an answer.

Ryan had just returned from voting in the basement of St. Viateur church, around the corner on Laurier Avenue, a place where for years of Sundays, he had encountered the likes of Camille Laurin and Jacques-Yvan Morin, apostles of independence, and exchanged pleasantries on the way out of church.

Trudeau knew this house, as he had known Ryan for more than thirty years. What Trudeau may not have known was that it was around the corner and up the street a few yards from the Nelson Avenue home of Guy Beaugrand-Champagne, the man who had introduced them all those years ago.

While Trudeau went in for a long cup of coffee, the man who would accompany him to the polls waited outside on the front lawn. As Trudeau's lawyer, it would be Michel Robert's task that morning to answer any challenge to the prime minister's claim of being domiciled at his federal riding office in Mount Royal. A few months later, Robert would again have the prime minister as a client at the September Summit of first ministers on the constitution. Later still, he would argue the federal government's case on patriation of the constitution before the Supreme Court. Had Robert arrived with Trudeau that morning, it would have presented an awkward moment at Ryan's front door. For a permanent rift had developed between Ryan and Robert, the man who had invited the publisher of *Le Devoir* to give the keynote at the Quebec Liberal policy convention of 1977. Robert had been a charter member of the Draft Ryan movement. It was at Ryan's insistence that he agreed to serve as chairman of the Pro-Canada Committee, the umbrella group of federalist forces which Ryan then forced him to fold by virtue of his effective veto of the committee's organization plan for the referendum. So like any other lawyer in a village, Robert went out and got himself another client.

Trudeau and Ryan may not have recalled why Beaugrand-Champagne, the man around the corner, had brought them together in the first place, thinking that they would be among the leaders of their generation. This prediction had been borne out by events, though the years had taken them on divergent paths. It was another man of their generation, René Lévesque, who had brought them to this day. It was Lévesque, finally, who brought the remedy of the ballot box to bear on the matter that consumed the best energies of their generation, and divided their loyalties as well as their friendships. From the federalist perspective, it was known as the constitutional question. From the vantage point of the *indépendantiste* camp, it was called the national question.

Trudeau, Ryan and Lévesque spoke to the question as the leaders of their generation. And whatever one thought of their ideas, one had to admire their purpose.

Each had gone into political life at a mature age, with a comprehensive political agenda, not to be someone but to do something. Trudeau was 46 when he went to Ottawa with Gérard Pelletier and Jean Marchand to assert their claims on the federal system. Lévesque was 37 when he abandoned his career as French Canada's leading broadcast journalist to become a Liberal candidate and minister in Jean Lesage's government in 1960, the administration that opened the doors to the Quiet Revolution. And Ryan, youngest of the three despite appearances, was 53 when he became leader of the Quebec Liberals in 1978, with the goal of finding a middle way between Trudeau and Lévesque. Each had gathered to himself a group of adherents who were remarkable for their ideas as well as their numbers. The Quebec of their generation, and the one that followed, had produced a quality of leadership out of all proportion to the importance of a little society of six million people.

"Quebec is Indiana," as Michel Robert observed, "with the same population and the same industrial base." Yet Quebec, in the pioneer activism of Trudeau's generation, and the political ferment of Robert's, had produced the dominant political personalities, engaged in the most interesting clash of ideas, on the Canadian scene. Perhaps this could be attributed precisely to the fact that Quebec was just a village, where everyone knew everyone. "You would expect people to know people better in a small nation more than in a large one," said Claude Forget, the former social affairs minister in the second government of Robert Bourassa, who had been a year ahead of him at the University of Montreal law faculty in the mid-1950s.

Gérard Pelletier had once had this discussion with John Turner, about how Quebec had thrown up so many leaders, when English-speaking Canada was so bereft of them. As Pelletier recalled it years later, Turner thought it was because the best people in English Canada gravitated to the private sector, the reverse of the trend in Quebec.

Michel Robert, standing out on the front lawn, belonged to the next generation, the generation that had split apart in college and university over the national question. They came out of the classical colleges, Brébeuf and Ste. Marie, and they went on to the law faculties of Montreal and Laval. Twenty years later, they emerged as the leaders of their generation. From Robert's time at the University of Montreal, there were the likes of Robert Burns, the brilliant parliamentarian and first House Leader of the Lévesque government; Pierre Marois and Bernard Landry, both future members of the Lévesque cabinet; and Francis Fox, who would become a Trudeau aide and later a cabinet minister in Ottawa.

At the same time, an even larger group of future public figures was flowering at Laval's law and social science faculties. In a mock parliament, the first leader of an independent Quebec was Jean Garon, later the jovial-looking agriculture minister in the Lévesque cabinet. The leader of the opposition was Brian Mulroney, head of a rather unusual rump of future Conservatives that included Michael Meighen, later national president of the Conservative party, and Mulroney confidants Jean Bazin and Michel Cogger. There were future Lévesque cabinet members such as Clément Richard and Denis de Belleval, as well as the odd future fed like André Ouellet. And those were just the public figures. Behind them stood a host of comers who would take over the Quebec public service, as well as making a name for French Canadians at the top of the federal civil service.

Between them at Montreal and Laval, they formed as tight a network as anything seen among the old school ties of English-speaking Canada. "It wasn't complicated," Mulroney said twenty years later. "Everybody knew everybody. There were only two law schools, Montreal and Laval. The McGill guys weren't on our route." Down the road, though they would become mortal political foes over the national question, the men and women of this generation remained personal friends.

They were almost the last of that old school of Quebec's closely linked political elites. By the end of the 1960s, the classical colleges were supplanted by junior colleges known as CEGEPs, and by the 1980s there were more than forty of them around the province. Where Laval and Montreal had been the two universities of consequence, the Université de Sherbrooke and the Université du Québec, with several campuses, grew by leaps and bounds in the 1970s and into the '80s. There would be no more generations quite like the one represented by the man who stood on Claude Ryan's front lawn on the morning of the referendum. Not only had students been dispersed throughout the education system, but by the end of the 1970s, they were going in for different things, crowding into the business faculties. It was no longer the Quebec of their fathers, for their fathers had changed it. Whatever the evening would hold for them on May 20, the men and women of Trudeau's and Ryan's and Lévesque's generation had brought the national question to a formulation, if not a resolution.

Trudeau had some thoughts on that, although he did not fully share them with Ryan. He said he wanted to move quickly on the constitution after the referendum. What he did not say, what no one could have imagined, what Ryan would have protested in the strongest terms, was how quickly. As Trudeau left Ryan that morning, it was really the end of their uneasy alliance. In the car on the way over to vote in Mount Royal, Robert asked him the question on everyone's mind that day: how would the vote come out? Trudeau was less optimistic for the prospects of a big No sweep than might have been imagined. His guess was that it would come in somewhere between 55 and 57 percent. Perhaps he was merely fearing the worst, since a 55 percent score for the No would have given the Yes a moral victory, a majority of the French-speaking voters. More likely, he was simply repeating Chrétien's prediction, based on federal polling data, of a 10 to 12 point margin of victory.

The man who had waved goodbye to Trudeau on the sidewalk in front of his house had experienced his own moments of uncertainty over the holiday weekend, la fête de la reine. In Quebec on Saturday morning, Ryan was visiting the No committee room in suburban Ste. Foy when he was called to take a phone call from his chief organizer, Pierre Bibeau, in Montreal. Bibeau had just received the leaked results of the final IQOP poll that would be published in the following day's edition of *Dimanche-Matin*. It was not good news. The IQOP survey, conducted at mid-week, projected a 52 to 48 win for the Yes, reversing a 52 to 48 lead for the No only the previous week. It hardly seemed possible that a four-point swing could have occurred in the space of a few days. And of course, it wasn't. But it gave Ryan a bit of a jolt. "He came back from the telephone," said Bernard Langevin, who was travelling with him, "white as a ghost." Ryan was very worried, as Liberal MNA Jean-Claude Rivest noted, "not about the poll so much as its impact." By the next morning, when the No organizers had a chance to examine the IQOP numbers and methodology, they were satisfied that it was wrong. But if anything, it seemed to have the salutary effect of a cold shower upon the No forces, who had been lulled by their optimistic canvassing, or pointage, which indicated a big federalist win in a range of 60 to 63 per cent. "You don't know how it woke people up," said Léonce Mercier, the one-time chairman of Raymond Garneau's leadership campaign who was on loan to the No committee from the Quebec wing of the federal Liberals, where he had become director general.

The other side had also received an advance copy of the IQOP poll from the company's president, Jean-Pierre Nadeau, the previous afternoon. But the generally demoralized Lévesque forces, who could have used a bit of a boost that weekend, didn't believe it either. The very best construction they could put on their own polling figures was a 52 to 48 loss for the Yes, and their more probable scenario called for a 58 to 42 win for the federalist forces. René Lévesque, in a Sunday afternoon news conference, was curiously subdued, even morbid, when he ought to have been jubilant at the latest poll results. Quite clearly, he did not believe it. Some people in the Yes camp may well have suspected that the polling numbers were cooked by the other side to scare a few swing voters back onside with the No.

For its part, the Ryan entourage suspected that the numbers had been manipulated to present the most favorable hypothesis for the Yes. Certainly Ryan would not have given himself all that trouble on the last full day of the campaign. Since April 13, he had not permitted himself a single day off. Now he was coming down with such a bad cold that he was scarcely able to talk. That afternoon, at his wife's adamant insistence, he would cancel his first event of the campaign, a meeting in the North Shore community of Louiseville some fifty miles east of Montreal that Robert Bourassa would attend in his place. Ryan would not even have got out of bed that morning to attend a church breakfast in suburban Laval, had he not been determined to show the colors and refute the conclusions of the IQOP poll. Very few, if any, reporters believed it. Their attitude was summarized by the CBC's Don MacPherson who asked one colleague: "How would you like to have shares in IQOP this morning?" More seriously, reporters asked themselves if they'd seen anything in the final week of the campaign to account for a four-point swing, other than the controversy over the federal government's advertising binge, which may have produced a small backlash, but nothing as significant as a four-point turnaround on a question of country. Still, they had their jobs to do, and that morning's assignment was to get Ryan's explanation.

Marc Lalonde stood off to one side and said he didn't believe it, either. "It can't be," Lalonde said, referring to private federal polls that indicated a No win on the order of 57 percent. Lalonde was on his way to Paris for a meeting of energy ministers, and he would spend referendum night in the company of Gérard Pelletier, listening to the returns on a hookup with Radio-Canada. At one point in the evening, Lalonde suggested they go over to the Maison du Québec, and have a glass of champagne that was being offered by delegate general Yves Michaud as his guests watched a color television feed from Radio-Quebec. "I have as much right there as anyone," Lalonde said. Pelletier had the impression that he was just kidding.

In any event, they stayed put, and a possible diplomatic contretemps was averted.

It was past midnight in Paris when the voting concluded in Montreal and around the province. All day, the people of Quebec had streamed to the polls in record numbers. Of the 4,367,134 names on the electoral list, 3,673,842 would answer the referendum question. It was an astonishing turnout of 85.61 percent. In the first hour and the last, the heaviest voting periods, long lineups stretched outside polling stations in church basements and school gymnasia. In some polls, particularly in the predominantly English-speaking West Island, where some voters claimed they were needlessly held up by Yes scrutineers, the final votes were not cast until long after the polls were officially closed.

Then the province, and the country, settled back to await the result. At 425 St. Joseph Boulevard, Ryan's house was full of his kids and their friends. By now, Ryan was beginning to shake off the effects of his cold, and he had recovered his confidence sufficiently to predict that the No side would triumph with a 62 percent score, the same guess he had made five weeks previously at a Garrison Club luncheon in Quebec with Bourassa and Jean Lesage. On that evening of evenings, he was surrounded by few friends and advisers. Bernard Langevin, secretary of the Ryan road show, was about the only outsider from the political entourage present in the Ryan home. The others waited for him at the No referendum-night headquarters in the old Verdun Auditorium, from Bibeau on down to Herb Laviollette, the Air Canada pilot who had been the captain of Ryan's charter DC-9, dubbed the "DC-Non."

At 24 Sussex Drive in Ottawa, Pierre Trudeau gathered half a dozen staff members and colleagues. Commons Speaker Jeanne Sauvé was there, along with Trudeau's principal secretary, Jim Coutts; cabinet secretary Michael Pitfield; de Montigny Marchand from the referendum core group in the prime minister's office; press secretary Patrick Gossage, and speechwriter André Burelle.

There were two television sets going in the Trudeau living room, one tuned to Radio-Canada and the other to the CBC, and a lively argument ensued among the guests whether they should turn up the volume in English or in French. Trudeau ignored the chatter around him, he was riveted on the results.

They weren't long in coming. From the earliest returns rolling in from the easternmost corner of the province, it was clear the No forces were building to a significant victory. Half an hour after the polls closed, the game was clearly up for Lévesque. Within another ten minutes, the CBC called Ryan and the No side as the winners.

At Montreal's Paul Sauvé arena, traditional election-night gathering place of the Parti Québécois, René Lévesque was curiously alone on the night of his defeat. Where he had been mobbed by tearful supporters on the night of the PQ election victory in 1976, he was now a solitary figure on stage except for his wife, Corinne, who clutched a single long-stemmed rose. Further upstage stood Lise Payette, the only member of Lévesque's cabinet who was there to face the music. She had committed the biggest blunder of the Yes campaign in March with a remark that sparked the Yvette movement, the most spontaneous occurrence of the entire campaign.

Lévesque had always been good in defeat. On another spring evening, a decade earlier, he had stood in the same place and tried to put the best face on his party's having only seven seats to show for its 23 percent of the vote in the 1970 election. That night, he asked if his people didn't see the moral victory of a new party winning even half a dozen seats. It was Lévesque at his best, defusing what might have been an explosive situation. Similarly on referendum night in 1980, he could take heart from the fact that 40.5 per cent of the electorate had endorsed his mandate question for sovereignty-association. "We have to swallow it this time," Lévesque began, conceding that "this hurts more than any election defeat." He acknowledged that clearly Quebecers wanted to give federalism another chance, asserting that the "ball is in the federal camp." On the whole, it was a moving and graceful concession speech, apart from his predictable attack on the "scandalous" entry of Trudeau and the feds into the campaign. Watching this in Ryan's dressing room at the Verdun Auditorium, Jean Chrétien muttered that Lévesque was "a goddamn hypocrite."

There was quite a different reaction to Lévesque's concession in the living room of 24 Sussex. Everyone in the room later said that Trudeau genuinely felt for Lévesque that night. When someone mentioned to the prime minister that he seemed touched by Lévesque's concession, Trudeau defended himself against his own feelings. "I would have felt a lot sorrier for him," Trudeau said, "if he had been defeated on an honest question."

As always, Trudeau had a way of concealing his thoughts and camouflaging his emotions. As the result became clear that evening, he turned to speechwriter Burelle and said: "If I understand it correctly, I don't need the text for the Yes."

There was such a text, and there still is, locked away in Burelle's files in Ottawa. Presumably it will be released some day, after the thirty-year embargo on state papers expires, after most of the principals of this generation are dead and buried. Only then will Quebecers and Canadians know what Trudeau would have said in the event of a Yes. Burelle would give only one hint. "It would have been consistent," said the former philosophy professor, "with the logic of the previous speeches."

As it was, Trudeau was not in the position of having to answer that question, though he was undoubtedly concerned to assist in the process of binding up the wounds. There was only one text for a No result, not one for 51 percent and another for 59.5 percent. In preparing it, Burelle said later, "we were only hoping that Lévesque could not use the argument that it was because of the English."

Reviewing the text, Trudeau decided to make no changes and only one addition. He got out a pen and in his broad hand wrote a single sentence across the top of the first page of the French text. "Never," he wrote, "have I felt so proud to be a Quebecer and a Canadian." It was his answer to Lévesque's opening remarks on the night of his victory in 1976, that he had never felt so proud to be a Quebecer. Trudeau was able to add, "and a Canadian."

With that, he got ready to go downtown and speak to the country from the National Press Theatre on Wellington Street, five minutes drive from 24 Sussex. But like the rest of Quebec and Canada he had to wait for Claude Ryan to finish talking. And wait and wait and wait.

On the two television sets in Trudeau's living room, Ryan was giving every appearance of being a sore winner. It wasn't his words so much as the way he delivered his victory speech. He appeared to have seriously misjudged the occasion, to be giving a raw and partisan stump speech, a harangue, rather than calling for a healing and reconciliation of Quebecers, as indeed he had planned to do. But between the time he left home, and the moment he climbed onto the stage in Verdun, something happened to Ryan that threw him badly off balance.

The organizers of the evening had planned that Chrétien would introduce Ryan, and had invited the justice minister there for that purpose. That was their first mistake, since it was an occasion on which only the heads of the three clans were expected to speak. Ryan had himself agreed to this on the telephone with Trudeau, earlier in the evening. Trudeau had said that Ryan should speak first for the federalist forces, since it had been his campaign, and Ryan agreed that Trudeau should have the last word, since he was prime minister of Canada.

Ryan was also sensitive to the perception that the feds should be seen as having won the day. He had already been annoyed earlier in the evening when he looked in on the television coverage by Radio-Canada and saw none other than Jean Chrétien sitting in as one of the network's panelists. For Chrétien, who had come down to Montreal after voting in his home riding of Shawinigan, it was an evening for a bit of vindication. "Ah, it's a beautiful studio," he had said on the way in, "in a beautiful building, built by the federal government."

Ryan was not amused to see Chrétien on television. "I felt that since we had worked as a team," he said later, "it was not at all appropriate that one member of the team should go and issue comments before the leader of the team had spoken. And I thought he should have cleared that with me before he did it, you know. And that was the beginning."

What happened next, below the stands of the old Verdun auditorium, was a scene that no one there soon forgot. Ryan arrived and began his customary round of handshakes and kissing the ladies, Solange Chaput-Rolland and Aline Chrétien among others, on both cheeks.

A few minutes after Lévesque's concession, Ryan was told by one of the organizers of the evening, an advance man named Pierre Brodeur, that it was time to go on. Chrétien would be up first, would say a few words, and introduce him. Ryan, still fighting off his flu, bone-weary from his non-stop campaign, did what any exasperated person would do in his place. He blew up. He was terribly sensitive to the perception that the feds had saved his campaign. Moreover his travelling secretary Bernard Langevin thought he detected a pang or two of jealousy on Ryan's part that Trudeau and Chrétien should be receiving so much credit in the closing days of the campaign. "I remember," Ryan said later, "I may have had a couple of harsh words with Chrétien."

He had more than a few harsh words. "No, no, no," Ryan told Brodeur. "Nobody but me will speak. I'm the head of the No forces. I will speak."

Chrétien, standing a few feet away, appeared crestfallen, and was told by his wife that, there, there, it was nothing. Ryan turned to him and told him he was the boss. "That's okay," Chrétien said, "it wasn't me who asked to come here." Much later, he minimized the importance of the incident saying that Ryan "was nervous that night." But the incident did reopen a sore between them, and in a larger sense between the two federalist camps. It also threw Ryan completely off stride. Instead of going out and saying that it was a time for healing, as he had planned to, he charged into the arena like an angry bull with his nostrils flaring. In the hall, he delivered

what appeared to be a strong partisan speech. On television, it was horrifyingly bad, and would haunt Ryan
afterwards. He sternly called upon the government to
observe "the lesson which the referendum imposes, a
useful lesson, it seems to me, to be faithful to the popular
will as it's just been expressed in the referendum." Ryan
was calling on the government to resign and face the
people in new elections to clarify the personality of Quebec's bargaining agent in the inevitable negotiations towards renewed federalism. Had he been at *Le Devoir*, this
would have been a perfectly logical conclusion for the
next morning's editorial. For a politician, it was a terrible
mistake. First, he was making news on a day when there
had already been quite enough news. Nothing more was
expected of him than to be a generous winner. He had
every intention of being one, but he left that speech in
the dressing room. It was the speech he had made at a
dress rehearsal the previous evening in Lachute, a strongly
bilingual town in his riding of Argenteuil, northwest of
Montreal.

There, on the eve of the vote, he had been able to
look beyond the tensions and turmoil of the long campaign.
He had looked within himself for the best in himself.
"One thing I learned at my mother's knee," he had said
the previous evening of the French and the English of
Quebec and Canada, "is that we are different, but that
we must love each other." And if you looked beyond the
austere image, there was an element of that message of
fraternity in his victory statement that was generally overlooked. "This evening in leaving my home to come here,"
he said at Verdun, "a young man of around eighteen
years came up to me. He said to me, 'Mr. Ryan, I voted
Yes today, but I want to congratulate you on the fine
campaign you've waged.' I thanked this young man, and
I said to him that his behavior was an example for all of
us."

He even tried to thank the women who had worked
in the campaign, the Yvettes "from Gaspé, from Rimouski,

from Sept-Iles, from Quebec, from Chicoutimi, from Valleyfield, from Joliette, from Trois-Rivières, from Shawinigan, from Sherbrooke, from St. Jean, from Ste. Hyacinthe
and everywhere across Quebec." There was the cadence
of a campaign speech, but the occasion was all wrong.
Looking at Ryan's rostrum-thumping speech, many Quebecers formed an opinion of him, or confirmed their worst
opinion of him.

For the battle for the hearts and minds of Quebecers,
to use the operative cliché, was far from concluded. In a
sense, even as he lost their minds, Lévesque won their
hearts as he led a chorus of *"Gens du pays,"* the Gilles
Vigneault song he had called "our national anthem by
anticipation." He then coined a new PQ slogan in his
parting words, *"à la prochaine."* Till the next time, he said,
raising his arms in a boxer's salute. No wonder Trudeau,
as his press secretary Patrick Gossage noted, "felt a certain
empathy for him."

And since Ryan was losing their hearts even as he
had won their minds, it was left to Trudeau to summarize
the occasion, as Ryan himself acknowledged, "gracefully
and beautifully."

"We are experiencing tonight," Trudeau said, "the
fullness of democracy, with all its joys and sorrows." It
was the healing gesture Quebecers on both sides had
waited for. And finally, Trudeau was something Ryan
was not, a political actor. As much as he had reproached
the PQ for lacking the courage of their convictions, he
now said he could not forget "all those Yes supporters
who fought with such strong convictions . . . . Their
disappointment prevents me from entering unreservedly
into the spirit of celebration."

And he continued: "To my fellow Quebecers who
have been wounded by defeat, I wish to say simply that
we have all lost a little in this referendum. If you take
account of the broken friendships, the strained family
relationships, the hurt pride, there is no one among us
who has not suffered some wound which we must try
to heal in the days and weeks to come."

And so the day, and the referendum era, passed into history. And the healing would begin soon enough. It had been the most remarkable time to be living in Quebec, between November of 1976 and May of 1980. For three and a half years, there had been an intense debate over a question of country. And through it all, most remarkably, not a single shot was fired in anger. As Ryan himself said many times, in many contexts: *Formidable, formidable.*

17

THE SILENT SPRING

L ater on, the pollsters and pundits would refer to the phenomenon as the depolarization of Quebec. This was a fancy way of saying that, in the voters' minds, the referendum was over, and with it the alignment of public opinion that crushed the PQ's option in 1980.

Nobody could be quite sure just when or how this happened, least of all Claude Ryan, because he refused to authorize the necessary funds for polling in the fall of 1980 and the winter of 1981. In a non-scientific but very much in an observable sense, the depolarization set in around the table of the Quebec family at Christmas of 1980. For the previous four holiday seasons, these reunions had been marked by the family divisions that plagued Quebec society as a whole during the referendum era. Now that it was over, the voters were clearly relieved that they could get on with the ordinary business of living. Something very noticeable happened early in the New Year. While people were fixing up their licence plates, they decided to take the Quebec, Quebec-Canada or Canada plate off the front of the car. More than a thousand polls, this should have signaled the end of the referendum period. But nearly everyone missed it.

Everyone, that is, except René Lévesque.

By February of 1981 Lévesque was talking about winning 72 ridings in the new 122-seat National Assembly. To most observers, it appeared the premier was either smoking funny cigarettes, or simply whistling past the graveyard. In fact, he had it from his pollster, Michel Lepage, that the PQ had successfully waited out the depolarization of the voters. As long as independence was not the issue in an election, and Lévesque had already seen to it within his own party that it would not be, then he had a good chance of winning. With the referendum issue settled, the electorate would be more likely to vote its satisfaction with the government, and its satisfaction with the Lévesque government was very high indeed. As for a beauty contest between Lévesque and Ryan, it was no contest. Lévesque enjoyed something Ryan did not. If the premier did not always live in a state of political grace, he had the capacity to obtain forgiveness. Ryan was increasingly perceived as a mean-spirited reminder of Quebec's priest-ridden past. A lot of voters were still bothered by his aggressive victory speech on referendum night.

In late 1980 and early 1981, the ground slipped from beneath his feet. And he didn't even know it.

For Ryan had developed an aversion to polls, or at least to spending the Liberal party's money on them.

"It's not wise, it's not smart," said Yvan Corbeil, president of the the CROP polling house in a prescient remark in late October of 1980. "I think Ryan is doing himself a disservice."

Normally, as Corbeil remarked, Ryan could expect a winkle from other polls, CROP polls for the federal government, or Sorecom surveys for the Montreal and Quebec newspapers. In the referendum period, Corbeil pointed out, "Ryan's entourage knew even if he didn't."

It was about this time that Ryan had a long argument in a parking lot outside a television station with Maurice Pinard, the George Gallup of Quebec pollsters. Pinard had not only called the PQ victory in 1976, at a time when the publisher of Le Devoir, Claude Ryan, made a point about keeping his faith in polls. Pinard had also called the referendum to within half a point of the outcome. As it would develop, he would also call the 1981 election in a range of 76 to 84 seats for the PQ, and the result would fall smack in the middle of that range. Pinard's 1981 projection was based on field work compiled by the Sorecom firm of Soucy Gagné, his old associate from the pioneering Social Research Group. In one of those coincidences that occurs only in Quebec, the Social Research Group had its offices at 425 St. Joseph Boulevard, and for a while Gagné lived upstairs. Later, Claude Ryan bought the house. So Pinard and Ryan went back a long way in professional and personal terms. And here they were having this bitter argument about the necessity and usefulness of polls.

The last information Ryan had to go on was the result of four by-elections on November 17, one in the Liberal fortress of Outremont, and three ridings in the Eastern Townships that had been held by the Union Nationale. The Liberals won easily, as you would expect, in Outremont, where the candidate, Pierre Fortier, looked like a reasonable facsimile of the Man from Glad. But though the Liberals gained the three Township seats, the PQ finished a very interesting second in two of them, Megantic-Compton and Johnson, losing Johnson by only a few hundred votes. When you looked at the results, as Lévesque and his braintrust did, the old *bleu* vote was in the process of crossing over to the PQ in a context where independence was not an issue. Ryan and his people took no apparent notice of this. They had run their by-election record to 11 to 0, plus the big win in the referendum. Why shouldn't they be feeling confident about the general election, whenever Lévesque dared to face the voters? It was then, in the period of late 1980 to early 1981, that the political climate changed. And Ryan, too headstrong to hire a political weatherman, was heading into a big storm.

In losing the last batch of by-elections, Lévesque only proved that he would have been cleaned in a general election that day, four years plus two days after his accession to power. Normally he would have called an election. It was his inclination that it was the right thing to do. He didn't like staying on past four years in office, even if he was going to lose. Now he would stay in power over the winter months, always the toughest political season in Quebec. And his prospects for re-election in the spring were decidedly gloomy. Still, Lévesque had two good reasons for hanging on, both of them called Pierre Trudeau.

It was Trudeau who had nearly tested the five-year constitutional limit of his July 1974 mandate, holding off the next election until the end of May, 1979. If it was acceptable for Trudeau to cling to office at one level, the federalist side in Quebec was in an awkward position to criticize Lévesque for doing the same thing at another level.

And then there was Trudeau's unilateral push on patriating the constitution with an amending formula and an entrenched charter of rights. Trudeau unveiled the package on the evening of October 3, just two weeks after the failure of the September Summit of first ministers in Ottawa.

To say that Claude Ryan was shocked was something of an understatement. As early as May 21, the morrow of the referendum, he had publicly cautioned Trudeau against moving with undue haste, especially before Quebecers had an opportunity to change their bargaining agent in an election. Ryan had some inkling of what the prime minister was up to from their conversation in the Quebec leader's study on the morning of the referendum vote. "He told me he wanted to move rapidly," Ryan said later. "He told me he was intent on patriating the document. I insisted there were some conditions that had to be met. We did not go much beyond that. It was a friendly conversation, but I could not have inferred from what he said that he would attempt to do it in the way he did."

The day after Trudeau's October surprise package began much as any other for Ryan. He left home at 9:30, hopped in the front seat of his government-issue Pontiac, and had the driver drop one of his daughters off at school. Under his arm that morning, he carried a briefcase bulging with the usual number of documents. Later in the day, he would have to face the press. He would have to say something on the one issue above all that engaged his mind and stirred the passions of his heart.

In the privacy of his Gilford Street office that day, he raged at the timing and thrust of the Trudeau package. In public, he was placed in the awkward position between his nominal ally, Trudeau, and his sworn adversary, Lévesque. "Don't worry about Claude Ryan," he told reporters, "I've been in a lot of tight corners before." But he would never emerge from this one. On the one hand, he deplored the unilateral nature of the federal package; on the other, he would have to applaud the Victoria amending formula, which assured Quebec of a regional veto, and the entrenchment of minority language rights in a charter, a cause for which he had been a tireless champion during his years at *Le Devoir*.

And, much as he deplored the unilateral aspect of the Trudeau resolution, much as he was horrified by the political timing of it, there was simply nothing he could do about it, for he was only the leader of the opposition in a provincial legislature. Before he could speak on behalf of Quebec, he would need a mandate, as he would put it, expressing "the sovereign will of the people." But for the time being, and until further notice, the bargaining agent for Quebec was René Lévesque, and the Trudeau package gave him the pretext he needed to hang on over the winter.

By Thanksgiving Weekend, the provincial premiers had met in Toronto and there were already the makings of a common front of six dissenting provinces, with Nova Scotia wavering but likely to move onside. To put that common front together, Lévesque would need time, and he would take it. For the next six months, right up to the election, the alliance of dissenting provinces would consume much of his energies. Of course, it was strictly an alliance of convenience, and would later crumble in the space of a single November night in Ottawa, while René Lévesque slept across the river in Hull. Lévesque himself would have a fair amount to answer for in signing the declaration of the eight dissenting provinces on April 16, 1981, only three days after his electoral triumph. In the April 16 manifesto, for the sake of unanimity, Lévesque abandoned Quebec's veto claims and went along with the Vancouver formula, which required the consent of any seven provinces adding up to 50 percent of the population. There would be an opting-out clause for provinces that didn't want to go along with changes, with full financial compensation, a key clause that was later dropped over Lévesque's protests.

So you had the irony of Trudeau, the centralizing devil, maintaining Quebec's veto in the Victoria formula, and the autonomist premier of Quebec giving up those claims in the Vancouver formula. It was not a position that any Quebec Liberal leader had ever advocated or ever could. In any event, all this would occur after an election in which Lévesque neither sought nor received a mandate for constitutional change, just as Trudeau had not requested a similar mandate in the federal election of 1980. All Lévesque said was summarized in his campaign slogan: *Faut rester forts*. It would be a campaign of brilliantly mounted images of the popular premier surrounded by strong ministers like Jacques Parizeau.

When Lévesque finally pulled the plug in the National Assembly on March 12, the Liberals began what they and most observers assumed would be a triumphal return to power. In fact, the election was a tossup at that point. In the view of senior Péquistes like Claude Charron, it could actually be won or lost in the campaign. Depending on the third-party splits, the PQ could form another government with as little as 44 percent of the popular vote. The Liberals, with their wasted English votes, needed at least a 51 to 45 spread over the PQ. Even before the campaign senior Liberal organizers like Jim McCann, though unshakable in their optimism, figured it was a close thing, something like a 52 to 44 proposition. In other words, with a five-point swing in the campaign, the results could favor the PQ by a 49 to 47 margin in the popular vote, with a comfortable Péquiste majority in terms of seats.

So at the outset of the month-long campaign, the election was in the bag for neither side. Instead, it was in the hat, and the outcome would depend largely on the campaign shakeout.

The PQ's principal campaign strategist, Michel Carpentier, had designed a campaign that took account of certain realities. First, while Lévesque was the undisputed star of the team, he was also 58 years old, and should be scheduled accordingly. Second, since the government was more popular than its option or even the party, maximum use should be made of popular ministers like Jacques

Parizeau and Pierre Marc Johnson. Where they had been practically invisible during the referendum, members of the Lévesque team suddenly turned up in television spots. Lévesque's electoral braintrust was also determined to improve the government's standing among women and rural voters, who had voted in decisive numbers against the government's mandate question in 1980. For the rural vote, it was enough to send agriculture minister Jean Garon on the road by himself, as Quebec's answer to Ottawa's Gene Whelan. Though Garon was an economist out of Laval, he projected the image of a country boy taking the city folks to the cleaners. For the women's vote, the PQ bombarded the airwaves in the afternoon with reassuring messages and reminders of all it had done for the status of women.

As for the premier, he was fighting his eighth campaign in twenty years, and he had learned how to pace himself. The typical campaign day would begin around 11 a.m. with Lévesque feeding a "Gainesburger" of a campaign promise to the hungry hounds of the press corps. Then, as at Laval on April 2, he would go into a luncheon with a target group—in this case about 800 senior citizens, every last one of them the soul of middle-class respectability. Lévesque would normally take some down time after lunch, with perhaps a photo opportunity in late afternoon, followed by a big meeting geared to regional press and militants in the evening.

In the first two weeks of the campaign, Lévesque used up a whole box of Gainesburgers. The most intriguing of all was his housing platform, in which he promised that a family with a child less than a year old would be eligible for a $10,000 low-interest housing loan, with a portion of the debt to be forgiven with the birth of each subsequent child. One French-language daily gleefully headlined the program as "The Revenge of the Cradle."

Instead of ridiculing Lévesque's barrage of promises, Ryan gave the appearance of trying to match them. In the second week of the campaign he went ahead with his own pre-planned progression of promises, including a housing plank that pledged $5,000 grants to persons buying homes valued at less than $50,000. He also had something for women, namely making family-allowance payments receivable from the time a women's pregnancy was confirmed by her physician. On a doctrinal level, this led to the obvious conclusion that a fetus is a living human being and should be treated as such. On a practical level, it would encourage women to visit their doctors early in pregnancy, and ultimately result in healthier babies. It was a thoughtful and interesting wrinkle, but it was received with derision. By this time, Ryan was perceived as being caught in a game of catch-up with Lévesque.

Ryan was also sending out confusing signals, after saying for months that hard times would require hard spending decisions by government. Given the barrage of promises made by both leaders in the first half of the campaign, one columnist was reminded of the axiom of Prince Edward Island elections: if it moves, pension it, if it doesn't, pave it.

Ryan's promises of Week Two weren't his first mistakes of the campaign. In the previous week, he had inadvertently played to the allegations of his meanness of spirit. It came in response to Roch LaSalle's taunt that Ryan had endorsed the PQ in 1976, and presumably followed his own advice in the polling booth.

In fact, the Union Nationale leader was grasping at straws in the wind, since Ryan had followed his own advice in 1976 in one of those ridings, Outremont, where the Liberals offered a "superior candidate," André Raynauld. Instead of making this point, or simply ignoring LaSalle altogether, Ryan ripped into LaSalle as "lacking the breadth and depth of view which must be expected of a political leader. I think I'm stating the obvious when I say that." And so he was. It would have been a perfectly normal observation for a newspaper editorialist, but coming from an opponent, and especially one with Ryan's image problems, it sounded presumptuous and pompous. More to the point, it was politically stupid. The Union Nationale was plainly going nowhere, so nothing was to be gained by attacking its personable leader. The old Union Nationale vote had to go somewhere, and if Ryan belittled the intelligence of the UN leader, what was he thinking of its clientele?

Ryan spent a few days shaking off this mistake and then blundered into another unforced error on the Thursday of Week Two when he said that the Assembly's deputy speaker had been ineffective in the chair, but you had to understand these things, "because she's a woman." Heaven knows what Ryan meant to say, and Louise Cuerrier certainly was ineffective, but Ryan's remark cost him a few more days' momentum. By then, the first polls were out, and he was really in trouble, suddenly trying desperately to catch up.

On March 28, the big Montreal Saturday papers hit the streets with the first public opinion polls of the campaign. Both were bad news for Ryan. The CROP survey for *La Presse* gave the PQ a surprising nine-point lead, at 41 to 32. The second survey, in *The Gazette* and *Le Soleil* of Quebec City was in a sense even worse. It was a Sorecom, analyzed by Maurice Pinard, and it put the PQ ahead 44 to 38, or 50 to 44 when the undecideds were adjusted. It meant that Ryan was not only not holding his own, he was steadily losing ground. The Liberals wasted no time convoking an emergency meeting of the campaign high command that very afternoon on Gilford Street.

Ryan's mood was solicitous. What did he need to do to win? He was told bluntly that Week Two had been a disaster for him. He was advised to try to force the issue of the PQ still being a separatist party, and he was urged to emphasize the Liberal team. It was also decided that weekend to put Madeleine Ryan back on the road with him.

For the remainder of the campaign, for the first and only time in his five years in politics, he put himself in the hands of the party professionals. He would do whatever they deemed necessary, and whatever he felt comfortable with, to win.

Two days later, on March 30, Ryan brought out the new line that the separatist menace had not receded with the referendum of the previous May. "A lot of people," he suggested on a Montreal hot line show, "seem to think that the problem of separatism was settled following the defeat of the Parti Québécois in the referendum. But the only way of saying with a clear, decisive voice, to the rest of Canada that we want to remain in the federal structure is to elect the only party with a clear federalist position." It was a day for even more global concerns. In the afternoon, Ryan was touring the Valleyfield area of western Quebec when the word came of the attempt on Ronald Reagan's life in Washington. For any North American politician, especially one exposed to the dangers of a campaign, it was a sobering moment. In their own small way, both Ryan and Lévesque were aware of it that evening as they campaigned, a few miles apart from each other on the South Shore of Montreal. Lévesque was surrounded by a beefed up contingent of four nervous bodyguards as he walked into a wild reception from 2,000 PQ activists in a Longueuil arena. It was a choreographed evening, with born-again testimony from five area residents as to why they were voting for the government. There was a slide show, followed by the premier's appearance. It mattered not what he said. The crowd cheered him to the echo. It had to do with the magic. He always had it. He still did.

And Claude Ryan never had, never would. That was the difference between them. When all other factors such as independence were effectively neutralized, and all other things being equal, Lévesque would be the winner of a beauty contest with Ryan. Madeleine Ryan, traveling for the first time with her husband on March 31, tried to make light of such a reference in a newspaper column. If this was a beauty contest between the two husbands, she said, then she felt sorry for Mme Lévesque.

Madeleine Ryan was talking near the beginning of the longest and, what proved to be, the most fruitless day, of her husband's campaign. It would take him some 2,200 kilometers by air, in a chartered Convair turboprop from Innotech Aviation in Dorval, on to Sept-Iles, the windswept Magdalen Islands in the Gulf of St. Lawrence, and back to the town of Gaspé before bedding down for the night in Chicoutimi. Everywhere he went, Ryan was trying to stop the bleeding. But as the day made clear, events were out of his hands; the polls were consigning him to defeat and developments on the constitutional front made clear that he was only a spectator. In Sept-Iles, he learned that the high court of Newfoundland had found for the provinces in their challenge of the Trudeau resolution on the constitution. In the Magdalen Islands, he ascertained that Ottawa had decided to refer the whole business to the Supreme Court. He should have been elated by the day's turn of events, for from the beginning he had argued that parts of the resolution were unconstitutional, as the Newfoundland court had found, and that the only way to break the deadlock was for Ottawa and the provinces to return to the bargaining table. Yet with Pierre Trudeau in retreat, Ryan seemed somehow removed from the process, as he stood on a runway in the Magdalen Islands, answering questions from reporters who had no hope of filing in time for the supper-hour deadlines. And when he finally came to rest in the Kingdom of the Saguenay, he would receive no respite. The next day, he was awakened by a telephone call from a Montreal radio station asking for his reaction to Trudeau's resignation. Ryan took the call seriously, and had to be reminded by his assistant, Pierre Pettigrew, that it was a *poisson d'avril*— an April Fool's joke. Typically, Ryan told the story on himself at a breakfast meeting with the traveling press corps, who did not seem to take it as evidence that he was sympathetic, only that he was naive. Later in the day, he went on to Roberval and Dolbeau, before flying home to Montreal. In the accounting of the campaign on election night, the Liberals would lose every last one of the ridings Ryan had visited in his grueling two-day swing around the province.

For Ryan, perhaps the cruelest joke of the campaign occurred on the plane that night when television reporter Ralph Noseworthy placed a newspaper cutout version of a papal crown on his head. Ryan laughed and everyone on the flight took the joke in the spirit in which it was intended. But instead of showing his human side, the newspaper photos of the reporter's prank seemed to illustrate the haplessness of a man with whom the press took liberties. In other words, a loser.

In the closing week of the campaign, Ryan drove himself harder than ever. On April 7, his bus rolled up Highway 20 from Montreal to Quebec, where his staff hoped Ryan would have his picture taken with Pierre Trudeau at the gala premiere of the film version of Roger Lemelin's Quebec classic, *Les Plouffe*. Somehow Trudeau was late flying in from Ottawa and Ryan had to leave the reception at the Château Frontenac before his arrival to attend a campaign event in Ste. Foy. Instead, Trudeau arrived on the arm of the film's star, Denise Filiatrault. It was the front-page picture in all the papers the next day, and it was the most eloquent testimony to the end of the referendum era and its associated divisions within the Quebec family. For on another opening night, November 15, 1976, Filiatrault had been one of the artists who ushered in the Lévesque era on stage at the Paul Sauvé arena in Montreal.

Ryan tried his own monster rally the next night at the Paul Sauvé. Like the Soirée Pierre Trudeau eleven months earlier, it was intended to be a show of strength in the PQ heartland of East-End Montreal. Because comparisons would be invited to the Trudeau meeting, it was important that the Liberal organizers fill the arena with an enthusiastic crowd, which they did without difficulty. But every one of the 9,000 activists in the arena that night could have been doing other things like knocking on doors. The rally was the usual case of a big risk for small gains, the sure sign of a losing campaign. The newly disciplined Ryan got on and off in the space of twenty minutes, and made one of the strongest speeches of his career, in plenty of time, for once, to be reported on the late news. The organizers could only hope the reports would be generally positive, creating the impression of momentum where none seemed to exist. "What else can we do? " asked senior organizer Jim McCann, defending the effort and resources that went into the meeting. "We need a break."

But they were not about to get any kind of break.

The Liberals approached the final weekend of the campaign with a grim sense of foreboding. It was not long before their worst fears were realized.

At the end of the afternoon on Friday, April 9, Pierre Bibeau sat in a corner of La Niçoise, a restaurant across the street from the Gilford office. He was about to receive advance information on the Sorecom poll that would be published in the next day's *Gazette*. And he had been warned it would not be good. Bibeau had been quoted at the beginning of the campaign as saying "we have better instruments than polls," referring to the party's system of supposedly fool-proof pointage. But he knew better. Besides, he also knew Sorecom was Sorecom, and that Maurice Pinard was not somebody off the street. He braced himself for the worst by beginning the conversation with a double scotch on the rocks. He soon had reason to order another. The Sorecom survey showed the Liberals trailing in every region of the province except the West Island. It was worse for the Liberals than the previous Pinard poll. Ryan had actually slipped a point in the last two weeks, to a 45 to 37 deficit. Pinard's analysis to appear in the next day's paper indicated the PQ was heading toward "certain victory," and probably a sweep in the range of 76 to 84 seats.

Bibeau accepted the news calmly, and did not seem unduly surprised. "There's no doubt," he said about his opponents, "that they've cleaned us in the campaign."

Still, he would not altogether abandon hope.

When they looked at the breakdown in the Pinard numbers the next day, they couldn't believe they were trailing by twenty-six points in the Ottawa Valley. If so, they wouldn't win a single seat on Monday (Pinard explained this aberrational situation as something that occurs in closely clustered groups of voters, and said the final figures were adjusted to reflect this fact). Bibeau and his people had another way of looking at it. They took the 45 to 37 PQ lead, and gave themselves the full four-point margin of error, which made it a 41 to 41 ballgame. They then gave themselves the usual two-thirds of the undecided vote, and figured they would come out ahead 51 to 45, crossing the finish line on empty, but nonetheless the winners. "Stop being so depressed," Bibeau cheered his troops on the Saturday afternoon.

As for Ryan, he finished the weekend, telling supporters in Longueuil to "keep your chins up."

In a reflective mood, Ryan sounded a dominical theme, telling supporters that the whole thing was now in the hands of a "superior force" and that "the Father's will be done in the final analysis."

It was a genuine statement of his beliefs, and it was a touching way of saying it was all out of his hands now. But when his political managers heard about it, they were horrified. It was the Hand of God business again.

On election day, Ryan was out to vote early in the first wave of pensioners and nuns at a school a couple of blocks from his house in Outremont. He ran into Maurice Sauvé, who had been chief organizer for Jean Lesage all those years ago. Sauvé showed Ryan the same optimistic way of working over the Pinard numbers, and figured it could still come out to a Liberal majority of about sixty-six seats. Ryan agreed with him.

It was the only time all day he would come out ahead.

Behind the scenes at a Montreal television station that night, Paul Desrochers was serving as a human backup for the CFCF television computer. Desrochers, with former party treasurer Claude Desrosiers, had already figured it out. In a Liberal party pamphlet with the pictures of all 122 candidates, he had already crossed off about 80 before the broadcast began. It was a night of a certain settling of accounts for Desrochers, whose services had been refused by Ryan. It was Desrochers who would "call" the election for the PQ about half an hour after the polls closed. The score was 49 to 46 in the popular vote, 80 to 42 in seats. The polls had been closed for more than three-and-a-half hours, and the election had been lost for more than two hours before Ryan finally turned up at his virtually deserted headquarters at the CEGEP Vieux-Montreal. By the time he got there, only a few dozen supporters were left in the room. The Liberals remained true to their tradition of leaving a sinking ship, as they had deserted

Bourassa in droves on election night in 1976. One thing you had to admire about the Péquistes: win or lose in every election and referendum since 1970, they always stayed till the end. Ryan, who had looked like a sore winner in the referendum, was a gracious loser on this April night. "I congratulate the Parti Québécois and its leader," he began, "and I wish them a fruitful mandate."

"We're still with you Mr. Ryan," Bibeau had assured him as he entered the hall after driving down from his riding in Lachute. Ryan knew better. As for his own future, he told the television audience, it would be discussed at the appropriate time with the competent officials of the party.

He didn't get a chance to finish. Across town, René Lévesque had heard enough, and decided to get on with his triumphal entry at the Paul Sauvé, and television went with the winner.

It was a time to recall that Paul Desrochers had been told by a wise old man in a rocking chair that whoever won the referendum would lose the election, such was the shrewdness of the Quebec voter in building a system of checks and balances into the ballot box.

Ryan himself had once been given the devil's own choice in a question as to which he would rather win. He had answered without hesitation: "the election." But now he had lost it. After all his work, he had lost everything, and won nothing.

18

RYAN:
THE FINAL DAYS

A fterward, when the ordeal of his leadership had passed, even Claude Ryan could not remember the moment he had decided to give up his losing battle to stay on.

"I can't say with any precision, I can't be sure in my own mind," he said as he left the tumultuous news conference where he officially threw in the towel. It was the afternoon of August 10, 1982. The scene was a jammed salon of the Queen Elizabeth Hotel in Montreal. Most of Ryan's friends, and a good many of his political enemies, were in the room. By quitting the leadership, six weeks before a scheduled review at a party policy convention, Ryan was recognizing the grim reality of the situation. The leadership review was lost. If Ryan insisted on fighting it, he would be humiliated. As his brother Yves had observed the previous winter, it was unthinkable.

In a sense, Ryan had been moving inexorably towards this decision since the night of his defeat, a year and a half before. He frankly acknowledged the leadership

Why is this man laughing? It is the fall of 1981. Ryan, who had told Bourassa he would rather lose the election without him than win with him, has seen that doomsday wish fulfilled. And Bourassa, untarnished by the defeat, has a clear run at the leadership whenever Ryan decides to face the fact that the party is determined to oust him.
(Photo by James Seely)

problem in his concession speech on election night, allowing as how his status would be discussed with those competent authorities within the party.

On the morrow of his defeat, there was hardly anyone in the party who did not consider himself qualified to give an opinion on the leadership question. Anyone who had knocked on a door during the previous weeks knew what the situation was with the voters. The professional *cadre* within the Gilford Street group was horrifed at the campaign Ryan had run, and mortified that he would not listen to their advice until it was too late. Looming already in the wings were the figures of Raymond Garneau and Robert Bourassa. Garneau, from his corporate perch as chairman of the City and District Savings Bank in Montreal, was nominally out of politics. But he hadn't forgotten his own bitterness after the 1978 leadership defeat, and Ryan's subsequent stand-offish treatment of him. As for Bourassa, he surely remembered Ryan's remark in 1979 that he should forget about making a comeback for the next ten years. Bourassa, despite his efforts on behalf of the referendum, had been unable to win Ryan's acceptance. Ryan still regarded him as superficial and obsessed with polls. On election night in 1981, Bourassa was in the fortunate position of having been rejected as a candidate by Ryan. Since the campaign had been built on Ryan's shoulders, it stood to reason that all the recriminations would now fall on his head.

So the ranks of the disgruntled on April 14 quickly became a cast of thousands, from the rank and file to the cousins in Ottawa, from the party pros in the Gilford shop to the unreconstructed Garneau and Bourassa loyalists, who had kept their mouths shut for years. It would not be long for a consensus to shape up that Ryan would have to go. Ryan himself was not averse to leaving, but he warned that he would not be pushed. "To be perfectly frank with you, I would be the first one to be relieved," he said privately in the autumn of 1981. But he added that he would permit no palace revolts. In a sense then, his mind was already made up.

But there were two other points on his agenda for the fall which, in his own mind, took priority over the leadership issue.

At a general council meeting of the party in September, Ryan was determined to return to the question of the Liberal constitutional perspective. For himself he was determined to return to some of the nationalist-federalist positions he had espoused during the *Le Devoir* years. It gradually came into focus for him during an actual summer vacation, his first in years, that he took on Cape Cod with his wife and family during the first two weeks in August. "A defeat forces you to return alone to yourself," he told Graham Fraser of the Montreal *Gazette*. "Then you are obliged to face your conscience, to look yourself in the mirror and say to yourself, 'Who am I? ' and you define yourself accordingly." Walking alone on the sands of the Cape, Ryan came to terms with himself. He would return to his own intellectual sources, and his own understanding of Quebec's role in Canada. On vacation, he wrote up the first 125-page version of the electoral post-mortem he would deliver the next month in Quebec.

As winnowed down to fifty-five typewritten pages, Ryan read it in his habitual style, head bowed over the text. For him, as always, the message was the medium. For those who took the trouble to hear him out on an objective basis, it was the most concise and logically rigorous explanation of why the Liberals lost. In spite of their internal reforms of finance and organization, in spite of increasing their share of the vote from 34 to 46 percent, they still got swept aside by the PQ. "We must face the following facts," Ryan said. "First, our clientele is older than the PQ's. Second, our clientele is more geographically concentrated. Around 60 percent of the people who voted for us on April 13 live between Montreal and the Ontario border. Third, our clientele is a strong majority among *anglophones* and the ethnic communities, but it's a minority among *francophones*. Fourth, our clientele is clearly in the minority among young people and unionized workers."

Ryan was making it brutally clear in electoral terms the party wheel horses would understand: the party was out of touch with the mainstream of Quebec voters. And so he came at length to the part of the speech that would be remembered for his *Québec d'abord* pronouncement that the party had to put Quebec and its interests first.

"We must perceive ourselves, think, act and take positions as a party that is fundamentally and resolutely *Québécois*," he said. For those who might have reservations about this, he noted that "the Albertans do the same." Render unto Ottawa that which is Ottawa's, and unto Quebec that which is Quebec's. Between the positions of the federal Liberals and the interests of Quebec, "the first loyalty must be to Quebec, and not to the federal Liberals."

The speech created a sensation, though not exactly of the kind Ryan had in mind. It clearly drew the lines in the party for the imminent battle over the constitution.

Just a week later, on September 28, the Supreme Court issued its ruling, 6 to 3 in favor of Ottawa's legal right to act unilaterally, but 7 to 2 on its moral obligation to consult the provinces as an unwritten part of Canadian constitutional convention. What did it mean? "Legally," said Michel Robert, by now Ottawa's lawyer on the case, "it means we won. Politically, it remains to be seen."

For the Ryan Liberals, it meant confusion, fear and loathing in the ranks for the remainder of what was for many of them, the longest week of their lives. By Friday, October 2, the National Assembly would vote on a government resolution calling Ottawa back to the bargaining table and opposing unilateral patriation. The resolution was mild and ambiguous. It could have been written in Ryan's office. It was certainly drafted with a view to obtaining his support. Ryan and thirty-two of his colleagues would vote with the government. Nine would not.

But the dissension in the ranks ran even deeper than indicated by the 33 to 9 split. By most inside accounts, about half the caucus was prepared to break with the leadership on this issue until House Leader Gérard D. Lévesque called every debt he had outstanding. In the process, for the first and only time during his quarter century in politics, Lévesque made some enemies in the party. He asked MNAs to vote with the leader not for Ryan's sake but that of the party. He pleaded, cajoled and threatened. All week long, all along the Liberal corridor on the second floor of the National Assembly building, the ferocious arm twisting and lobbying went on. "You won't believe the pressure I'm under," said John Ciaccia, the dissenting MNA from Mount Royal which, federally, just happened to be Pierre Trudeau's riding.

For Ryan, the choice was between the cousins and the larger interests of Quebec. For the dissenting MNAs, the choice was defined by their constituents as between Pierre Trudeau and René Lévesque.

With the constitutional conference of the "last chance" in November, the Quebec Liberals again found themselves irrelevant to the constitutional process. They found Lévesque using the October resolution, "adopted by all parties in the Assembly" as one of the Quebec delegation's talking points. Meanwhile, as the talks went on and there was the suggestion of a straight swap of Ottawa's Charter of Rights for the dissenting provinces' Vancouver amending formula—the one which accorded a veto to no province, Ryan found himself reduced to sending a telegram to Lévesque warning him urgently not to give up the veto. It was a message for posterity rather than the present. Lévesque, ditched by his erstwhile provincial allies in the middle of the third night of the conference, did not have to give away the veto. He simply lost it. For Ryan, the November accord reopened the constitutional bitterness. Again he was squeezed between the feds and the Péquistes. For he supported the basic minority-rights package of the charter; he supported mobility rights; he was prepared to define reasonable compensation in the opting-out clause of the amending formula. But he also thought none of this should be imposed on Quebec, and he could make a very good argument that Quebec's veto claims constituted part of the constitutional convention as defined by the Supreme Court, since both Jean Lesage and Robert Bourassa had exercised *de facto*, if not *de jure*, vetos in the past.

Once again, the Quebec Liberals were torn. Once again, Trudeau had put Ryan in a bad position. In the end, Trudeau extended financial compensation to the cultural and educational fields, as demanded by Ryan and a good part of his own Quebec caucus in Ottawa. This represented a kind of victory *in absentia* for Bourassa, who had once coined a slogan called "cultural sovereignty," which was what the refined amending formula amounted to for all the provinces who chose to exercise it.

For Ryan, there were no moral victories, only more hard times in the National Assembly. He could at least be thankful that the November accord turned the PQ on itself in a runaway December convention that gutted "association" from the party platform, renewed the emphasis on independence and suggested that a simple majority of seats in the next provincial election would be enough to set the process in motion. Lévesque was forced to threaten his own resignation and finally had to waste months running a junk-mail "Renérendum," which reaffirmed the PQ's commitment to gradualism, fair treatment of minorities and the need to obtain a clear majority of votes rather than seats in a general election before setting the independence process in motion.

During this period, the Liberals resumed their discussion of the leadership issue, and over the Christmas holidays, Ryan had a long look at it himself.

As whenever he was faced with an important career decision, Ryan convoked a family council with his brothers, Mayor Yves and Judge Gerry. And as always between these three plain-spoken men, there was straight talk.

"You have a very steep hill to climb this year," said Yves, for twenty years the mayor of Montreal North, and by far the most colorful and pragmatic of the three brothers. "I think you can do it, but you have to know, is it still possible?"

And the way of measuring that, Yves continued, was to go back and see if the people who were with him at the beginning of his leadership could still be counted on. If they were still there, Ryan must fight. If they weren't,

Yves conceded, it would be "an abject situation" to see his brother go down at a convention.

When you cut through it all, Yves said later, it comes to two choices: "either he stays or he quits."

It was the best and most forthright advice Ryan would receive, and in the end he would stick by it. But in the winter of 1982, he wasn't quite ready to quit. "There are two notions of political action that confront one another in the Quebec Liberal party," he said, just before another general council meeting on the last weekend of January. "The first is to demolish your opponent and win elections. The second concept is one of ideas, and the putting together of a program that you would apply in power. On all the evidence, I represent the second. If there's no room for that, then I have no place there, but I won't leave without a fight."

There was a contemptuous edge in Ryan's voice as he talked about those of his critics who asked for anonymity in their dealings with the press. That, he said, "I find reprehensible." For the rest, he betrayed none of the sadness and bitterness he must have felt from his defeat. "If he had no bitterness, he's no Ryan," his brother Yves said in a revealing appraisal. "If he had bitterness and didn't show it, he's a Ryan."

By the spring of 1982, Ryan had developed a certain sense of humor about his predicament. After a Canadian Club speech in Montreal in May, a reporter asked him if he felt like taking the Métro, a standing joke from the days when Ryan used to boast of meeting people on the subway. "Not today," he answered with a laugh. "Maybe when I return to private life, which some people would like to see sooner rather than later."

It would be sooner, but the problem was coaxing Ryan to resign rather than pushing him out, to make him see that it was his duty as well as in his best interest to quit.

The summer of 1982 would prove decisive. By Labor Day, the party delegates would be chosen on a slate basis for the leadership review. Ryan had to make the fight or know that he didn't have the numbers. And so he would have one last go round at seeing what had become of the

Draft Ryan forces of 1978. If he could put them together, he would stick it out. If not, he would leave.

In late June, an informal committee formed around Ryan in a last-ditch attempt to ascertain whether he had the votes on review.

There was Guy Saint-Pierre, the former trade minister in the Bourassa government, who had served as president of Ryan's leadership campaign. There was Jacques Lamoureux, the whiz-kid organizer, who had been pushed out by Bibeau in the reorganization that followed the convention. Now, at Ryan's request, he was back. As André Ouellet's organizer on the federal level, he also had an idea of where the sympathies of the feds' lay. There were two loyalists from the caucus, Thérèse Lavoie-Roux and Pierre Fortier. There was John Parisella, former West-End organizer who would see how the non-*francophone* rank and file shook out. There was Jean Corbeil, the mayor of suburban Anjou and his son Michel. There was Ryan aide Michel Gaudette and Jean-Pierre Hogue, an industrial psychologist, and husband of Ryan's private secretary, Claire.

On Wednesday, August 4, the loyalists went through it with Ryan one more time. The outlook was decidedly gloomy, even worse than at the beginning of the summer.

"The assessment a month ago was that it could be turned around," Saint-Pierre observed. Now they had the individual and collective tasks of reporting that Ryan's support had collapsed in virtually all segments of the party. Saint-Pierre, for one, had taken on the assignment of persuading prominent Liberal personalities outside active politics to sign a petition in support of Ryan's continued leadership.

In fact, the names on Saint-Pierre's list said something about the real nature of his assignment, which was to present Ryan with the starkest reality possible, and nudge him ever so gently to the decision he finally took.

There was no way, for example, that André Raynauld was going to sign. He had quit politics a year before, quite bitter about Ryan's treatment of him dating back to the period of the Draft. There was no way that Claude

Forget, who had left the previous fall, would sign either, or he wouldn't have left in the first place. But the big surprise was Claude Castonguay of Quebec, former social affairs minister in the first Bourassa government, and a man who now collected corporate directorships the way some people collect wine. He wouldn't go along. Castonguay was at once the symbol of the party's intellectual establishment, the leader of the Grande Allée crowd and a man with entrée into every boardroom in Montreal. He had always enjoyed a cordial relationship with Ryan—in 1978 they had an understanding that one wouldn't run for the leadership against the other.

Saint-Pierre reported that he came up empty, dead empty, in his quest for prestigious names. Ryan, taking notes, said nothing. But he was shaken to the marrow by Castonguay's refusal to sign.

Saint-Pierre was not the only one to bear gloomy tidings. Lavoie-Roux had the job of rounding up caucus support. She had only four names out of forty-one, other than Fortier and herself: Herb Marx of D'Arcy McGee and Reed Scowen of Notre Dame de Grace, neither of whom reflected the sentiment of his riding association; Christos Sirros of Laurier and Daniel Johnson of Vaudreuil-Solanges. Sirros was devoted to Ryan and Roux, but again did not reflect the sentiment of his predominantly Greek, Italian and Portuguese rank and file. Johnson was genuinely loyal to Ryan—"I always said I would support him for as long as he stayed"—but he was also suspected of protecting himself from the accusation that he was grasping for the throne.

Here again, one name stood out by its absence, Gérard D. Lévesque, the House leader who had faithfully stood by Ryan as he had stood by Robert Bourassa and Jean Lesage before him. Gérard D., the ultimate party man, wouldn't sign. If there was going to be a battle, he would stay above it. But there would be no battle, as it became brutally clear to Ryan. Just as his support had collapsed within the establishment and the caucus, John Parisella had had no luck with the leadership of the English-speaking community.

The only note of cautious optimism was struck by
Gaudette, who thought the constituency battle was shaping
up reasonably well. But Ryan was not blind to the evidence
of two meetings that had already been held in July, in
Charlevoix and Rimouski. In North-Shore Charlevoix, he
mustered only four of sixteen delegates. If Ryan decided
to press ahead with the process, it was clear he was in
for a series of humiliations, whatever the final result.

They could put off the decision, and take one more
run at rounding up support, Saint-Pierre ventured, but
he didn't think it would change much. "Let's face it,"
Saint-Pierre said later, "if he had decided to go ahead,
he would have had to go through to the first of September."

Sometime before he went to bed that night, Ryan
decided that he couldn't and wouldn't. He had followed
Yves's advice to the letter, and found it wasn't there.
"The inner circle," as the younger brother later observed,
"started to show cracks. That's what did it."

The older brother had another way of appraising the
situation. "You have to consider the popular will" he told
Brian Mulroney, one of the people who was urging him
to hang in. Ryan still remembered the fourteen-point
handwritten checklist of do's and don'ts for a leadership
campaign that Mulroney had written up for him in 1978.
And while he was undoubtedly gratified by Mulroney's
supportive advice now, Ryan was too much of a realist
to carry on much further.

On the morning after the round table at the Bonaventure hotel, Ryan had one last round of phone calls and
consultations in his study, where only four years before
a stream of visitors had come on bended knee to beg him
to run for the leadership. Ryan's mind was probably made
up, though he didn't altogether let on to visitors like John
Ciaccia. But Ryan knew he was short of a bare majority
of delegates, to say nothing of a strong majority on review.
"Unless you can rally the support of a good majority,"
he told Ciaccia, "that's too high a price to pay."

The same evening, Ryan went to visit his 82-year-old
mother, Blandine, at the Berthiaume du Tremblay nursing
home in the North End of Montreal. He informed her of

his decision and then went over for a visit with Yves, the man Gerry Ryan still called "the baby brother."

There, in the mayor's elegantly appointed office, the middle and youngest brother spoke as friends and confidants. "I might as well tell you I've taken my decision," Claude began, "It's finished. I'm going to resign. I just have to work out the modalities."

Ryan's first instinct was to put the word out to the press immediately, leaving the caucus and party to fend for itself. Yves prevailed on him to do it the right way, with elegance, to avoid the taint of bitterness. "You've got to take the most gallant, the most civilized way out," he insisted. He even urged his brother not to slam the door on remaining as interim leader, in the unlikely event he was asked to stay on.

At his office on Friday, Ryan informed the members of his leadership defence committee and his two private secretaries, Claire Hogue and Josette Poliquin, that he was quitting. The rest of the staff, including his chief organizer, Pierre Bibeau, were left to learn about the decision in an exclusive story in the Saturday edition of *La Presse*. It was not a story written based on rumors. It had a hard, authoritative edge to it, and carried the by-line of Michel Roy, now editorial page editor of *La Presse* but formerly Ryan's editor-in-chief at *Le Devoir*. Maybe Ryan felt he owed Roy one for past loyalties. Maybe Roy just happened to call Ryan on this Friday afternoon for a chat. In any event, he had himself a big story, and the whole town started running at midnight Friday to catch up. One unfortunate *Gazette* reporter, rousted from his bed by the desk, was given the unenveniable of assignment of waking Ryan for confirmation at 2:30 in the morning. Ryan would neither confirm nor deny, but he was not amused about being called in the middle of the night. For the rest of the weekend, he went into seclusion. On Sunday morning, a few journalists who knew Ryan's habits turned up on the steps of St. Viateur church, around the corner from his house in Outremont. Ryan wasn't there. He and Madeleine went to Mass instead at the Carmelite convent on Côte St. Catherine Road.

But by Monday, he was ready to receive visitors. And they came in a steady stream. Gérard D. Lévesque, summoned from his holidays, was informed he would again have to assume the interim leadership.

Ryan told him he knew he would do his duty, even if it meant sacrificing whatever ambitions of his own he might entertain for the leadership. Another caller was Daniel Johnson, back from a Maine vacation, who did have leadership ambitions of his own. "You're not ready," Ryan told him bluntly, although he did not rule out his support if Johnson were to emerge as the stop-Bourassa candidate.

"How do you feel?" Johnson asked.

"It's done, it's finished," Ryan replied.

Another visitor was journalist Jean Rivard, who had been a defeated candidate in 1981. On the morrow of the defeat, Ryan commiserated with him, telling him he felt like he'd been hit by a two-by-four. Now Ryan said he was leaving unfinished his goal of reforming the party. "With another year I could have come through that, and transformed this party," he said.

It was perhaps his one great regret, even more so than the sadness over losing the election.

Yet even those who had turned against Ryan, partly because he had turned against them, maintained that he was the right choice at the time, the man the party needed for the referendum battle.

August 10, 1982: Claude and Madeleine Ryan on their way to the news conference where he will announce that he is giving up the battle to remain as Liberal leader. He had known it was pointless to fight on when members of the inner circle, such as Gérard D. Lévesque, wouldn't sign a pledge of allegiance to the leader. At right is the party's chief organizer, Pierre Bibeau. (Photo by Michael Dugas)

In this perspective, there was a good deal of rationalization, of people explaining why they were for Ryan then, and weren't now. Then, he had been chosen to give the party a new image of intellectual and financial rigor; as a man of the middle, the third option, between Quebec and the status quo. He was all of that and more, though it never occurred to people then that the cause could carry the day on its own. Just as his importance was magnified by the leadership process in 1978, so were his faults enlarged in defeat. He had brought much of it on himself, by his inability to command the continuing loyalty of the very people who had begged him to come into the game. By the time he left in the summer of 1982, only a scattered remnant of the original organization remained. Only Pierre Mercier would say, when it was over, "I still think he's the best man for the job." And Mercier was fighting his own battle, a losing one, for his life. Three months later, he was dead after a long struggle with cancer.

And so Ryan came at last to the difficult moment of facing the media and announcing his resignation. In the crowd were some of his former staff who had come back, his executive assistant Pierre Pettigrew, who had gone on to become an official in Trudeau's Privy Council Office. His former press secretary, Michèle Bazin, and former MNA Solange Chaput-Rolland. Jacques Lamoureux was there, acknowledging he'd told Ryan it was too late. And Guy Saint-Pierre and the others. They were not with him any more, but they would see him to the door, give him his hat, and wave goodbye.

At least there was that much dignity to the occasion, and Ryan invested it with a good deal of his own. "I doubt that the support on which I could count," he said frankly, "would have sufficed to ensure an affirmative vote of confidence in my leadership at the policy convention in September."

So he was giving his notice, quitting before they could fire him, as of the end of the month.

He said he felt "serene and free," and he looked it. When the press inquisition was over, he made his way out of the room as he had hundreds of times, kissing women on both cheeks, and grasping men's hands in that pumping movement of his.

Except he wasn't campaigning any more. He was just going out in his own way, in his own good time.

19
BOURASSA REDUX

On summer evenings, you could hear the voices drifting up from the river as a tour boat went by Robert Bourassa's country home on the St. Lawrence at Ste. Anne de Sorel.

"They used to announce that this was the summer residence of the premier, and then everyone would boo," he said one August evening in 1979. "Now they say it's the summer residence of the former premier. Only nobody boos anymore."

He told the story with that ironical sense of humor he had always reserved for unguarded moments with his family and friends. And he also told it with just the slightest trace of satisfaction. The murmurs from the river were Bourassa's own private poll, and they told him that summer that the mood of the province was shifting. The same voters who had dumped him without ceremony in 1976, were developing a nostalgia for his administration less than three years later. Where they had seen him as weak and irresolute, they now began to acknowledge the difficulties of governing in Quebec. Even René Lévesque, the darling of the trade unions, had been hit by tough

. . . this time Bourassa was not the choice of the Liberal establishment. This time, he had got there on his own. If they wanted to stop him they would have to beat him, and from beginning to end, they do neither. (Staff photo by John Mahoney, *The Gazette*)

public service negotiations that would culminate in a disastrous hospital strike in November of 1979. Even Lévesque's administration, for all its "favorable prejudice" toward the trade union movement, would not be able to prevent mid-winter transit strikes in Montreal.

As for Bourassa, in the summer of 1979 his name began to be associated with happier economic times, and with the boom and the pride of the mammoth James Bay construction project, which he had nurtured along in the early to mid-1970s. There had been horrific cost overruns, bringing the job in at $16 billion. And there had been big trouble on the worksite, going back to March of 1974, when a man named Yvon Duhamel bulldozed a power generator to the ground. Bourassa had appointed a high-powered inquiry led by Judge Robert Cliche of the provincial court, and the spectacular proceedings of the royal commission introduced the public to one of its members, a young Montreal labor lawyer named Brian Mulroney.

The Cliche Commission hearings into the late winter of 1975 reinforced the impression that the government was weak and losing control of the province. The cost overruns of the Montreal Games in 1976 also did not improve the Bourassa administration's prospects for re-election in that Olympic year of 1976. Driven from office by the voters in November, defeated in his own East-Central Montreal riding of Mercier, Bourassa seemed well advised to take a long and probably permanent rest from public life. He went to Europe, to study the workings of economic federalism in the common market. He went to teach in Paris. This period in his life was described then and later as an exile. And so it was.

But it was not a wandering, aimless exile. It was a planned and purposeful sojourn, and it was meant to create a space for Bourassa in the referendum, whenever it came. He told his wife as much on the night of his defeat: he would be back for the referendum. And then, in suite 2100 of the Queen Elizabeth Hotel, the defeated premier made a second decision. He went to bed. Andrée and Robert Bourassa couldn't have gone home anyway that night. There was a steady procession of horn-tooting cars past their modern stone house on Maplewood Avenue in Outremont and the occasional beer can was tossed in the general direction of the driveway.

The next few weeks were hard on Bourassa. He did his best to give Lévesque a smooth transition. Ten days after his defeat, he paid a final courtesy call on the lieutenant governor, Hugues Lapointe, and left Quebec City in the back seat of a rented Pontiac. The premier's Cadillac would remain behind in a government garage. Gone were the other trappings of office, the executive jet, the bodyguards and the remainder of the entourage, for which Bourassa could be grateful. Only one man rode with him, Jean Prieur, his 35-year-old chief of staff and close friend, who would take much of the defeat on his own shoulders. A year later, when the stigma was lifting, Prieur wryly insisted that "the blame is all mine. I refuse to share it with anyone else."

But in those first weeks, it seemed Bourassa was entirely to blame, blamed by the party for risking and losing power in an unnecessary election, blamed by the federalists for putting the country at risk, and blamed by the intellectuals like Claude Ryan.

He had been able to live with the scorn of his contemporaries, but he was disturbed in those weeks that he would be forgotten by his friends and neglected by historians.

"It's a funny thing," he said, four weeks after the defeat. "My phone doesn't ring as much as it used to."

He was sitting in a private salon of the Chez Son Père restaurant on Park Avenue, the same room that had always been reserved for him during his premiership on Mondays and Fridays when he was in Montreal. Now, over a three-hour lunch and unusually copious amounts of wine and cognac, Bourassa finally unburdened himself to a small and sympathetic audience of two friends.

One of them offered meaningful solace. For Brian Mulroney was still feeling wounded and abandoned from his own defeat in the Conservative leadership in February of that year. In the days after his defeat, he received a call from Robert Bourassa inviting him to lunch. The premier did his best to console him with the fact that he had run well for a longshot and nearly won, and that there might yet be another day. Now it was Mulroney's turn to wave aside Bourassa's concern that, in the flower of Péquiste euphoria, he would be forgotten by history. "Give it time, Robert, you've got to give it time," Mulroney said. "In a few years, compared to these guys, you're going to look pretty good."

It seemed like the kind of unfounded Irish optimism for which Mulroney was known to his friends. But by the summer of 1979, Mulroney's words of solace were beginning to have a prophetic ring to them. Compared to these guys, Bourassa *was* beginning to look pretty good, and he hadn't yet started seriously to rehabilitate his name. To his surprise at first, and then to his gratification, he found that the voters remembered him, and linked his name with the prosperity of the Bourassa years rather than the troubles which had beset his administration.

Not only had they stopped booing, they were cheering at the James Bay site when Bourassa walked unannounced into the workers' cafeteria on the morning of October 27, 1979. It was the kind of ovation most politicians would like their advance men to rent with the hall, foot-stomping, whistling, with people standing on tables. "Well received?" snorted his friend Jean Drapeau, who knew how to read

April, 1971: On the first anniversary of his election Bourassa unveils the James Bay energy project that will eventually launch his second career in politics. Eight years later, he will be cheered at the inauguration of the LG-2 damsite. Paul Desrochers, the eminence grise who was never far from Bourassa in his first mandate, is with the man he helped make premier of Quebec. (Montreal Star photo)

a room after nearly a quarter century as mayor of Montreal. "More than well received."

It was the inauguration of the huge LG-2 damsite, 600 miles north of Montreal, that would eventually produce 5,200 megawatts of electricity. Bourassa had been the political patron of James Bay, had dubbed it the "project of the century" when unveiling it in 1971. He had celebrated his fortieth birthday at the site in 1973. All the blame for the labor troubles and the cost overruns had been heaped on him when James Bay was looking more like the white elephant of the century. So it stood to reason that he would not be forgotten now that his seemingly misplaced faith in the project was about to be vindicated.

Amazingly, in one of the more brazen attempts at political highway robbery, the Parti Québécois administration tried to steal all the political credit for itself. It was too much even for the government's many admirers in the Quebec news media. Memories weren't as short as all that. It was only in 1973, after all, that the PQ was scorning hydroelectricity as a thing of the past and hailing nuclear power as the wave of the future. In the fall of 1979, Rene Lévesque's braintrust tried to hitch James Bay to the PQ's referendum wagon. Needless to say, they weren't offering Robert Bourassa a ride.

At first, there were rumors that he wouldn't even be invited to the opening ceremony. In the event, he was placed in the eleventh row of VIPs in the workers' arena, where Lévesque walked onstage like some kind of Ed Sullivan to open a really big show. But by then, Bourassa had stolen the show, simply by turning up at the press room that morning, and in the cafeteria that noon. The previous day's newspaper supplements had been full of stories. "Bourassa's dream comes true," *The Gazette* proclaimed over eight columns of a full-page feature on the origins of the project, and the former premier's return from the land of the political dead.

But back to what? He was still only forty-six years old in the fall of 1979, and it was hard to determine where he could play a useful role in the affairs of the Liberal party. Only the previous March, Claude Ryan had point-edly suggested that he might think about a comeback in about ten years. That seemed to foreclose the possibility of his seeking a seat in the next election. In those days, Bourassa would wistfully observe that it was too bad Canada did not have a tradition like England, where a former prime minister could sit as a private member, as Edward Heath did in the British House of Commons. Ryan, who was riding high in those days, was more likely to point out that Heath had been left out of Margaret Thatcher's cabinet upon the Tories' return to office in May of 1979.

But there was nothing Ryan could do about the way Bourassa had positioned himself for a role in the refer-endum debate, and rehearsed his arguments with student audiences.

From the beginning Bourassa had staked out for himself the issue of monetary policy and the territory of the college campus. The issue was too arcane for most politicians, the territory considered too hostile for most federalists.

Bourassa had recognized early on that the question of monetary union was one of the structural flaws in the PQ's program of sovereignty-association.

Lévesque would be asking for a mandate for a sovereign nation which, through a monetary union with Canada, would not have control of its money supply, one of the most important features of a sovereign state. And he ridiculed the proposal in a way the ordinary voter could appreciate. In the name of pride, he said in the referendum debate, Quebecers were being asked to create a country which would have the Queen of England on its money. Eventually, Lévesque felt the heat, and not without some annoyance he assured Quebecers that they'd still have the Queen on their precious dollars for a few years yet. Parizeau felt the heat, too, in a debate with Bourassa at Collège L'Assomption in his own riding east of Montreal in January of 1980.

Parizeau arrived looking harried and distracted from the heavy concerns of the finance minister's day. Bourassa arrived looking serene and ready. It was a moment for which he had been preparing for three years and more. The cameras rolled, the students listened, the two of them talked, and soon the perspiration was glistening on the brow of the normally unflappable Parizeau. Sovereignty, he blurted out at one point, wouldn't cost the average voter any more than a case of beer a year.

He was referring to the transfer payments that would be lost from Ottawa, and if he was trying to vulgarize the issue, he succeeded. That night at least, the witty and urbane Professor Parizeau was no match for the more intellectually rigorous Professor Bourassa.

For while Parizeau spent his days closeted with his officials, Bourassa had been leading the life of a visiting professor here and there, here at Laval and the University of Montreal, and there at the Fontainebleau of Paris and Johns Hopkins in Washington. Students found him well informed, forthcoming and surprisingly sympathetic. At Laval, teaching a course on political economy, he was voted the most popular teacher in his faculty. One thing he was discovering as he went along, and that was Quebec students were intensely interested in the referendum issue, and were not necessarily a monolothic bloc of voters for the Yes.

But if he had developed an appealing style and a quick rapport in the classroom, Bourassa was moving into the bigger lecture theatre of the referendum campaign. From the federalist perspective, there was not much competition for these podiums, not from the cousins in Ottawa and not from Ryan's people down on Gilford Street. Certainly neither federalist clan was in a hurry to send someone else in against the likes of a Pierre Bourgault, who may have mellowed with the years, but had lost none of his eloquence or his ability to carry a hall with his cries for an independent Quebec.

"I fought hard and alone," Bourassa said later, "in all those places that were considered more or less hostile territory".

No CEGEP was too remote, no service club too small, to receive a visit from Bourassa. One night he was driven home from Chicoutimi, some 250 miles northeast of Montreal. He slept in the back of the car during the overnight drive, and went out to do an event a few hours later.

On a spring afternoon in 1980, passengers on the five o'clock train from Quebec to Montreal noticed the former premier sitting at the back of one coach, his feet up on a facing chair, munching on an apple, and correcting term papers. It was April 17, and Bourassa was coming from a news conference where he had at once been welcomed to the ranks of the referendum leaders, and restored to respectability in the Liberal party.

Sitting alongside Jean Lesage, Bourassa heard the virtues of his administration extolled by the current leader, Claude Ryan. The former leaders were held to be living examples of how the Liberal party had built the modern state, financed generous social measures, and brought prosperity to Quebec, all under the Canadian federal system which they had constantly striven to improve.

It was Lesage who stole the show, at his first news conference in nearly ten years, and the last one of his life. For the most part, Bourassa was content just to be there, as part of the continuity and tradition of the Liberal party. From that day, he needn't have worried about his welcome on any referendum stage or party function.

On the three-hour ride to Montreal, Bourassa left no doubt that the No forces would prevail, in spite of the winds then blowing in the other direction. "We should have a good 58 to 42 score," he said. He turned to the mood in the universities. The students he saw were in a mood to listen, and his pitch was to ask why they should renounce a larger Canada for a smaller Quebec, when "the quality of freedom in Canada, the quality of social progress, the quality of our economic well-being makes it one of the very best countries in the world." He had openly challenged students to name a better country, and none had been able to do so. This was Robert Bourassa, the man who had so often stood accused, not without reason, of practising checkbook federalism, of being in it strictly for the transfer payments. It was also recalled that Rene Lévesque and a few others had met in the basement of Bourassa's Town of Mount Royal townhouse in 1967 to discuss the possibility of breaking away from the Liberal party.

Bourassa had broken with them that night, partly because it made no economic sense, and partly because it did not correspond to the political path he had chosen for himself. After Lévesque's departure, he would remain in the Liberal party, and within three years he would be its leader and premier of Quebec. He won an election in 1970, with a campaign the media called "profitable federalism," but he won no hearts. And he remained under suspicion in the federalist clans for the remainder of his premiership. To the other side, he looked like a marionette of Ottawa, especially after the October Crisis of 1970, when Pierre Trudeau, nominally at Bourassa's request, sent the armed forces into the streets of Montreal. For his part, Trudeau evidently shared the former perception, especially after the constitutional talks at Victoria in June of 1971, when the premier of Quebec reneged on a patriation and power-sharing agreement that would have been the centrepiece of the prime minister's first mandate. It was not over something significant like an amending formula that Bourassa rejected the deal. The Victoria amending formula—with its veto for any province, such as Quebec or Ontario, with 25 percent of Canada's population—accorded a veto to Quebec without granting it special status, thus giving both Trudeau and Bourassa what they wanted. The disagreement came over the sharing of powers and funding of social programs, and the 37-year-old premier acceded to the advice he was receiving from two quarters—Claude Morin, the deputy minister of intergovernmental affairs, and Claude Ryan, the publisher of *Le Devoir*. Bourassa, mindful of the image of the puppet dangling on Ottawa's string, decided at the last minute not to sign. It was the most serious misjudgment of his premiership, for as later events were to demonstrate, it was one thing to exercise a *de facto* veto, as Bourassa had done and as Jean Lesage had done before him, and quite another to claim a *de jure* veto which the Supreme

Court would not uphold, as was the case with René Lévesque in 1982. The approach advocated by Ryan and the others had been an unbending insistence that there could be no agreement on patriation and an amending formula until the new power-sharing arrangements were worked out.

But in retrospect it is clear that had Bourassa signed the Victoria accords of 1971, he would have gone into the history books as the man who secured Quebec's veto claims. He could at least maintain that he had upheld the veto by his action, as René Lévesque would lose it by his.

Bourassa's pragmatic approach to the problems of an evolving federal system seemed to satisfy no one in the 1970s, not the cousins in Ottawa, and not the nationalists in Quebec. Nor did his language law of 1974, although some English-speaking citizens developed a nostalgia for the easier strictures of Bill 22 after Camille Laurin came along with Bill 101 in 1977. A majority of English-speaking Quebecers still seemed to resent Bourassa as the author of their present misfortune, the man who had caused them to live the Lévesque experience, with their neighbors and children moving out of the province. Few of them would have believed their ears to hear Bourassa in the universities in the spring of 1980, attacking the harsh interdictions of Bill 101 as to the language of outdoor advertising and signs, which were to be only in French. Bourassa pointed out that it was ridiculous to prevent people from putting up bilingual signs in English-speaking neighborhoods. Federalists of all persuasions, French as well as English-speaking, might have been surprised to hear Bourassa defying students to name him a better country in the world for the quality of its freedoms and the permissiveness of its dissent. There wasn't a society in the world, he would say, that had made as much social and economic progress as Quebec in the last generation.

This was a striking departure from the careful approaches to the problems of federalism that had marked his premiership. In the referendum campaign, he spoke for the first time with conviction as to the quality of Canadian life and the opportunities of Quebecers to flourish within it. Bourassa was finding out something that spring, namely that the *appartenance canadienne* was a sentiment that even many students felt more deeply than was generally acknowledged. There was even room for it among the "soft Yes" voters. For while 59.6 percent of Quebecers would say no to Lévesque's mandate question, fully 75 percent of the respondents in Maurice Pinard's referendum poll answered yes to a question as to whether they felt strongly attached to Canada. It was this hidden attitudinal data that told the tale of the referendum vote, and Bourassa was seeing it everywhere he went.

In the beginning, Bourassa had imposed himself on the referendum debate, but by April of 1980, he was one of the star performers on the "B" team. Ryan, despite his unflagging efforts, could not be everywhere with the "A" team at once. Only once did Bourassa share the spotlight with the president of the No committee, and that was on a May 6 swing to James Bay. They held a joint news conference where Bourassa went to considerable lengths to state that electricity had not been invented by the PQ. The reporters were more interested in asking Ryan whether he would encourage Bourassa in making a comeback. Ryan, already somewhat annoyed by this question, simply said it was too early to discuss it. But he was prepared to recognize Bourassa's contribution to the referendum cause, and did not hesitate to make use of his talents. And Bourassa, as always, was available.

He was most assuredly available to appear on Radio-Canada's referendum-night broadcast. "It's your victory," said his fellow panelist Pierre Bourgault. In a small way, it was, just by the fact of his being there.

On an afternoon in September of referendum year, Robert Bourassa and Claude Ryan went for a walk together. It was no simple Sunday stroll. They were deep in conversation. There was a by-election coming up in Outremont, the seat Robert Bourassa should have grabbed in 1976, the chance he wanted to grab now. Then he had given it to André Raynauld, his most prestigious recruit for the losing 1976 campaign. Raynauld, an independent-minded person, had grown weary of Ryan's authoritarian style. Within weeks of the referendum, he had resigned his seat to go back to teaching at the University of Montreal. All through the summer, Ryan had been annoyed by speculation in the press that Bourassa would attempt a comeback in the historic Liberal riding where the mountain met Côte St. Catherine Road, where the Liberal bourgeoisie rubbed shoulders uneasily with the Péquiste professors from the university, and where Michel Tremblay could find enough material for a dozen plays just by listening in behind the curtains of the swankier salons of Outremont. It was not just another riding, it was a cabinet seat, where the voters expected a candidate to be ministerial material. There was no doubt that Bourassa was a cabinet possibility and for Ryan that was a problem.

Even if Bourassa assured him that he had no higher ambition, what was Ryan to do with a former premier in his caucus who was nearly ten years younger than himself and two terms more experienced at running a government? Bourassa had tried to make the case that he could help Ryan, as finance or energy critic, and in any other way the leader deemed useful, even as a simple private member. Ryan had thought about it, was bothered by it, and clearly wished Bourassa would just go away. He was like the mother-in-law tagging along on the honeymoon, Ryan would say in an unguarded, unkind moment.

Finally at their September meeting, Ryan let him have it straight, so that there could be no confusion and no misunderstanding between them. "I would rather," Ryan said, "lose without you than win with you."

For Bourassa, not running in the November 1980 by-election, and the April 1981 general election, turned out to be the best thing that never happened to him.

As it became clear that the 1981 campaign was going badly, it was equally clear that Bourassa could not be blamed for it. On the contrary, he was more in demand than ever in ridings where the local candidate and organization didn't want to see Ryan. And all along the way, as he had in the referendum campaign, Bourassa was picking up IOUs for the future. In the context of Watergate, he had often been compared to Richard Nixon, by which he was not greatly flattered. But he acknowledged a striking similarity in the way Nixon had been out campaigning for the Republicans in the 1964 presidential election and the 1966 congressional campaign, so that by 1968 he had made himself the first choice for president of the party's rank and file.

Bourassa knew that he would have to wait for his opportunity until the end of Ryan's prospective premiership. But then in the spring campaign of 1981, it developed that Ryan was in danger of losing an election that should have been in the bag. After his own experience of defeat, and his own travels of the province in the 1981 campaign, Bourassa knew that Ryan's own leadership would be in serious jeopardy if the Liberals lost. On April 13, Robert Bourassa wasn't going anywhere near a television studio. He stayed at home, watched the results on television, and talked to a few friends on the telephone. One of them was Raymond Garneau who, considering the way he had been treated by Ryan, could be forgiven if he had fallen down laughing.

Once, in the days when Ryan was riding high, Bourassa had asked a friend to assess his chances of making any kind of comeback in politics. Maybe one percent, he was told. Bourassa said he put it at five percent himself, but even if it was one percent he would never stop working for it. He was a political animal, and there was no use pretending he was anything else.

Even on vacation in Rome with his wife, exactly one month after the election, Bourassa could not resist going to an outdoor rally climaxing Italy's referendum campaign on abortion.

On the way over, he thought he would stop by St. Peter's Square and take in the Pope's weekly outdoor audience. Bourassa was standing in the seventh row behind the barricades as the Polish Pope rode into view and then, from only a few feet in front of him, the shots rang out. He recognized the sound and the smell of gunfire. And he saw that Carol Wojtyla was hit.

"I was no more than ten feet from the assassin," Bourassa would recall. "He was in the third row, a few feet to my left." Bourassa asked himself if this could really be happening, if someone was really trying to kill the Pope. He watched as enraged pilgrims wrestled the gunman to the ground, and saw the police hustle him away. Bourassa stumbled on to the pro-abortion rally, where the crowd was informed the meeting was canceled because of the attempt on the Pope's life.

When Andrée Bourassa heard the shocking news back at their hotel, her first thought was that her husband had been somewhere in the crowd at St. Peter's Square. He has a way, she thought, of always being where things happen.

20

FROM BOURASSA
TO BOURASSA

I f they wanted to stop Robert Bourassa, they would
have to beat him.

He had begun his journey in politics as the protegé,
if not the child, of the Liberal establishment. But somewhere along the way, they left him off at the side of the
road. If he was ever going to make it back, he would
have to get there on his own. No longer could he count
on the Outremont and Westmount crowds. They were
looking for someone else, Anyone But Bourassa, and they
would do everything in their power to thwart his designs
to regain the leadership he had forfeited with the inglorious
defeat of 1976.

The prospect of a Bourassa comeback was not regarded
with great enthusiasm by the cousins, or by the business

*In the spring of 1982, Brian Mulroney introduces his
old friend Robert Bourassa at a labor relations symposium
in Montreal. One month after the 1976 defeat, Mulroney
told him: "You've got to give it time. In a few years,
compared to the PQ, you're going to look pretty good."
At the time this picture was taken, both men were still
private citizens. A little more than a year later, they
would be the leaders of their respective parties, posed to
become prime minister of Canada and premier of Quebec.*
(Staff Photo by Bill Grimshaw, *Canadian Press*)

elites of St. James Street, or by the significant English-speaking element of the party, or by the remnants of the Ryan crowd, or by a good majority of the caucus. He would simply have to wear down their resistance, or go over their heads to the rank and file.

For even before Ryan threw in the towel in the summer of 1982, Bourassa correctly sensed the mood of the party's activists. This time, they were determined to make the choice themselves. The convention would be won in the ridings, not in the bar of the Ritz-Carlton, or the third floor dining room of the Club St. Denis, not in the Caucus bar of the Quebec Hilton or the snooty salons of the Grande Allée in the provincial capital.

While the Liberal elites of Montreal and Quebec still considered that they knew what was best for the party, they had lost control of it. For it had changed in several respects.

First and foremost, the establishment no longer controlled the party finances, and so was no longer in a position to call the shots from Montreal. Second, Ryan had built new regional structures for the party, putting permanent organizers in place around the province, and party activists had begun to experience and enjoy a degree of autonomy from the office on Gilford Street. Third, Liberal militants around the province came to the conclusion that maybe the party elites to whom they had always deferred weren't so smart. The establishment had given them Bourassa in 1970, when he was clearly too young and inexperienced for the job. The elites had drafted Claude Ryan in 1978 with their decree that the party needed an outsider, untainted by association with the discredited Bourassa regime, to fight the coming referendum wars. In the end, in the 1981 election, the Ryan experiment had been worthy enough, but a failed one all the same. In the year following his defeat, there was an unmistakable grass roots consensus that the party should turn to a seasoned professional politician. It might well be Bourassa, it might be Raymond Garneau, or it might be Daniel Johnson if he showed himself to be a fast learner in opposition.

But first the party would have to settle the question of Ryan's leadership. In Bourassa's mind, there was never any doubt about which way that one would go. He knew the party, and he knew the way it had turned on him after 1976, as it had turned on Jean Lesage after 1966. "They'll get him out of there," Bourassa said privately on the afternoon of April 13, 1981, a few hours before Ryan's defeat.

As it became clear that evening that Ryan was indeed going to lose, the leadership was suddenly within Bourassa's grasp again. No longer was Ryan in a position to dash his predecessor's hopes for a comeback. All Bourassa had to do was avoid a vulgar display of grasping for the throne. All he had to do was keep on with what he had been doing, attending Friday night dances, Saturday night socials and Sunday brunches, raising money for the party at the riding level, as he did in the fall of 1981.

Five years to the day after his defeat, Bourassa was invited to one of those Sunday events at the Holiday Inn in Longueuil in René Lévesque's riding of Taillon on the South Shore of Montreal.

The room was packed with some 400 card-carrying Liberals, who accorded Bourassa a prolonged standing ovation as he left the podium. "It wasn't like this five years ago," he whispered to Nicole Petit, the president of the local riding association who had introduced him.

But the period of recriminations and critical appraisals had finally come to an end. Only the previous week, the last of three Lévesque-appointed inquiries had come up empty where Bourassa was concerned. Like the Malouf inquiry into Olympic costs and the Keable inquiry into the activities of the Mounties, the Duchaine inquiry into the October Crisis was able to find no evidence of wrongdoing or bad faith on the part of the former premier.

The process of rehabilitation was complete. The comeback had begun.

Bourassa would never win a charisma contest, and he had never delivered a memorable speech in his life. But one thing he had learned in his exile was how to be himself. His critics might submit that he still talked in cassettes, that he was still a packaged product, but at least he was now doing his own marketing. In uncounted university lectures and service club speeches, he had finally acquired the self-confidence to speak with nothing more than few notes, or none at all. He had never been able to read a prepared text anyway, and now that he had no choice but to extemporize, he found that he was reasonably good at it. He had always been good at making debating points, he had always been good at boiling down complex material into simple home truths, and he had always been possessed of the kind of singleminded determination that had brought him this far in life.

It was not as if he were to the manor born. The Bourassa story is a kind of Horatio Alger saga, told twice over.

He was born on Bastille Day, July 14, 1933, the second of three children of Aubert and Adrienne Bourassa, and their only son.

Half a century later, he would admit to having been "pretty well" spoiled by his mother and sisters, Marcelle Morin who was five years older, and Suzanne Labelle, two years younger than himself. "There was nothing to prevent me from studying," he would say. "I wasn't in the kitchen. At least, I would be the fourth one, the last one, in there."

They lived as tenants on the ground floor of a greystone triplex on Parthenais Street, at the corner of St. Joseph Boulevard. "It wasn't luxurious but it wasn't poor," he would recall. "I would say it was a lower middle-class neighborhood."

His father was an accountant, in all but name, with the National Harbours Board, a minor federal functionary who got into the civil service through his own father. Toussaint Bourassa had been captain of the Port of Montreal.

His grandson attended primary school at St. Pierre Claver, a couple of blocks from home at the corner of St. Joseph and De Lorimier streets. At the age of eleven, still in grade school, Bourassa remembered attending his first political meetings in the 1944 provincial election that saw the ouster of Adélard Godbout's Liberals, the triumphant return of Maurice Duplessis and the Union Nationale, and the emergence as an electoral force of the nationalist Bloc Populaire.

The Bloc Populaire, as Bourassa put it, "were the Péquistes of the day," and he remembered going to a meeting near his house where André Laurendeau, the candidate in the adjacent riding of Laurier and the future editor of *Le Devoir*, was the principal speaker. The platform was lined with like-minded orators. "They were real good speakers," Bourassa would recall, "they made a good change from the Union Nationale, who were a bunch of showmen."

Bourassa's interest in politics did not come from either of his parents. Politics was neither talked around the table, nor banned from discussion in the home. His parents just weren't interested. He could never really say where he picked it up. He decided quite on his own to attend meetings, and listen to speeches, "because in those days meetings were attended, you went to them, but I decided those things on my own."

In the fall of 1945, the 12-year-old Bourassa was enrolled as a day student at Brébeuf College, the training ground for the elites that the Jesuit fathers had set up at the western approach to Outremont. While Brébeuf may not have been in Outremont, it was very much of Outremont, and the sons of the bourgeoisie, and those who would be, went through there. Robert Bourassa was neither from Outremont, nor of it, but because of the low cost of being a day student, no more than a few hundred dollars a year, his parents were able to afford it. And like Pierre Trudeau a decade before him, he acquired all the intellectual discipline, and learned all the tricks of logic, for which the Jesuits were justly celebrated.

And then in May of 1950, just as he was finishing up the first year of his baccalaureate studies, his father died of a heart attack. He was only 57 years old, and there had been no warning of it.

"He died suddenly," Bourassa would say many years later. "It was his first heart attack, and his last. It was a shock. It's one of the things that marked me the most in life. You always remember it."

Neither had the teenage Robert ever known his grandparents, either on his father's side of the family, or his mother's, whose maiden name was Courville.

The sudden death of his father "could have created a bit of insecurity," Bourassa acknowledged, but it did not interrupt his studies. It may have drawn him closer to his family. In the way of people who didn't necessarily see each other often, they always remained quite close. In her failing years, his mother lived in the Berthiaume-Tremblay home for the aged on Gouin Boulevard in the North End of Montreal. He would go and sit with her for hours. And as long as her health permitted, he would fly her down to Florida in winter with one of his sisters and family to spend a couple of weeks at his oceanview apartment in Bal Harbour.

As he worked his way through college, and later through law school, Bourassa held down about ten summer jobs. One year he was a toll taker on the night shift on the Jacques Cartier bridge. In those days, the tolls were calculated by the number of passengers, but it was not arduous work. "There was hardly anyone at night," he would say, "we could have slept for hours."

Another year he worked in a textile plant, one of the sweat shops for which Montreal's rag trade was still noted more than a quarter of a century later. And for those who always thought Bourassa reminded them of a bank teller, he actually worked two or three summers in a bank, as a teller. When he entered the law faculty at the University of Montreal in 1953, he immediately went to the head of the class, even as he plunged into student politics. It was a strong faculty in his year. His classmates included Antonio Lamer, who would go to the Supreme Court when he was still in his forties. And there was Jacques Mongeau, later a leading education administrator in Montreal, and an interesting collection of future business and law leaders in Quebec. Bourassa was first in his class every year, and on graduation won the governor general's medal.

On the student activity side, he wrote for the student newspaper, *Le Quartier-Latin*, was the youth representative to the France-Canada Association, and was extremely active with the young Liberals.

In 1956, as he was finishing his legal studies, Bourassa plunged into the provincial campaign, and became involved to the point where he was sent out to debate Paul Sauvé, the elegant youth minister and heir apparent of Duplessis, who would become premier briefly after the death of *le Chef* in 1959, only to die in office himself four months later.

The *assemblée contradictoire* was being held in Ste. Scholastique in Sauvé's own riding of Deux-Montagnes. It promised to be an old-style meeting, packed with truck drivers jeering his unfortunate Liberal opponent. The Liberal candidate came down with a diplomatic illness, a mysterious case of laryngitis. Bourassa was asked to go in his place.

There was a third person who wished to speak, on behalf of the Quebec wing of the socialist CCF. His name was Pierre Trudeau.

"What do we do with the guy from the CCF? " Sauvé asked his young Liberal opponent. "We don't have any time to listen to those thinkers."

And so, Bourassa recalled many years later, "We made a deal so that Trudeau wouldn't speak. He was very angry, and wrote a long article about it in *Le Devoir*." It may have been a poor omen for their relationship.

It was on the student council at the university that Bourassa met his future wife. she was the representative of a women's faculty, *pédagogie familiale*, which was later phased out.

And she came from a different world. She was the eldest child of Edouard and Orise Simard of Sorel. They were, to say the least, prominent citizens of the shipbuilding town thirty miles east of Montreal on the south side of the St. Lawrence. Simard's brother, Joseph, had built Marine Industries there from a small shipyard into a going national concern. The brothers did well enough before the Second World War, and their wartime building of ships and armaments for the federal government made them wealthy men. They made a formidable team. Joe Simard was the guiding genius, as reclusive as his brother was gregarious, who hated politics as much as his brother reveled in it, who despised politicians as much as his brother enjoyed their company. The wedding of any of their children—Joe had seven and Edouard had four— was bound to be a big event in Quebec. Hundreds of guests spilled over Edouard's great expanse of lawn down by the river at Sorel for the wedding of Andrée Simard to a 25-year-old graduate student, Robert Bourassa of Montreal.

After their marriage on August 23, 1958, they went over to England where Bourassa completed his economics and political science studies at Oxford.

He had made it there on his own, with a $5,000 scholarship from the Royal Society and a grant from the Mackenzie King Foundation, and he would obtain a master's degree the next year. That first year of their marriage, they lived the bohemian life in a Victoria Road flat with three kinds of heating—gas, electricity and coal. From Oxford, Bourassa moved on to Cambridge, the one in Massachusetts, where Harvard awarded him a grant from the Ford Foundation to study for a second master's degree in tax and corporate law. During the winter and spring of 1960, they lived in a small apartment on Robinson Street near the university. Andrée Bourassa was pregnant with their son, François, born that year in Montreal.

And then the Bourassas settled down for the next four years in Ottawa, where he worked as a fiscal adviser for the Department of National Revenue, and taught economics and taxation at the University of Ottawa, not far from their house on Rideau River Drive.

He later recalled that period as the years of decline leading to the fall of John Diefenbaker's government. And every month, on the day the unemployment figures would come out, Bourassa would arrange to be in the galleries to watch the Liberals go after him. "They had the four horsemen," he recalled, in Lester Pearson, Jack Pickersgill,

Lionel Chevrier and Paul Martin, and when one had finished, the other would stand up and fire away." It was
the proof that you don't need fifty members to bring
down a government. "It was parliamentary debate at its
best."

By 1963, Bourassa was turning thirty, growing bored
in Ottawa, and looking for a way to get back home and
into politics. By then, he said, "it was a question of how
and when, not whether. In the early days, I might have
ended up as some kind of senior civil servant."

Marcel Bélanger provided the how, Jean Lesage provided the when.

Bourassa had been doing some work for the federal
government's Carter Commission on taxation. In Quebec,
Lesage was in the process of appointing his own inquiry
into fiscal policy under Marcel Bélanger. Lesage and Bélanger were looking for a general secretary and research
director for the commission. One of the people Bourassa
had run into around Ottawa was Carl Goldenberg, the
famed labor lawyer and constitutionalist, who was one
of those well-connected Montrealers around the federal
capital. He also had occasion to settle the odd labor dispute
for Lesage, and recommended Bourassa as secretary to
the Quebec inquiry. Since Bélanger also wanted him for
the onerous job, that just about clinched it.

The work of the Bélanger Commission did not make
many headlines, for it was not about constitutional or
cultural matters, the great preoccupations of the age. And
Bourassa would be the first to acknowledge that much
of its work was "as boring as the rain." But it was an
epic inquiry, and as Bourassa discovered it touched on
every level of public policy in Quebec, from school levies,
to municipal taxes, to personal and excise taxes. "It gave
me a good chance to deepen myself in everything," Bourassa said twenty years later. It also gave him the chance
to travel into every corner of the province, as the inquiry
completed the public phase of its work. It was the origin
of his network in the Liberal party.

When the work was done in 1965, the young secretary
of the commission delivered a copy of the report to the

home of *Le Devoir's* publisher on Garnier Street in East-Central Montreal.

It was one of the first extended conversations Bourassa would have with Claude Ryan, but it would not be the last. "Two days later he had read the whole report, and published the only intelligent editorial on it, he 'Ryaned' it," Bourassa recalled with some admiration.

Ryan would have been one person who read the Bélanger report, and Premier Lesage was undoubtedly another. By this time it had been agreed that Bourassa would run for the Liberals at the next election, which Lesage was impatient to get out of the way before the celebrations of Expo year in 1967. In the spring of 1966, only three-and-a-half years since his previous election, Lesage summoned his cabinet to a cabana at the Surf Club in Miami Beach. The election would be held on June 5, a Sunday, and the Liberals had every expectation of winning big.

For Bourassa, it came down to a choice of two seats, St. Laurent in the West End of Montreal and Mercier in the East End. St. Laurent was by far the easier bet, but with its predominantly English-speaking population, it would make a difficult and delicate base for an aspiring politician with higher ambitions. It was René Lévesque who warned Bourassa not to run there, if he entertained hopes of seeking the leadership someday. "Lévesque was the big star," Bourassa said, explaining that he had been recruited by Lesage, but approved by Lévesque. And so a word of advice from the most popular minister in the government was not to be taken lightly.

"But if Lesage had asked me to run in St. Laurent, I would have," Bourassa said. "He had asked his organizers to free a good riding for me, and Mercier was rather safe in those days."

It was safe enough for Bourassa, because the Liberals were maintaining their hold on the cities even as the tide was going out for them in the rest of the province. Union Nationale leader Daniel Johnson had been out in the boondocks for years, and his Irish charm made a refreshing change from the Gaullist pretensions of Lesage. Moreover, the pace of the Quiet Revolution had been rather too hectic for the liking of many rural voters.

And so on June 5, the people reelected Lesage and threw him out at the same time. He had a majority of the popular vote, but Johnson had a majority of seats. Since there was something in this for everyone, the new premier pointed out with considerable mirth, everyone should be happy.

The Liberals, who had acquired some dynastic airs during Lesage's two terms of office, were now nothing more than rulers in exile. For Lesage, the next three years would be the most difficult period of his leadership, when as he later confided to one friend, he had his back to the wall to make sure there wasn't a knife in it. But when caucus members would sometimes gather to discuss the leadership, kicking names around a table, they would all feign disinterest. Bourassa's name never occurred to anyone, except René Lévesque. "You're forgetting one guy," Lévesque told a group of colleagues, showing them a paper with Bourassa's picture. For Lévesque, Bourassa had it written all over his face.

For Bourassa, the big preoccupation in the first year after the Liberal defeat was keeping Lévesque in the party, or trying to. "I tried to build bridges between Lesage and Lévesque," Bourassa said in 1984. "For me, René was a bit like Nye Bevan in the British Labour party, a bit left but a good caution against the bourgeois faction."

Bourassa, who regarded himself as a social democrat in those days, went so far as to have serious discussions in the summer of 1967 with Lévesque and a few friends as to the possibility of forming their own party, not unlike the Mouvement Souveraineté-Association which Lévesque later founded when he walked out of the Liberal party at its autumn convention. Bourassa always maintained that what he really wanted was to keep Lévesque in the embrace of the Liberal family, that it was "better to have him inside than outside." In any event, Bourassa told Lévesque, his ideas of sovereignty-association wouldn't work, that his proposal for a monetary union was so much wishful thinking. Then as later, Lévesque waved off this objection as "plumbing," the sort of thing you could worry about when the time came. Jean-Roch Boivin, another participant in those discussions, would leave the party with Lévesque and eventually become the premier's chief of staff after 1976.

When Lévesque left, the Liberals lost a prospective heir apparent, certainly one who would have been a serious contender at any leadership convention if he and the party had been able to achieve a satisfactory resolution to their differences over the federal link.

And then former Education Minister Paul Gerin-Lajoie, who got tired of hanging around waiting for Lesage to retire, left provincial politics to accept an appointment from the new Trudeau administration in Ottawa. By 1969, the party establishment lacked a candidate at the very time Lesage had decided to pack it in. Paul Desrochers, recruited by Lesage to rebuild the organization after the 1966 defeat, had conducted a survey as to what the voters were looking for in the 1970s, and the answer came back: jobs. The party needed an economic profile, and Bourassa, with his social-technocratic background, fit the description down to the ground. He didn't have Pierre Laporte's two terms of experience in government, and he didn't have Claude Wagner's way with words. But on the afternoon of January 17, 1970, he had something more important—votes.

Even as a freshman member, he had made a favorable impression as the party's whiz-kid finance critic, and even in those days, he had been available to travel the province on behalf of the party, and was often remembered and well thought of from his days on the Bélanger Commission. But when it came down to the crunch, it was the appointed delegates-at-large who gave Bourassa his 53 percent majority and first ballot victory. Or as he said himself many years later: "Lesage had decided it would be me."

And so it was. Premier Johnson's Unioniste successor, Jean-Jacques Bertrand, unveiled a phantom budget in March and called an election for April 29. Bourassa would triumph, with 45 percent of the vote, to the UN's 19 percent, and the PQ's 23 percent, giving the Liberals 72 seats in the 108-member National Assembly, while the UN remained as the opposition with 16 seats; the Créditistes won 12, and the PQ had only 7 ridings to show for their efforts.

Bourassa's campaign proved to be a triumph, with its single slogan: "100,000 jobs."

But at the outset, the election had been considered too close to call at Liberal headquarters. "We couldn't measure the impact of the PQ," Bourassa said many years later. "At first, we didn't know how it was going to come out."

The first Bourassa administration was marked by political crisis and an economic boom. As a 37-year-old freshman premier, he had to live through the October crisis in his first year in office, the Victoria constitutional dustup in his second year, and the Common Front of public employees in his third year. But in 1973, a year of phenomenal economic growth, he decided to go back to the people. He did so on October 29, just before the effects of the new Arab oil politics, tripling the price overnight, could be measured by voters in the western economies. Bourassa started that campaign with a 55 to 30 lead in the polls, and finished there on election day. It was very much a personal triumph for him. For contrary to the commonly held view that Paul Desrochers was calling all the shots, the premier's special adviser was suffering from a bout of depression that fall, and was not involved in the daily affairs of the campaign. It was really run by Jean Prieur, with help from party treasurer Claude Desrosiers, and Richard Mongeau, the young lawyer from the social affairs minister's office.

It was a great and splendid victory. It was also the beginning of the end.

Ten years later, on August 15, 1983, Bourassa officially began his second campaign for the leadership of the Liberal party. His defeat and exile were hardly mentioned, least of all by his campaign staff, who dealt with it in two lines in the biographical sketch they distributed to reporters. "Following the 15th of November, 1976, after ten years in active politics," it read, "Robert Bourassa began a period of study and reflection."

The study and reflection was of the way back. By the summer of 1983, he had the leadership convention locked up before the first delegates were elected in the ridings. He had made the seemingly impossible appear ridiculously easy.

But it was no mean achievement. He had done it by hard work, and by and large, by himself. He had done it by getting out in front and staying there, so far in front that his prospective serious rivals never came into the race.

From the beginning, Bourassa later acknowledged, the strategy was "to keep them home."

It might have been Raymond Garneau for a while, and then it might have been Gérard D. Lévesque, and there might have been a federal candidate acceptable to the Quebec party, a Francis Fox or an Yvon Pinard, presentable ministers who had not been scarred by the constitutional debate, or did not carry the paternalistic baggage that weighed down other Quebec ministers in Ottawa. Any of the above could have counted on the ABB factor, on substantial caucus support, on votes in the anglophone ridings, and on the cousins.

Garneau had a look at it and said no in the summer of 1982, and no again in May of 1983, and no a third time in the month of June. He could have counted on important caucus backing, not to mention the support of the feds. Trudeau had Raymond and Pauline Garneau around to lunch at Sussex Drive in early June, urging him to run. With this kind of encouragement, Garneau was obliged to have another look at it. But two weeks later, he received a poll of the party rank and file conducted for him by some friends in the business community. It showed Bourassa leading him by 34 to 25 percent, with Gérard D. Lévesque back at 10 percent, andDaniel Johnson at 8 percent. It indicated Garneau's strength around Quebec City and the West End of Montreal, but pointed to Bourassa's strong lead among francophone and youth delegates. Garneau could have forced a second ballot, but it was by no means clear that he would win. It was a big risk for a man who was just settling in as chairman of the City and District Savings Bank in Montreal, who had a chauffeur at his front door in the morning, a membership in the exclusive Mount Bruno Country Club, and a house on Edgehill Road, near the summit of Westmount, with a commanding view of Montreal's twinkling crown of lights.

Garneau was 48 years old, still young enough to have a future in provincial or federal politics, at a time more of his own choosing, when he had provided for his financial security.

After thinking about it over the St. Jean Baptiste weekend, he finally said no for the last time. This time, his people believed him, and they began making their way to the Bourassa camp. Marc-Yvan Côté, the whiz-bang organizer from Quebec who had himself just been elected to the Assembly in the Quebec-area riding of Charlesbourg, moved over as Bourassa's chief organizer. The entire Grande Allée crowd moved onside within a week. The resistance within the caucus collapsed. Garneau turned over his privately-commissioned opinion-poll to Bourassa, and promised his support. When Garneau finally said yes to John Turner in the 1984 federal election, he may have regretted doing so.

It was over. It was not as if the establishment had not had a few meetings, as Philippe Casgrain who had attended a few in his time, acknowledged to Bourassa in the summer of 1983. There was still an ABB movement but by this time, nobody was willing to go public anymore. Bourassa had achieved his primary goal, "to reply to the establishment guys getting together at the Ritz. When they saw my strength, they had to back down."

Even the feds began to change their tune. Trudeau, in Montreal on personal business in mid-June, happened to be lunching at the University Club the same day Bourassa was there with Jim Robb, a lawyer who had long advised him on matters relating to the English-speaking community. Trudeau walked over to Bourassa's table and they had a light-hearted exchange. But Trudeau also gave an interview to *Le Devoir*, in which he sounded less than enthusiastic about the prospect of a Bourassa comeback, finally allowing as how he would prefer Bourassa over René Lévesque. "Between cancer and the plague," Bourassa said angrily after seeing the interview, "he'll take me."

This was one difference between the Bourassa who was returning to the leadership and the man who had relinquished it. He had developed a memory, and he had decided that no one would ever again take liberties with him.

As for the feds and their meddling, he would later say that "they went just a bit too far to try and stop me." He was not unaware that the new Conservative leader, Brian Mulroney, had sent word to Trudeau through a mutual friend to call off the dogs. Mulroney made it quite clear that Bourassa was going to win, and that he was prepared to help him win if it came to that.

There was another brief bubble rising over Ottawa in the month of July, when Marc Lalonde kept hearing from people that he should have a run at it. But he knew better, and besides, he was the federal finance minister and the most powerful figure in the national capital after the prime minister himself. There was no compelling reason for him to enter a provincial race, and no guarantee of winning. If anything, a Lalonde candidacy would have sparked a family quarrel between the Quebec Liberals and the cousins that would have torn the party to pieces. It was never on. But at least Lalonde had enough political acumen not to make stupid public statements about Bourassa, as André Ouellet and Jean Chrétien had done.

Lalonde angrily told them at a Liberal caucus meeting in June that they had missed an important opportunity to shut up. Ouellet had gone so far as to say Bourassa had been given his chance, and blown it. Bourassa waved him off as the personification of insignificance in politics, to the delight of many of Ouellet's own colleagues. As for Chrétien, they patched things up over a dinner at the home of Paul Desmarais. By this time, Chrétien was looking to his own prospects at succeeding Trudeau, and it would not help him in his home province to make an enemy of the man who was going to be leader of the Quebec party.

Bourassa had two adversaries, but no opponents, in the 1983 leadership race.

Daniel Johnson was the first to declare himself in the middle of July. He was clearly the candidate of the establishment and the Ryan crowd, or what was left of either. He did not expect to win, but he had every expectation of finishing second.

Pierre Paradis, who achieved the ripe old age of 33 in the summer of 1983, was the candidate with everything to gain and nothing to lose, just by being in the race.

A lawyer from Bedford in the Eastern Townships, Paradis burst on the scene to win the party's nomination in a 1980 by-election in the riding of Brome-Missisquoi. He had nothing to recommend him for the leadership except a personal network of friends from the Townships and his days at the University of Ottawa law school, as well as the interests of pork farmers he represented in his law practice.

But he was not short of moxie. The country lawyer sashayed into town on August 9, to announce his candidacy from the Oval Room of the Ritz, filled to overflowing with enthusiastic supporters decked out in his red and grey badges. When they poured out of the hotel onto Sherbrooke Street, it looked like a convention of Métro-Richelieu dealers going back to the grocery store.

Paradis arrived with a bouncy campaign jingle and the slogan, *Enfin,* as if the whole province had been waiting for his arrival. It was quite a nervy performance, and a very good one. From the beginning to the end of his campaign, he played a cassette about three themes, individual rights, economic recovery and federalism, all dear to the hearts of Liberals. In the crowd that day, somebody observed that the booming, self-confident Paradis sounded like a cross between Ronald Reagan and Camil Samson.

There was a distinct difference between Paradis and Johnson. Paradis had the flair without the finish. Johnson had the finish without the flair. Paradis might in time acquire the finish. But flair is something you're born with, and the 38-year-old Johnson didn't show much in the summer of 1983. From the beginning, his campaign was terribly organized, thematically confused, based on the naive assumption that the establishment could still call a few shots, and going nowhere fast. Johnson and his campaign team took what should have been a respectable second-place showing and turned it into a disastrous third-place finish. He opened his committee room with a crane hoisting his name on the sidewalk outside his downtown storefront headquarters on Sherbrooke Street, and with a slogan calling for "A New Liberal Leader." In case the significance of this escaped anyone, he made a rather sharp attack on Bourassa for having led the party into the wilderness.

Bourassa, as if swatting flies, replied that Johnson had been in the party of his father in 1976, and that long-time Liberal activists had no lessons to take from him.

And at his own campaign launching at Montreal's Holiday Inn Centre Ville on August 15, Bourassa made it clear that reporters should no longer be familiar with him. What did he say, asked Radio-Canada's Jean Larin, to those who said he was still surrounded by the same people. "Yes," Bourassa replied, without missing a beat, "I see we're still together."

The audience of supporters roared with appreciative laughter. To another question, this time in English, as to whether on the night of November 15 he had ever dreamed of making a comeback, he gave a simple reply: "Yes."

He promised that he would run a campaign "with no zig-zagging and no gadgets," and reporters were quite welcome to take his picture from any angle they pleased.

"I'm getting jowls like Joe Clark," Bourassa had said merrily at a private dinner a week before his 50th birthday in July of 1983.

"It's funny," he said. "I don't feel 50. When I was 20, I used to think that at 50 I would be in my grave."

Bourassa had grown older since his years as premier, without growing old. He had filled out a bit, and his suits

no longer fit him like a coathanger. He had even put
aside some of his pin-striped, double-breasted suits for
more casual and becoming blazers and slacks. Occasionally,
he would even show up at a party function wearing a
windbreaker over a turtleneck or open shirt.

So he no longer had the underfed aspect that in the
old days had caused matrons to take pity on him. Still,
he watched his weight by swimming every day, a quarter
to a third of a mile. And he still watched what he ate,
generally a piece of fish at noon and a steak in the evening.
Bourassa's one self-indulgence would be a glass of Chablis
with his lunch or Cabernet Sauvignon in the evening.
Among close friends, he might have a Cognac after dinner.

What he had learned in seven years was nothing more
or less than the chastening experience of defeat. "You
know what power is when you've lost it," he used to
say, "And you know what you would do differently."

He had also been the beneficiary of something denied
to those who exercise power: time to think.

"I will be a candidate for the leadership of the Quebec
Liberal party at its convention in Quebec on October 14
and 15," Bourassa began, reading from a prepared
statement.

This was an appropriate declaration for a meeting
held in a Holiday Inn, with a slogan of "No surprises."

Bourassa had a double-tracked program, proposing
economic priorities for his party, and attacking the party
in power.

His five-point program emphasized high technology,
opening Quebec to new investment, reducing the interventionist role of the state, making peace with Ottawa,
and civilizing relations between Quebec's public employees
and the citizenry.

That was the motherhood side of his platform, which
he would detail in a series of position papers in the coming
weeks. Clearly, he was setting the agenda, rather than
allowing the media to do it for him. And he attacked the
Lévesque administration with a surprising degree of
vengeance and scorn. "Dream merchants," he called them,
"who so recently had all the answers, now have nothing

but problems. Their ideology foundered on contact with political reality . . . . Once a source of pride and trust, the Quebec government has been discredited; the major projects are idle, or almost; taxes are higher than elsewhere; the public purse is depleted; regimentation abounds and young people have nowhere to turn.''

Andrée Bourassa, one week short of her silver wedding anniversary, watched her husband with a mingling of pride and resignation. Any sense of dread may well have been shared by their 23-year-old son, François, by now a student at the McGill Conservatory of Music. His 17-year-old sister, Mimi, was more at ease and in a sense better prepared for this day. For she had been too young to know the scorn and contempt that François had endured from his classmates during their father's first time around. She was a perfectly normal, gregarious, boy-crazy teenager, who had a well-developed aversion to schoolwork and had her father wrapped around her finger.

They had all known this day would come again, and they were prepared to face it together. Andrée Bourassa, with her interests in art history and classical music, had never been fond of her public role as the premier's wife, and she was not anxious to become public property again. But she was prepared to do it, to the extent that it was necessary, and in the brief two months of the leadership campaign, she sometimes insisted on appearing at her husband's side, as she did on this August afternoon. She was even prepared to have herself elected a delegate, along with her husband and two children, in his old riding of Mercier.

By then, on September 6, the delegate selection process had been under way for a week, and the Bourassa juggernaut was already rolling. There were 24 delegates, 12 men and 12 women, including 8 youth, from each of the 122 ridings, for a total of 2,928 delegates to be elected over the three-week selection period. In every riding, it was the Bourassa slate versus the others. No matter how much the other two campaigns teamed up, they could not stop him. When the process was over on September 18, even Johnson acknowledged openly that Bourassa had piled up a huge and probably insurmountable lead of 1,500 votes over his nearest rival. "I'm still confident I can turn the tide," Johnson declared bravely at a September 19 news conference. But the tone of the day was set by CBC reporter Don MacPherson, who asked if all this wasn't Johnson's way of admitting that his campaign was in a shambles.

By the time the leadership campaign rolled into Quebec in the days after Thanksgiving weekend, the only suspense was who would finish second. By Saturday, October 15, it was clear that Pierre Paradis had caught up with Daniel Johnson and passed him.

He had indeed come from no place to second place, with 353 votes to Johnson's 343. As the numbers were being called out, the victor was visiting the boxes of the two vanquished candidates, and he arrived back at his own end of the Quebec Coliseum just in time to hear his own numbers called out. Robert Bourassa, 2,138 votes, or 75 percent, the biggest winning margin in the history of the Liberal party, eclipsing Lesage's 1958 mark of 71 percent.

For Bourassa, it had been a long road back, and it had taken him through every riding in the province. Even when he was running well ahead in the winter of 1983, he cancelled a trip to Florida to make a fund-raising swing through the snowbound Gaspé. Even when there had been a province-wide power failure on the previous December 14, Bourassa insisted on going ahead with an appearance in Rivière-du-Loup, where he found that 350 people had waited four hours for him. There was still no power, so they had a very late candlelit supper. Bourassa later said it was the most moving moment of all his years in politics. And into the summer and the fall, he had run the same kind of campaign as his friend Mulroney had on a national level in the spring, down in the boondocks, with no media entourage and no hype. *À la Brian*, Bourassa said in the summer. And he too, would go all the way.

Now it came time to claim the victory and Bourassa, in the obligatory crush of cameras, guards and delegates, made his way to the stage. *Oui à un Québec Canadien*, he had said in his main address earlier in the day. But this was the more important speech, for the manner in which he took over the party again. Many people in the arena remembered the awkwardness between Ryan and Garneau.

They needn't have worried. The affairs of the party were again in the hands of a professional politician. Besides, by the nature of the contest, there were not many wounds to be bound up. And the vanquished candidates played out their scripted roles as gracious losers, while Bourassa sounded the gracenotes of a generous winner. Johnson referred to Bourassa as "my leader," while Paradis asserted that it was a great and open party that allowed a young man of humble origins to seek its leadership. Bourassa praised them both, and then in the clearest statement of his federalist convictions, said "we have to fight for Canada," for in doing so they would build a better Quebec.

Finally, he went out of his way to acknowledge his wife and two children, "for agreeing to the return to politics." When he had finished, the sound system boomed out the beat of his convention theme song, "Flashdance: What a Feeling." He wouldn't have seen the summer's hit movie of 1983, but he would appreciate the main lyric of the song: "Take your passion and make it happen."

This was exactly what he had done, against rather forbidding odds. Now he was beginning a second honeymoon with the voters. A Sorecom survey published on the day of the convention gave the Liberals a 61 to 29 lead over the PQ. A month later, the gap in another Sorecom poll had widened to an incredible forty points, at 67 to 27. "That worries me a bit," Bourassa would say in February of 1984. He knew it was too high, knew it would have to come down, but was determined to maintain the floor figure of 50 percent he needed to win an election.

Indeed, a CROP poll taken in the last days of February and published in *La Presse* on March 11 indicated that the PQ had finally bottomed out, and narrowed the spread to 61 to 31. Yet Bourassa maintained his high approval rating, for the moment at least, at 61 percent compared to 35 percent for Lévesque.

But a subsequent Sorecom survey in June gave Bourassa an incredible 69 to 23 lead over the PQ. Even among young voters, the Liberals led by a 3 to 1 margin. Reviewing these findings as he sat in the sun one day in mid-June, Bourassa simply shook his head in amazement.

For himself, he was in no hurry to get into the National Assembly before the autumn session of 1984 at the earliest, and if he could avoid the place, he would stay away from it altogether until the election expected in 1985. He had nothing to prove as to his parliamentary abilities, for he had already been there. Besides, the National Assembly was hardly ever in session more than four months of the year. Bourassa could put that time to use back out in the boonies, in the places he had just come from, and in putting his caucus in shape to provide a systematic op-position, and he began the job that October night in 1983 in Quebec with a couple of roundhouse swings at the government.

From the stage, he went upstairs to do a round of television interviews with the people in the glass booths, and then off into the night, appearing at a party at the Hilton, and another one at the Château Frontenac. A little after midnight, he went home to bed at the Môtel Universel, a rather nondescript place down the street from the swim-ming pool at Laval University in Ste. Foy, where the owners had been nice to him during the years in exile, and where no one would ever think to look for him. On the Monday, he would have his first caucus meeting there. The mountain would come to Muhammad.

The next morning, Bourassa walked into an efficiency room adjoining his own, carrying a small bottle of FBI orange juice. "See if you can open this for me," he said to an aide. In this respect he hadn't changed; there was no old or new Bourassa, only the real one, with shaving cream under one sideburn and his shirt tail hanging out. Room service had sent up a mess of bacon and eggs on a cardboard plate, with plastic knives and forks and coffee in a styrofoam cup. Bourassa wolfed it down and made his way out to a car, where a pair of his ever-present rubbers was on the floor of the back seat. In his first political life, someone once pointed out to him on an airport tarmac that he was wearing two pairs of rubbers. He promptly heeled and toed his way out of the other pair, and left them right there on the runway.

"You and your goddam rubbers," somebody mentioned to him.

"You never know when you'll need them," he replied a bit sheepishly.

Bourassa was going down to the Château Frontenac for a triumphal news conference, and on the way down the Grande Allée, the Bunker came into view. "A bad place," he agreed of the forbidding fortress that housed the premier's office, sounding as if he intended never to set foot in it again.

But if his lead in the polls and his determination held up, he would become premier again, as only Maurice Duplessis had done before him. Already, he had regained the leadership of his party, which no one in Quebec or Canadian politics had ever done before him. "I'm the tenth leader of the party and the twelfth," he said a few months later. "I replaced my successor."

And whatever lay ahead, he had been given what comes to few people, in politics as in life: a second chance.

October 15, 1983: The winner, with 75.6 percent of the vote on the first ballot, is the future former leader of the Quebec Liberals. He had two adversaries, Daniel Johnson and Pierre Paradis, but no opponents. . . . (Staff Photo by John Mahoney, The Gazette)

LIST OF INTERVIEWEES

Lina Allard
Alycia Ambroziak
Jean Bazin
Michèle Bazin
Pierre Bibeau
Georges Boudreault
Robert Bourassa
Andrée Bourassa
Albert Breton
Claude Bruneau
André Burelle
Robert Burns
Philippe Casgrain
Thérèse Casgrain
Réal Charbonneau
Jean Chrétien
John Ciaccia
Dominique Clift
Michel Cogger
Yvan Corbeil
Tim Creery
Paul Desrochers
Richard Dicerni
Jean-V. Dufresne
Evelyn Dumas
Claude Dupras
Gérard Filion
Claude Forget
Diane Fortier
Michel Fournel
Jean-Pierre Fournier
Bill Fox
Francis Fox
Jacques Francoeur
Soucy Gagné
Raymond Garneau

Louis de G. Giguère
Louise Gilbert
Carl Goldenberg
Eddie Goldenberg
Patrick Gossage
Gilles Hébert
Daniel Johnson
Pierre Juneau
Marc Lalonde
Jacques Lamoureux
Bernard Langevin
Thérèse Lavoie-Roux
Gérald Leblanc
Jean-Claude Leclerc
Pierre Lefebvre
Claude Lemelin
Gérard D. Lévesque
Reford MacDougall
Marcel Masse
Jean Masson
Jim McCann
Robert McConnell
Robert McCoy
Robert McKenzie
Léonce Mercier
Pierre Mercier
Jean-Pierre Mongeau
Claude Morin (Ottawa)
Jason Moscovitz
Brian Mulroney
Ross Munro
Jean-Pierre Nadeau
Peter C. Newman
Pierre C. O'Neil
Pierre O'Neill
André Ouellet

Jean-Pierre Ouellet
John Parisella
Denys Pelletier
Gérard Pelletier
Pierre Pettigrew
Laurent Picard
Maurice Pinard
Guy Potvin
André Raynauld
Louis Rémillard
Jean Rivard
Jean-Claude Rivest
Michel Robert
Louise Robic

Guy Rocher
Michel Roy
Claude Ryan
Gerald Ryan
Madeleine Ryan
Yves Ryan
Lucette St. Amant
Bernard St. Laurent
Guy Saint-Pierre
Jeanne Sauvé
Maurice Sauvé
George Springate
Larry Wilson

INDEX